Sunset

YOU CAN

Trimwork

by Jeanne Huber and the
Editors of Sunset Books

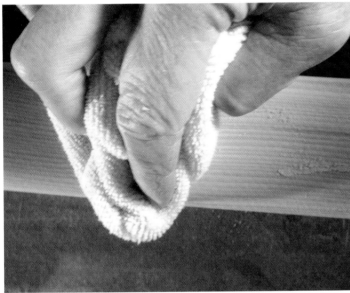

Sunset Books
VP, Editorial Director: Bob Doyle
Art Director: Vasken Guiragossian

Staff for This Book
Managing Editor: Ben Marks
Design & Production: Hespenheide
Design—Laurie Miller, Randy Miyake,
Gabe Manchego
Principal Photographer: Jeanne Huber
Principal Illustrator: Greg Maxson
Proofreader: Jennifer Block Martin
Indexer: Marjorie Joy
Prepress Coordinator: Eligio Hernández

Front cover photography by Mark
Rutherford, styling by JoAnn Masaoka
Van Atta

10 9 8 7 6 5 4 3 2 1
First Printing January 2009
Copyright © 2009, Sunset Publishing
Corporation, Menlo Park, CA 94025.
First edition. All rights reserved,
including the right of reproduction
in whole or in part in any form.
ISBN-13: 978-0-376-01270-8
ISBN-10: 0-376-01270-6
Library of Congress Control Number:
2008932404
Printed in the United States of America.

For additional copies of *You Can Build:
Trimwork* or any other Sunset book, visit
us at www.sunsetbooks.com.

Note to readers: Almost any do-it-yourself project involves risk of some sort. Your tools, materials, and skills will vary, as will conditions at your project site. Sunset Publishing Corporation and the editors of this book have made every effort to be complete and accurate in the instructions. We will, however, assume no responsibility or liability for injuries, damages, or losses incurred in the course of your home improvement or repair projects. Always follow the manufacturer's operating instructions in the use of tools, check and follow your local building codes, and observe all standard safety precautions.

How to Use This Book

You Can Build: Trimwork is organized by chapters, of course, but we have also created a number of repeating features designed to help you successfully and safely complete your trimwork project.

What It Will Take

As with the Degree of Difficulty, the time it takes to complete a trimwork project will vary with your skill level and experience, but this should help you plan for a quick trimwork project that can be completed in under an hour or a weekend-long one.

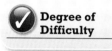
Skill Level Required

Most trimwork projects are Easy, but some are Moderate and a few are downright Challenging. The actual Degree of Difficulty will depend on your experience and skills.

Preparation Help

Having the tools you need on hand before you begin a project saves multiple trips to the home improvement center, so give this box a quick glance before you begin to trim.

Shopping Guides

In some cases, you can use the information in these boxes as the basis for your shopping list before you head off to the home improvement center. In other cases we offer tips and advice to help you shop smart.

For More Info

To save you a trip to the Index, we've placed Related Topics boxes on many pages in *You Can Build: Trimwork*. You may want to consult these pages before you begin a project, just in case your trimwork job is a bit of a hybrid.

YOU CAN BUILD

Degree of Difficulty
● Moderate

Stuff to Buy
LUMBER Casing material, shims
BASIC SUPPLIES 15-gauge 2½" nails, 18-gauge 1½" nails, latex caulk

Time Commitment
Weekend, including painting

Tools You'll Need
Brad nailer
Drill
Nail set
Power miter saw
Power nailer
Putty knife
Tape measure
Utility knife

Related Topics
Choosing a style, 26–27
Hammer & nails, 62–63
Make it straight, level, and plumb, 74–75
Trimming a window, 102–107

...an-style

...alls for simple butt joints at the
...e-basics flourishes. For example,
... plus a two-piece apron.

Contents

1 The Principles of Trimwork

Trimwork Makes the Room 8
Trimwork Defined 10
Learning from History 12
Choosing the Right Shapes 14
Door & Window Trim 16
Fireplace Surrounds 18
Wainscot & Wall Paneling 20

Stairway Trim 22
Ceiling Trim 24
Choosing a Style 26
Colonial & Colonial Revival 28
Neoclassical 30
Victorian 32
Arts & Crafts, Craftsman 34

Country 36
Art Deco & Modern 38
Choosing Materials 40
Details Make the Difference 42
Lumber for Trimwork 46
Sheet Products 48

2 Getting It Done

Power Miter Saws 52
Making Curved Cuts 56
Circular Saws 58
Table Saws 60
Hammers & Nails 62

Other Tools You'll Need 64
Setting Up Shop 66

3 Ten Rules of the Trim Carpenter

Rule 1: Mind Your
   Measurements 70
Rule 2: Minimize Math 72
Rule 3: Make It Straight,
   Level, Plumb 74

Rule 4: Check Every Angle 76
Rule 5: Make It Fit 78
Rule 6: Use Back Bevels 80
Rule 7: Match Your Project
   To Your Skills 81

Rule 8: Use Reveals 82
Rule 9: Give Yourself a
   Second Chance 84
Rule 10: Know When To Fudge . . 86

4 Trimwork for Windows & Doors

Pass-throughs 90
Trimming a Pass-Through 92
Mitered Trim for Doors 94
Trouble-shooting Mitered Trim . . 98
Plinths & Corner Blocks 100
Trimming a Window 102

Traditional Window Casing 108
Picture-frame Windows 112
Mitered Returns 114

5 Installing Running Trim

Baseboard, Chair Rail, Crown . . 118
Working with Horizontal Trim . . 120
Baseboards 122
Coping Inside Corners 124
Other Baseboard Techniques . . 126

Choosing Horizontal Trim 128
Choosing Crown Molding 130
Preparing for Crown
    Molding 132
Installing Crown Molding 134

Mitering Crown 136
Built-Up Crown 138
Making Your Own
    Molding. 140

6 Trimwork & Built-ins

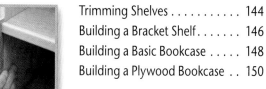

Trimming Shelves 144
Building a Bracket Shelf. 146
Building a Basic Bookcase 148
Building a Plywood Bookcase . . 150

Recessing a Bookcase 152
Embellishing a Bookcase 154
Wall & Base Cabinets 156
Building a Window Seat 158

7 Columns & Ceilings

Columns & Ceiling Trim 164
Box Beams 166
Faux Posts. 168

8 Custom Trimwork Projects

Bead-board Wainscot 172
Installing Bead-board
    Wainscot 174
Bead Board Around Windows . . 176
Other Bead-board
    Techniques. 178

Planning & Sizing Wall
    Frames. 180
Installing Wall Frames 182
Trimming a Basement
    Ledge 184
Trimwork for Fireplaces 186

Fireplace Surround & Mantel . . 188
Prehung Doors 192
Hanging a Door 196
Installing Bypass Doors 198
Installing a Pocket Door. 202
Handrails 206

9 All about Finishes

Choosing a Finish 210
Primers. 214
Fillers & Caulk. 216
Preparing to Paint 218
Prefinishing Trim. 220

Masking Surfaces 222
Working in Sequence 224
Painting a Window 226
Painting a Door. 228
Applying Clear Finishes 230

Metallic Effects 232
Patching Drywall 234
Resources & Credits 236
Index 238

1

The Principles of Trimwork

In this chapter, we help you get a handle on trimwork terminology and the classical proportions that still guide trimwork installations today. We also show you a variety of trimming options when it comes to doors, windows, fireplaces, ceilings, and walls; help you choose the style that's right for you and your home; and give you the information you need to shop for everything from solid wood to sheet products.

Chapter Contents

Trimwork Defined
page 10

Door & Window Trim
page 16

Fireplace Surrounds
page 18

Wainscot & Wall Paneling
page 20

Stairway Trim
page 22

Ceiling Trim
page 24

Colonial & Colonial Revival
page 28

Neoclassical
page 30

Victorian
page 32

**Arts & Crafts,
Craftsman**
page 34

Country
page 36

**Art Deco &
Modern**
page 38

**Choosing
Materials**
page 40

**Lumber for
Trimwork**
page 46

Trimwork Makes the Room

Paint, furniture, and window treatments go a long way toward infusing a room with a certain mood or spirit, but the substance of a room's style is usually built-in through the targeted use of trimwork.

Style Meets Function

It's trimwork that defines a room as Victorian, regardless of whether the window coverings are lace or wood. Similarly, square-edge, flat trim signals Craftsman or related styles, and sleek, stripped down trim looks modern.

But style was not the original purpose of trimwork. It was invented to serve practical purposes, such as plugging gaps in construction and protecting walls from dents and cracks. Modern building practices solve some of these issues, yet our fondness for trimwork endures because of its ability to make a room feel polished and complete.

An assymetrical design enlivens the wall surface above a pass-through door in this house.

Whether columns serve a structural purpose or are purely decorative, they divide a big, open area into distinct spaces without completely walling them off. In this light-filled house, trimwork over the columns and the windows also serves a dual role. It caps the entablature, or beam-type piece over the columns and window trim, while providing display space.

One of the wonderful things about trimwork is its ability to give a home a distinctive look even as it solves practical problems. In this house, slats with circular cutouts partially screen a work-space tucked into one side of a dining room. Light streams through the cutouts, making the openings seem almost like crystal beads.

Trimwork in this living room includes chair rail, wall frames, and a mantel with dentil, or "tooth," molding. Chair rail, as the name implies, helps protect walls from dents when people pull out chairs or lean back in them. The wall frames and the mantel trace their roots to the wood paneling commonly found on fireplace walls in Colonial homes in the United States.

Although trimwork can be elaborate, simple designs can also have a huge impact. Flat panels, flat baseboards, and flat base caps work together to create a serene look in this house.

Trimwork Defined

Bare-bones rooms sometimes have just two kinds of trimwork: baseboards and casing around doors and windows. But a wealth of other options also exist.

What's in a Name?

If you were to consult an architectural dictionary, you might think there were hundreds of different types of trim available to you. The variety is great, but not that great. That's because you can often use several terms to describe one part, depending on which linguistic tradition you're tapping and whether you are describing shapes or uses. For example, elaborate trim on the top of doors or windows can be an "entablature" or a "cornice and frieze," all of which are terms derived from classical architecture. That same cornice, though, might also be called a cabinet head, which, not surprisingly, is a term that's frequently used by cabinetmakers.

How to Talk the Talk

There are many ways to classify trim other than its use in a room. Carpenters typically distinguish between "running trim," which includes baseboard, chair rail, and crown molding, and "standing trim," which consists mostly of door and window trim. The categories have nothing to do with motion or the number of trips the installer needs to make to a miter saw. They have more to do with shopping.

With running trim, you just add up the total lengths you need, add a safety margin of 10 to 20 percent, and buy that many linear feet of molding. With standing trim, you must keep track of the specific lengths you need, not just the total. Two 9-foot trim pieces, for example, aren't enough to case a doorway whose sides are 7 feet tall and top is 3 feet wide, even though the two pieces of trim

Trimwork on a Stairway

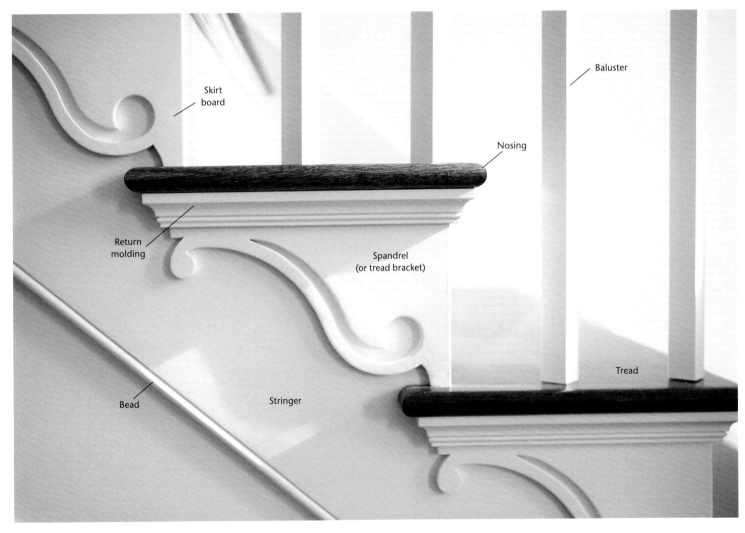

Skirt board

Baluster

Nosing

Return molding

Spandrel (or tread bracket)

Tread

Bead

Stringer

Trimwork in a Room

Box beam

Crown molding (or cornice)

Capital

Pilaster

Casing

Bracket shelf

Window stool

Window apron

Baseboard

Plinth

Trimwork by a Window

Cabinet head (or architrave)

Frieze

Crown molding (or cornice)

Casing

Wainscot cap

Wainscot

Stool

Apron

Bed molding

Baseboard

add up to 18 feet and the job requires only 17. But you could get the job done with a 10-footer and an 8-footer.

You can also group trim according to whether it will have a clear finish or be painted. While this might seem like an issue that you need to consider only at the end of a job, it also affects installation. You must be far more precise if you're installing material that will have a clear finish than material that will be painted because you can't plug gaps with caulk. Paint-grade trim is available in many materials these days, from natural wood to several kinds of plastic. To learn more about the pros and cons of various materials, see pages 40–49.

And, of course, there are stylistic issues, which is the focus of this chapter. Whether you should use molding with the elliptical curves favored by the Greeks or the round shapes used by the Romans may seem like an esoteric nuance if you are shopping for trim at a store with a limited array of molding. But understanding the history behind the shapes and the families they belong to does help you select a harmonious array of molding for a room or a house.

Dentil detailing give crown molding a classic look.

Learning from History

Though the heredity may not be obvious, most trimwork in the United States evolved from styles worked out by ancient Greeks and Romans. They used various "orders," or sets of proportions, to determine the size of beams, columns, and bases.

How Parts Relate

Even today, these proportions influence the way we pair up crown molding, wainscot, baseboard, and other types of trim. You don't need to follow every nuance of the traditional patterns unless you're aiming for historical accuracy, but understanding the architectural roots can save you from installing a combination that looks awkward or unbalanced. Here are a few key points:

- **Extend out at the top** The cornice, the uppermost part of the entablature, was there to shed rain and deflect it from the building underneath. Likewise, crown molding, which is also called cornice, usually looks best if it projects out farther than other elements.

- **Create a solid base** Just as pedestals were wide to create a good foundation for columns, plinths and base molding should stand proud of whatever surface is directly above. That means plinths are thicker than door casing, and baseboards are thicker than base cap molding or wainscot.

- **Support loads** When molding mimics parts that used to carry the weight of a building, the shape should look like it could do that. High on a wall, molding should flare out at the top, just as a bracket would. Near the floor, molding should flare out toward the bottom, as a buttress does.

- **Establish relationships** Even if there's no set architectural name for a style you pick, make sure there is a clear hierarchy for trim elements. For example, if you want a fancy baseboard cap, pair it with fairly wide baseboard. If you choose wide, elaborate crown and base molding, avoid thin door and window casing.

- **Stick with a style** If you want to make one or more rooms fancier than others, maintain architectural harmony in your house by varying your basic trim style, rather than establishing a new one. For example, you could omit crown molding in the more private rooms.

The Roots of Modern Trimwork

Actual columns are rare in houses today, but trimwork still hints at the traditional parts and proportions of Greek and Roman buildings.

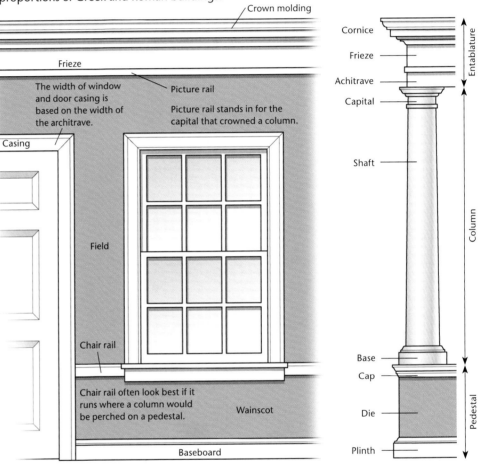

Crown molding

Frieze

The width of window and door casing is based on the width of the architrave.

Casing

Picture rail

Picture rail stands in for the capital that crowned a column.

Field

Chair rail

Chair rail often look best if it runs where a column would be perched on a pedestal.

Wainscot

Baseboard

Cornice
Frieze
Achitrave
Capital — Entablature

Shaft — Column

Base
Cap
Die — Pedestal
Plinth

How the Proportions Work

The illustration above is based on the Doric order, a Greek style that calls for making pedestals 2¾ parts tall, columns 8 parts tall, and entablatures 2 parts tall. To determine what a "part" is, you'd divide the room height by the total number of parts (12¾). For a room with a ceiling 10 feet tall, that works out to 9.41, or 9⁷⁄₁₆ inches. Thus, the best heights are 25⁷⁄₈ inches for the pedestal, 75³⁄₁₆ inches for the column, and 18⁷⁄₈ inches for the entablature. Doric columns are relatively squat, so their proportions give a husky, powerful feel to a room. Craftsman proportions tend to be Doric in origin. Victorian proportions are usually Corinthian, a style that stretches out the upper elements, creating an airier, more graceful appearance.

Though trimwork in the United States usually implies wooden moldings, it was made of stone in ancient Greek and Roman buildings. Evidence of this heritage persists in details such as the mock keystone at the top of this arch.

Choosing the Right Shapes

Moldings come in a seemingly endless variety, but they are based on just a handful of shapes: straight bands that are narrow or wide, and curves that go inward, outward, or both.

Basic Guidelines

- **Create shadow lines** When you shop for molding, you'll notice nuances in the shapes across the face. But after you install the pieces, the shadow lines separating the shapes will be far more significant. Flat spaces and tiny grooves create deep, crisp shadow lines, while curves create softer shadows. Aim for a combination. Too many crisp lines can look harsh; uninterrupted curves slur together.

- **Avoid monotony** Repeating identical shapes looks boring. It's like using three or more words where one would do, wrote C. Howard Walker in his 1926 classic, "Theory of Mouldings." If you are combining trim pieces to build up a crown, for example, incorporate one large cove and one smaller one, rather than two the same size. Or go with opposite curves: a cove and an ovolo. In either case, separate the curves with a tiny curve or flat space (a bead or a fillet).

- **Use detail where it counts** The wider the trim, the bigger you need to make details if they are to have a useful effect. If you want to incorporate fine detail, put it at eye level—on a fireplace surround, for example, rather than on crown. Molding with carved or pressed-in designs usually looks best paired with unadorned molding, rather than on its own.

Consider the Viewing Angle

The basic molding shapes are at their best when you look straight at them. But once the molding is installed, you'll look down on base molding, across at chair rail, and up at crown. So molding for each use is shaped so the design tilts to simulate a front-on view. Check the effect at the appropriate angle when you shop for material. Also factor in the way distance affects apparent size. Narrow molding gets even skinnier when it's nailed next to the ceiling.

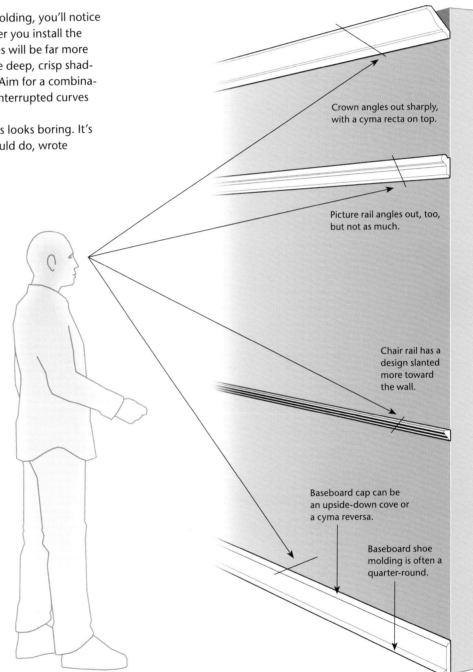

Crown angles out sharply, with a cyma recta on top.

Picture rail angles out, too, but not as much.

Chair rail has a design slanted more toward the wall.

Baseboard cap can be an upside-down cove or a cyma reversa.

Baseboard shoe molding is often a quarter-round.

Why Ovals or Circles?

If you own a period house and are aiming for historically accurate trim, pay attention to the curves included in molding. Greek shapes are elliptical, and Roman shapes are circular, a difference that shows up in architectural styles in the United States.

If your home was built in the first 100 years of the country, the trim probably has elliptical shapes. Greek traditions were celebrated then because Greece was the birthplace of democracy. It's why the Oval Office in the White House isn't round.

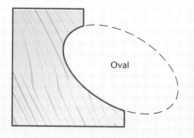

Oval

In the mid 1880s, several influential architects fell in love with Italy and began to adopt Roman elements. As the Victorian era blossomed, round shapes became more and more common. Buildings in one of the Victorian era's styles, Romanesque Revival (1870–1900), feature round arches and round towers, as well as round molding profiles.

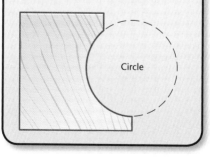

Circle

Learning the Lingo

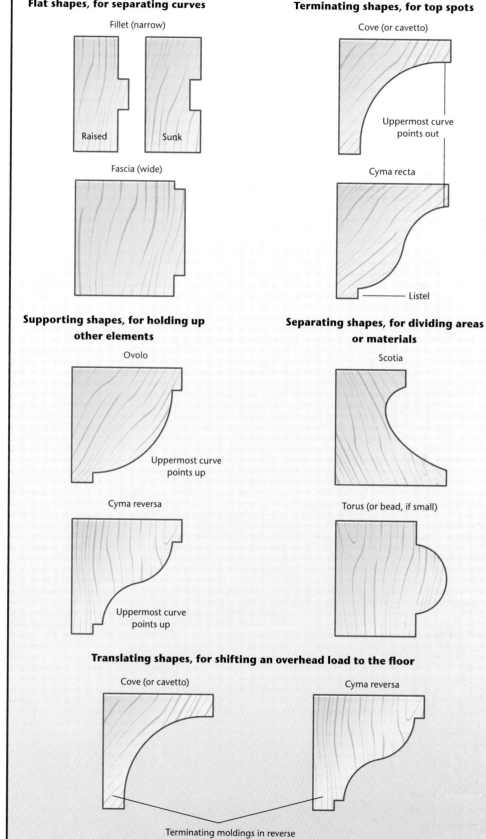

Flat shapes, for separating curves

Fillet (narrow)

Raised · Sunk

Fascia (wide)

Terminating shapes, for top spots

Cove (or cavetto)

Uppermost curve points out

Cyma recta

Listel

Supporting shapes, for holding up other elements

Ovolo

Uppermost curve points up

Cyma reversa

Uppermost curve points up

Separating shapes, for dividing areas or materials

Scotia

Torus (or bead, if small)

Translating shapes, for shifting an overhead load to the floor

Cove (or cavetto)

Cyma reversa

Terminating moldings in reverse

Door & Window Trim

Except at the bottom, window and door trim use the same basic components. Lining the opening on either side and perpendicular to the wall are the jambs; a head jamb bridges the top. Facing the room, trim pieces known as casing frame the opening.

Know Your Options

For obvious reasons, doors don't have trim at the bottom, although you can dress up the trim where a door's side casing meets the floor by resting it on a thicker piece of trim known as a plinth.

Windows always need a bottom treatment. You can continue the treatment that's on the sides—a style known as picture-frame trim—or install a shelf-like piece, known as a stool, and a support underneath, known as an apron.

Stool-and-apron trim was developed when windows came in frames that slanted out at the bottom so that the sill (the exterior equivalent of a stool) would shed water. Stool-and-apron trim looks especially good with double- or single-hung windows, which slide up and down. This style creates the most traditional look but uses more material and takes more time to install than picture-frame trim.

Picture-frame trim is a modern invention that pairs nicely with the square framing on many modern windows. Picture-frame molding looks great with casement windows, which swing out. It creates a more modern look and integrates better with some window coverings. But it doesn't make as much of an architectural impact—if you paint picture-frame trim the same color as the walls, it seems to disappear.

When several windows are close to each other, you may need to alter a standard design to solve stylistic and practical problems. These windows have traditional stool-and-apron trim, but the head casing of the lower windows also functions as the apron for the windows above. That double role explains the extra width of that trim piece. Conveniently, it's also the width needed to cover the framing around the upper and lower window assemblies.

Comparing the Parts

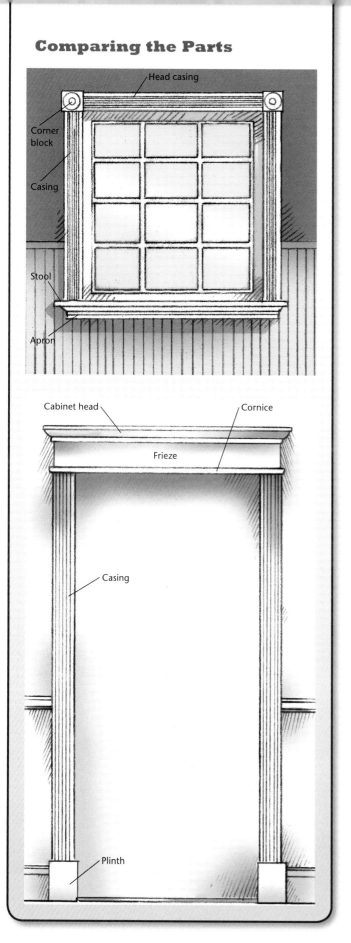

Head casing

Corner block

Casing

Stool

Apron

Cabinet head

Cornice

Frieze

Casing

Plinth

Components of Window Trim

Although window trim is designed to frame a view, it also covers actual framing and the rough edges of drywall. Understanding where the framing lies helps you aim trim nails accurately. There are usually two studs on each side of a window for a total width of 3 inches, but only one stud, 1½ inches thick, underneath, so you need to fasten the apron near its top. The header over the window is thick enough so you shouldn't have to worry about hitting framing there.

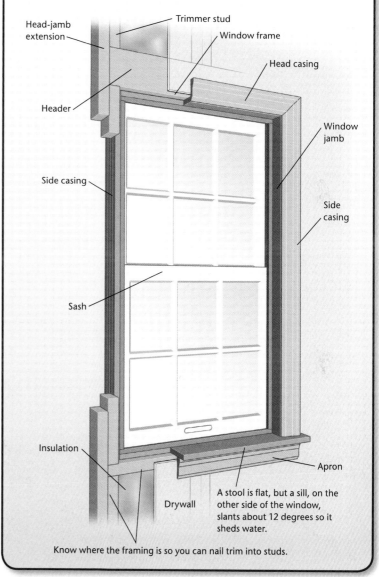

Head-jamb extension

Trimmer stud

Window frame

Header

Head casing

Window jamb

Side casing

Side casing

Sash

Insulation

Apron

Drywall

A stool is flat, but a sill, on the other side of the window, slants about 12 degrees so it sheds water.

Know where the framing is so you can nail trim into studs.

Design Tip

A room, and even an entire house, usually looks best when the window and door trim are variations on a single theme, with the same moldings and corner joints throughout. If you want variety, consider embellishing the door trim at the top but keeping other parts the same. You'll need different bottom details for doors and windows, of course.

Fireplace Surrounds

There are two basic ways of trimming a fireplace: You can install a basic shelf on top, or surround the fire box with trim that's topped by a shelf.

To emphasize an over-mantel shelf, make it taller than nearby wainscot or picture rail.

How to Do It

If you choose a shelf alone, you can mount it on hidden fasteners so it appears to float on the wall, or you can install brackets and rest the shelf on that. Or, if the fireplace projects from the wall, you may be able to set the mantel shelf directly on the brick or other material that surrounds the firebox.

If you opt for a full surround, you'll see a striking resemblance to a miniature Greek or Roman building, with legs or pilasters that stand in for columns, topped by flat and curved sections that resemble an entablature.

Although the legs of the surround may appear to be flat pieces attached to the wall, they're usually built like three-sided boxes. One side is not as deep as the other so it straddles the fireplace material; the opposite side is deeper so it butts tightly to the wall. The facing piece is a great place for decorations. The two vertical boxes usually hold up a third horizontal box, which forms the entablature. At the top, the mantle shelf should project out past all the other elements, just as a roof would.

Safety Tip

To reduce the risk of a house fire, a wooden fireplace surround needs to be set back from a firebox. The International Residential Code (2006 edition) requires a setback of at least 6 inches when a surround projects into a room ¾ inch or less. A deeper surround needs 1 inch of setback for each additional ⅛ inch of projection. Wood and gas fireplaces have identical setback rules.

Components of Fireplace Trim

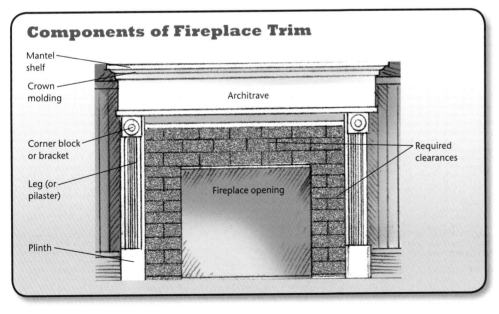

Mantel shelf
Crown molding
Architrave
Corner block or bracket
Required clearances
Leg (or pilaster)
Fireplace opening
Plinth

Comparing the Parts

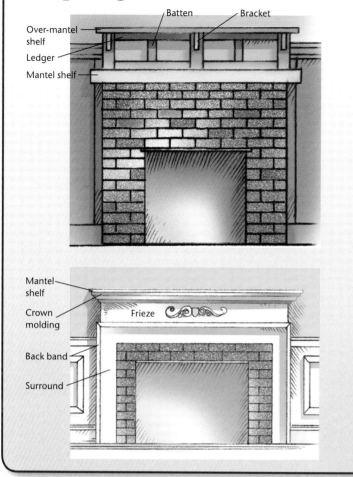

Over-mantel shelf
Batten
Bracket
Ledger
Mantel shelf

Mantel shelf
Crown molding
Frieze
Back band
Surround

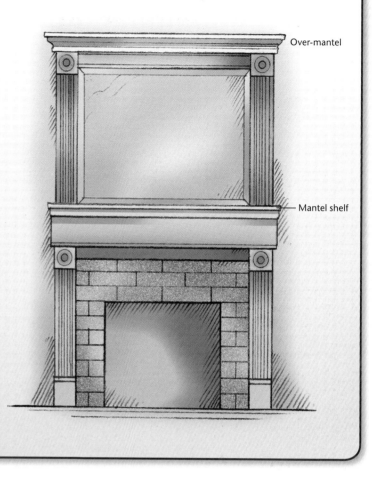

Over-mantel
Mantel shelf

A deep back band divides this fireplace surround from the adjoining wainscot. Edge trim like this is an easy way to add visual depth to flat trim around a fireplace that's flush with the wall.

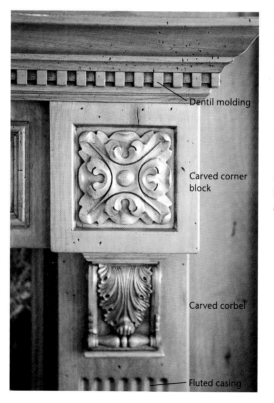

Dentil molding
Carved corner block
Carved corbel
Fluted casing

Because it's at eye level and where people linger, a fireplace surround is a good place to splurge on ornate details. This showpiece features dentil molding under the cornice, carved corner blocks, carved corbels (the brackets that help support the thick corner blocks), and fluted casing on the pilasters.

Wainscot & Wall Paneling

Traditionally made to cover plaster walls, wainscot is a sturdy wood skin that protects the lower portion of walls from dents and cracks. It also adds texture and a great deal of charm to surfaces that are otherwise just plain and flat.

Origins of the Style

Early builders didn't have plywood or other sheet materials, so to cope with the inevitable expansion and contraction of solid wood as humidity changes, they often used frame-and-panel construction techniques, similar to those found in fine furniture. The time and skill needed to install it meant wainscot was an option for only the finest rooms of a house. When bead-board (boards milled with interlocking edges) came along in the mid-1800s, the cost dropped. Since Victorian times, wainscot has been common to kitchens, hallways, mudrooms, and other utilitarian spaces.

Today, many people create a similar look by installing battens or wall frames. The other main type of wainscot uses bead-board or paneling with vertical grooves. Whatever the basic style, wainscot needs a cap to cover its top edge. There is usually molding on the bottom, as well. That helps with the transition to the baseboard or floor.

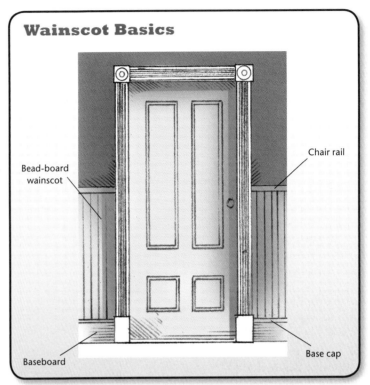

Wainscot Basics

Bead-board wainscot

Chair rail

Baseboard

Base cap

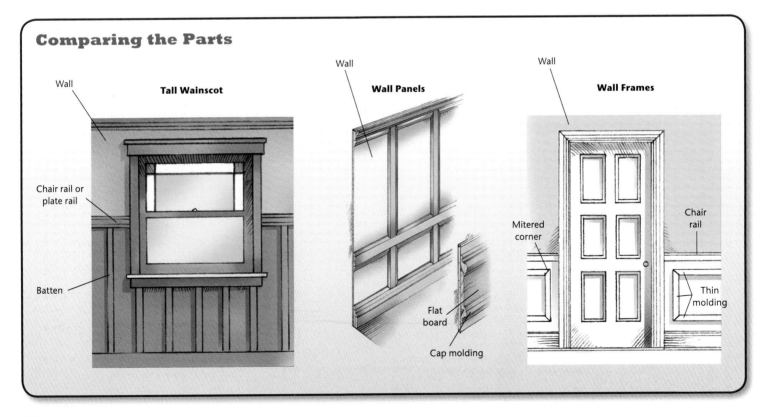

Comparing the Parts

Tall Wainscot

Wall

Chair rail or plate rail

Batten

Wall Panels

Wall

Flat board

Cap molding

Wall Frames

Wall

Mitered corner

Chair rail

Thin molding

Frame-and-panel wainscot is built in sections. The raised center panel enhances the authentic look, and the beveled edge helps deal with the inevitable expansion that occurs in solid wood as humidity changes. The bevel is thin enough at the edges for the panel to slide freely in a groove cut into the side of the framing. This allows the panel to expand and contract without cracking. Yet, the overall dimensions of the wainscot barely change because wood swells and shrinks mostly in width.

Tall wainscot consisting of narrow panels defined by battens, or strips of flat trim, is a distinguishing feature of Craftsman and Craftsman Revival houses.

These wall frames are made of wide, flat trim paired with skinnier but more ornate trim. The frames create a wainscot look that fits well in classically styled houses. The effect is similar to traditional frame-and-panel wainscot but doesn't require fancy joinery.

Picture-frame trim, made of simple molding joined with mitered corners, decorates walls of a dining room almost as effectively as complex wainscot. The frames define spaces that can be embellished with faux or decorative paint effects that would be too overwhelming to install on entire walls.

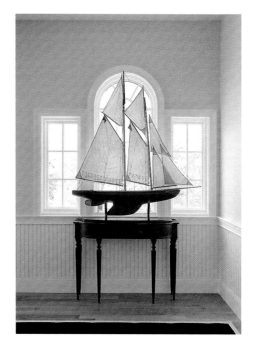

Because bead board was a relatively inexpensive wainscot material, it showed up often in beach cottages. The association is so strong that installing bead-board wainscot is now a prime way to establish a nautical theme in a room.

Stairway Trim

A stairway has only two essential components: treads, the pieces you step on, and stringers, the notched supports. Most stairways also have risers, which cover the gaps from tread to tread. Other than a handrail, that's all you really need.

Beyond the Basics

Of course, a stairway can be so much more. If the stairway is open on one side, you will want a balustrade, complete with balusters and a rail. Newel posts usually anchor the balustrade at the foot and top of the stairs. And there are numerous opportunities to add trim, such as a skirt board, which itself can be trimmed with decorative spandrels.

About Handrails

A handrail that simply ends at the top or the bottom of a stairway without turning back to a wall or balustrade is not only uninteresting from a design standpoint, it can also be dangerous. An open-ended handrail can catch on clothing, which could cause someone to trip. To learn how to replace an open-ended handrail with one that has mitered returns, or ends that angle back to the wall, see pages 206–207.

Stairway Components

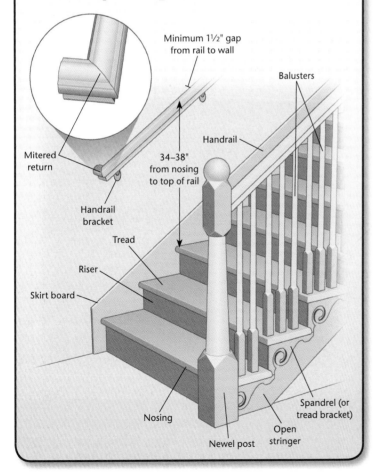

Minimum 1½" gap from rail to wall

Balusters

Mitered return

Handrail

34–38" from nosing to top of rail

Handrail bracket

Tread

Riser

Skirt board

Nosing

Newel post

Open stringer

Spandrel (or tread bracket)

Safety Requirements

Some stairway details need to be very precise. Here are a few of the requirements of the most recent (2006) International Residential Code.

- Minimum stairway width: 36 inches
- Minimum stairway headroom: 6 feet 8 inches
- Minimum tread depth (nose to nose): 10 inches
- Maximum riser height: 7¾ inches
- Maximum variation in risers or treads: ⅜ inch
- Handrail height (from nosing to top of handrail): 34 to 38 inches
- Minimum hand space between wall and handrail: 1½ inches
- Maximum handrail projection: 4½ inches
- Maximum gap between balusters: 4 inches

Turning Corners

When stairs reach an open landing or make a turn along the way, there are more trimwork details to work out.

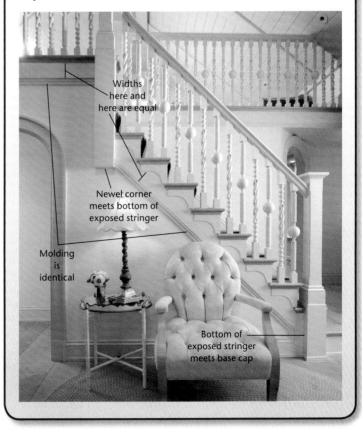

Widths here and here are equal

Newel corner meets bottom of exposed stringer

Molding is identical

Bottom of exposed stringer meets base cap

Newel Post Upgrades

A newel post's main job is anchoring a balustrade. But it can also be the key design feature of the staircase. There several ways to ramp up the style of a plain newel post.

Dress up a plain newel post with layers of molding, mitered at the corners. Top with several progressively smaller flat squares of wood and a turned ornament. Secure the turning with a hanger screw, which is threaded on both ends, or with two dowels and glue.

A crystal glass ball also makes a great finial for a newel post.

Contrasting paint sparks up a simple balustrade. It has a bench cleverly built in on the back.

Balusters

Most older stairways have two balusters per tread, but most new ones have three—the easiest way to meet the code width requirements of at least 10 inches for treads and less than 4 inches for gaps between balusters. But at three per tread, evenly spaced balusters lose their lighthearted look and begin to look like prison bars. Here are a few ways to avoid that.

Group balusters to create a more varied pattern On this stairway, trios of balusters are linked by pairs of cross-braces at their tops and bottoms.

Create a lattice that has openings of two sizes Here a grid of straight-sided stock is interrupted by round dowels to meet the 4-inch-gap requirement.

Install parallel rails Note how molding has been added along the tops of the treads and risers so a 4-inch sphere can't fit under the bottom rail.

Ceiling Trim

Many people never think of installing trimwork on a ceiling, even though it's usually the largest surface in a room. Yet installing trim above your head can create a powerful design statement.

Looking Up

Ceiling trim makes a room seem more stylish and complete. It can make an overly tall room feel more human-scale and intimate. In some situations, it can be used to help define and anchor a space. For example, in a house with an open floor plan, a ceiling frame can be installed to identify the dining area and turn it into a room of its own.

Some options for decorating ceilings, such as coffered and barrel designs, need to be framed in before drywall is installed. But other options consist only of trimwork, so you can create them any time. One of these is box beams, which simulate the look of functional, solid-wood beams. Another approach employs framed sections, similar to the faux wainscot you might apply to a wall. The frames can either divide the ceiling into a grid of smaller sections or set off a single area or two.

Design Tip

Box beams often look best if you add details at the walls so the beams appear to be carrying the weight of the floor or roof above.

Ends of these box beams rest on the vertical trim pieces, which stand in for the posts that hold up beams in traditional timber-frame construction.

The ends of box beams can also rest on hefty brackets. Many traditional building styles, including Southwestern adobes, use brackets to hold up ceiling beams.

Components of a Ceiling Frame

Cove or quarter-round molding

1×2 and 1×3 flat molding

Coped or mitered joint

Crown molding

Components of a Box-beam Ceiling

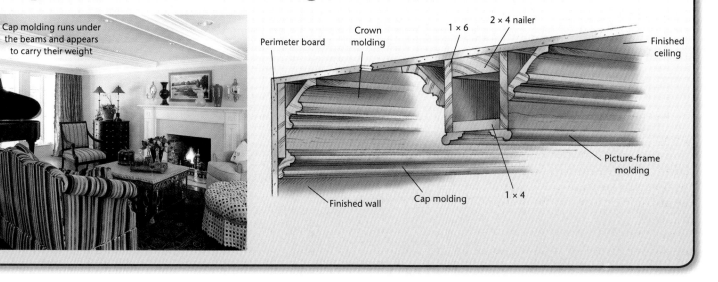

Cap molding runs under the beams and appears to carry their weight

Perimeter board

Crown molding

1 × 6

2 × 4 nailer

Finished ceiling

Picture-frame molding

Finished wall

Cap molding

1 × 4

An alcove becomes almost an independent room when its ceiling looks different from what's in the main room. Bead board or similarly styled paneling that's slightly flexible adds character.

To create a sunburst pattern like this, you could glue thin strips of molding to the ceiling, or use decorative drywall products such as corner beads designed for making ceiling trays.

Choosing a Style

With trimwork, style is all about relationships: which pieces are thicker or thinner, which overlap or lie side by side. Smiles and frowns—the shapes of curves—matter too, but more in their overall context than in each individual expression.

At Home with Trimwork

When a home has well thought-out trimwork, choosing a style for new trimwork may be as easy as paying close attention to what's already there. Even if you decide to try something different, you might want to make it a variation on the existing theme, not an entirely new style. If most of the trim is square-edged and butt-joint, for example, it would look strange to have an ornately curving crown molding. But if most of the trim is ornate, it's certainly not essential or even advisable to make sure all the curves match precisely. Even if you did go to such trouble, the pieces wouldn't look exactly the same anyway because people view molding at different angles as they move through a house.

ABOVE: In pre-World War II neighborhoods across the United States, there are many Tudor Revival houses. Designed to resemble old English cottages with thatched roofs, they tend to have small rooms, narrow doorways, and ceilings that slant because they're tucked under steep roofs. You can pick up this detail and create stylized pendants to give exposed roof framing a distinctive style that borrows from the past. BELOW: You might also want to have some fun with pendants if you're adding onto or remodeling a Tudor Revival cottage or other space with ceilings tucked into a sloping roof.

Dark wood paneling, wide crown molding, and bead-board wainscot are all features of Victorian-style trimwork. By using the same materials in slightly nontraditional ways, such as installing the bead board at a 45-degree angle, you can create a room that looks a bit more modern but still feels Victorian.

For Homes with Little Trim

If your house has hardly any trim, you can sometimes choose a style and start fresh. Borrow one of the historical styles shown on the following pages or create your own, perhaps by adapting several that you like best.

Federal-style trim often includes a pediment—a triangular piece over a door or window—that is meant to represent the gable end of a building. This stripped-down version merely hints at a roof peak, giving it a modernist look. For another variation, see page 38.

Subtly shaped mitered casing fits well in many recently built homes because it's not overly ornate. Although the joinery and molding shapes work fine for Colonial style, using light-colored wood and a clear finish creates a style that meshes equally well with country, Shaker, and Scandinavian styles.

Trim in Modern Homes

Before you go all-out to change or add trim to a house that has very little, make sure it wasn't designed that way. Many homes from the mid-20th century get their style from their clean lines and minimal decoration. In such houses, excessive trimwork would probably look odd and out of place. That's why, in homes where the trim style is "less is more," you'll do better to focus your trimwork efforts on elegant built-ins with interesting angles and textures.

Modern houses often emphasize materials and the textural contrasts between then, such as the smooth wood, pebble flooring and painted board paneling in this small bathroom.

Colonial & Colonial Revival

Authentic Colonial houses, built before 1776, tended to be quite basic. Constructed entirely with hand tools, they reflected the building traditions of the countries of the people who emigrated to the original 13 colonies.

Elements of the Style

Most of what we consider "Colonial" today actually comes from the Colonial Revival movement, which began in a burst of patriotism as the United States marked its first centennial. It was the Victorian era then, and factories were turning out millwork made from the magnificent trees in the West. The Colonial style became fancier, but it was still simple in comparison to other design trends of the day.

Colonial details are rooted in practical solutions to problems faced by early builders and reflect the fact that they shaped most trimwork with hand planes. These tools, which dedicated woodworkers still use, excel at creating crisp curves and fillets.

Simple handmade touches, such as the bracket shelf over the doorway, work well in Colonial style houses. The original homes were small and didn't have closets, so families often found creative storage solutions.

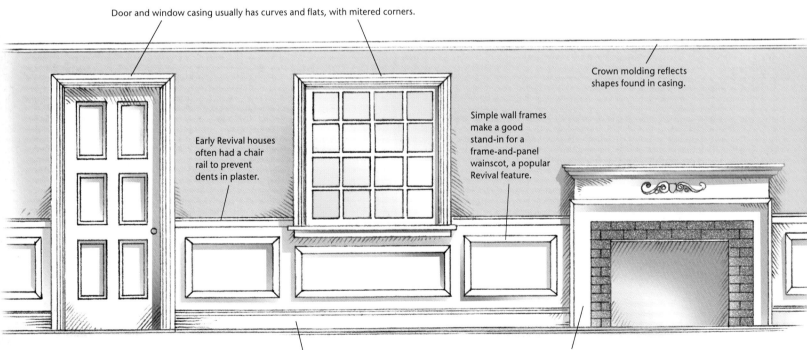

Door and window casing usually has curves and flats, with mitered corners.

Crown molding reflects shapes found in casing.

Simple wall frames make a good stand-in for a frame-and-panel wainscot, a popular Revival feature.

Early Revival houses often had a chair rail to prevent dents in plaster.

Baseboard often has a shaped top and shoe molding, reflecting details that were originally used to stop drafts.

The fireplace surround (see pages 188–191) is a classic Revival feature.

Colonial Molding Profiles

It's easy to create curved shapes with hand planes, so Colonial houses often incorporate pleasing shapes on every detail of trim.

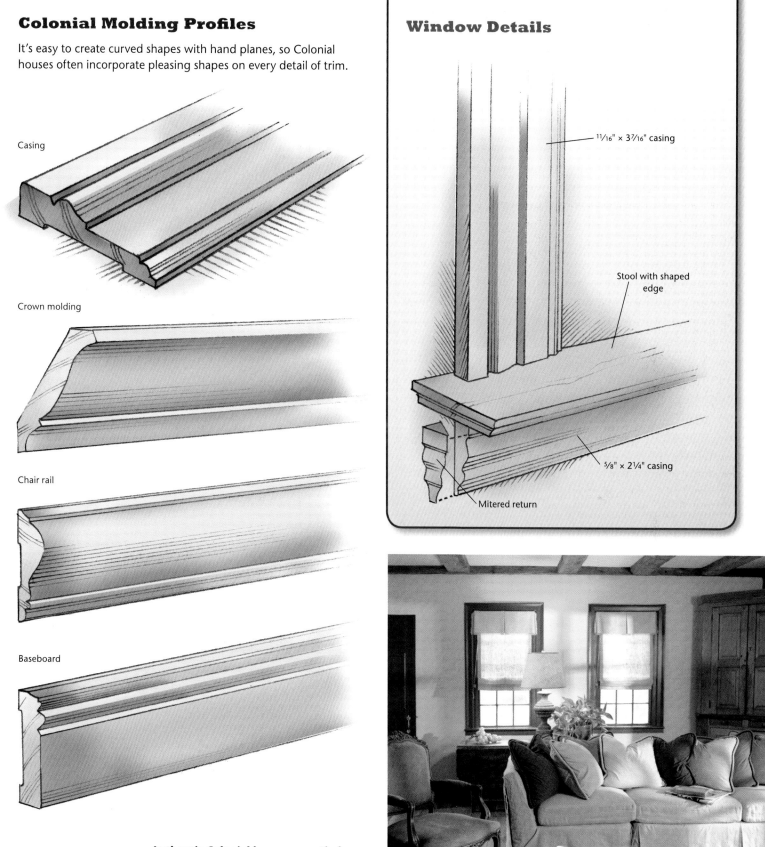

Casing

Crown molding

Chair rail

Baseboard

Window Details

$^{11}/_{16}$" × 3$^7/_{16}$" casing

Stool with shaped edge

$^5/_8$" × 2$^1/_4$" casing

Mitered return

Authentic Colonial homes were timber-frame structures, with the framing usually left exposed on the interior. Exposed ceiling beams help create a similar look today.

Neoclassical

As the Colonial period ended, demand for grander houses grew. Builders complied, resulting in the progressively more imposing Georgian (1740–1790), Federal (1790–1830), and Greek Revival (1820–1860) styles.

Elements of the Style

Neoclassical details reinterpret Greek and Roman design elements. There are obvious design links to the column-and-beam construction of ancient buildings.

Alternate Casing Styles

There are many ways to vary Neoclassical window and door casing. You can join the side and head pieces with butt joints or miters, and the top piece, often called a cabinet head, can be simple or decorated with ornate molding or applied carvings.

This dining room's trimwork is rich with Neoclassical details, from the pediment over the fireplace to the doorway columns and entablature. Mock columns on either side of the fireplace appear to carry the weight of the crown molding.

A lugged, or eared, architrave—the top piece on the door and window casing—mimics the outside edge of a capital, the top portion of a column.

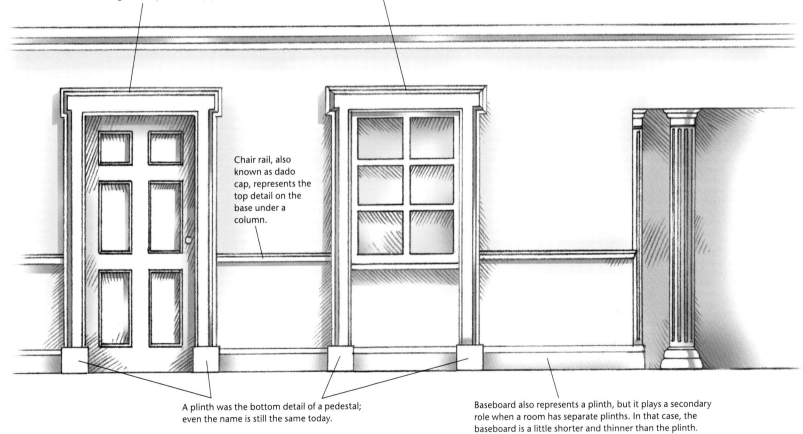

Chair rail, also known as dado cap, represents the top detail on the base under a column.

A plinth was the bottom detail of a pedestal; even the name is still the same today.

Baseboard also represents a plinth, but it plays a secondary role when a room has separate plinths. In that case, the baseboard is a little shorter and thinner than the plinth.

SIMPLE CABINET HEAD

⅜" × 2⅛" lattice

1³⁄₁₆" crown molding

1 × 8 flat stock

⁷⁄₁₆" × 1¹⁄₁₆" doorstop molding

CABINET HEAD WITH DENTILS

¾" × 2⅝" cap molding

1⅝" × 4" dentil molding

1 × 8 flat stock

1¹⁄₁₆" × 3½" casing

Attach plastic dentils with construction adhesive.

FLAT CASING WITH LUGGED HEAD

1 × 2 mitered around perimeter

Filler block

1 × 6 flat stock

Door or window jamb

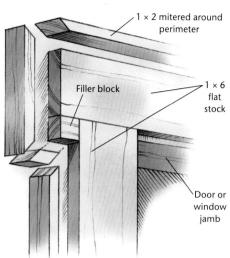

Columns & Pilasters

These pieces can be purchased ready-made at home improvement centers and lumberyards. When selecting a pilaster (a square-edge column), look for a base that's at least as high as your baseboard. Some columns have sliding capitals and bases. Others have three parts: a base and a capital that you install first, then a shaft that you shim and toenail into place.

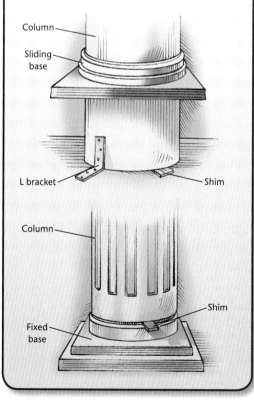

Column

Sliding base

L bracket

Shim

Column

Shim

Fixed base

CABINET HEAD WITH FLUTED CASING

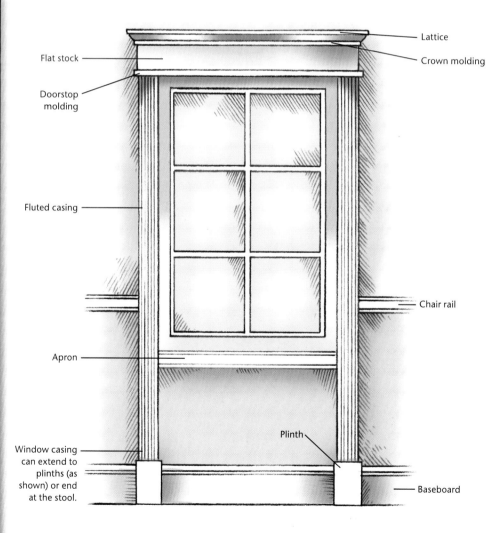

Flat stock

Doorstop molding

Lattice

Crown molding

Fluted casing

Chair rail

Apron

Plinth

Window casing can extend to plinths (as shown) or end at the stool.

Baseboard

Victorian

Architects in the Victorian era branched out beyond the designs inherited from the ancient Greeks and Romans. Borrowing medieval and Gothic elements, they designed complex houses rich with trimwork that factories were only too happy to supply.

Elements of the Style

Publishers spread the word about Victorian style through pattern books that showed numerous ways of detailing door and window trim, crown molding, and cabinetry. The feast of options fit perfectly with the Victorian aesthetic that "more is better," leading to some of the most magical and ornate homes ever seen in this country. Victorian style is actually a range of styles. Among them, Gothic Revival (1830–1875) features steep roofs, gables, castlelike parapets, and lots of gingerbread trim. Italianate (1840–1890) is boxy, vertical, and symmetrical. Queen Anne (1870–1910) is asymmetrical, with towers, turrets, and wraparound porches.

Homes built in the Victorian era generally had high ceilings and tall windows and doors, so there was room for multiple bands of horizontal trim. If your house has low ceilings, consider skipping the picture rail, or install it directly under the crown molding, with just enough room between so you can slip in hooks to hang pictures.

Trim Details

Victorian molding tends to be wide and features ornate details, including bulging curves, thin beads, and sharply defined flats.

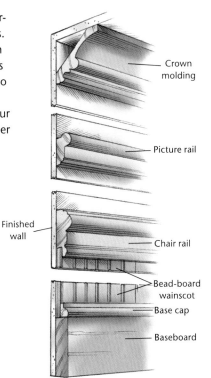

Crown molding

Picture rail

Finished wall

Chair rail

Bead-board wainscot

Base cap

Baseboard

Design Tip

Ornamental brackets show up in many Victorian houses. You can add them to corners of an open doorway to create the effect of an arch. Or use them to support shelves (see the bracket shelf project on pages 148–149).

The space between the crown and picture rail, often called a frieze band, may be highly decorated with paint or embossed wallpaper.

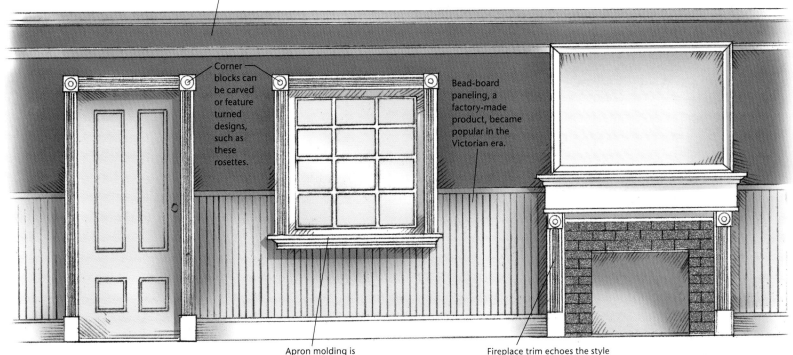

Corner blocks can be carved or feature turned designs, such as these rosettes.

Bead-board paneling, a factory-made product, became popular in the Victorian era.

Apron molding is shaped, not flat.

Fireplace trim echoes the style of door and window casing.

Elaborate molding supports the Victorian "more is better" decorating approach in this stairwell. Wide crown molding, tall head casing over doors, a wainscot treatment on the walls, and intricate but delicate balusters are paired with ornate wallpaper to create a great backdrop for period artwork and lighting fixtures.

Repetition and careful alignment of parts bring order to Victorian trim and help keep it from looking too busy. Here, the corner blocks and casing shape on the window trim are repeated in the fireplace surround. Notice how the picture rail lines up with the top of the overmantle.

Light and calming colors give Victorian-style trimwork a fresh, modern look.

The pendants, or drops, at the top of this photo are the bottom detail of upper-story newel posts in this Gothic Revival house.

Arts & Crafts, Craftsman

The Arts & Crafts movement, which originated in England around 1890, and then blossomed into the Craftsman style in the United States, was a rebellion against industrialization, as well as a campaign to renew respect for local craftsmen. It emphasized simpler, hand-crafted trim made with local materials.

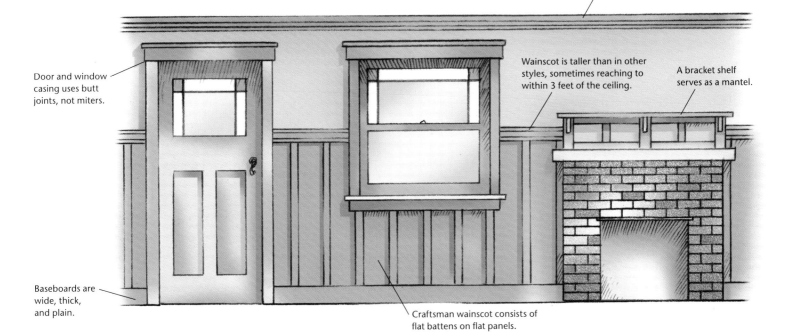

True crown molding is rare in Arts & Crafts homes; when present, it's often flat and nailed to the wall.

Door and window casing uses butt joints, not miters.

Wainscot is taller than in other styles, sometimes reaching to within 3 feet of the ceiling.

A bracket shelf serves as a mantel.

Baseboards are wide, thick, and plain.

Craftsman wainscot consists of flat battens on flat panels.

Elements of the Style

Arts & Crafts and Craftsman styles focus on materials rather than fancy shapes. In the United States, the most popular woods associated with these styles have been clear, vertical-grain fir and oak. When the wood is painted, white, sage green, or olive green are the colors of choice. Trim pieces are usually flat, but different sizes are used within a room so that there is variety and dimensional hierarchy.

In this country, Arts & Crafts ideas were picked up and reinterpreted by architects including Frank Lloyd Wright, whose Prairie style focused on low, horizontal houses, and California architects Charles and Henry Greene and Bernard Maybeck, who used wood trim with details adapted from Spanish and Japanese designs. But the most influential force was probably Gustav Stickley, whose magazine, *The Craftsman*, provided free plans for simple Bungalow-style homes and furniture. The trimwork in these houses had pleasing proportions but didn't require tricky joinery, so do-it-yourselfers of the day could install it successfully.

Window Details

Craftsman head casing was often a full 1 inch thick. To duplicate it, order "five-quarter" lumber, which was $1\frac{1}{4}$ inches thick when initially cut. Side casing is the standard thickness, nominally 1 inch but actually $\frac{3}{4}$ inch thick. Or you can downsize components proportionally and use nominal 1-inch boards for head casing and thinner stock for sides.

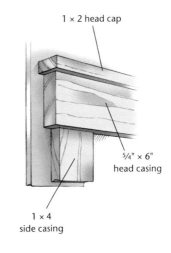

1 × 2 head cap

$\frac{5}{4}$" × 6" head casing

1 × 4 side casing

Wainscot Details

True Craftsman wainscot consists of a flat panel topped by square-edge battens. But you can duplicate the look with the battens alone, especially if you plan to paint the wall. Glue the battens to the wall with construction adhesive and drive finish nails to secure them until the adhesive sets; don't use nails alone unless you align the battens only over studs.

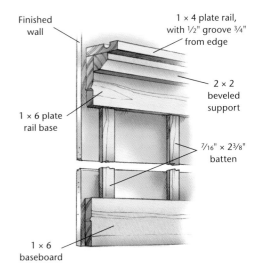

Finished wall

1 × 4 plate rail, with $\frac{1}{2}$" groove $\frac{3}{4}$" from edge

2 × 2 beveled support

1 × 6 plate rail base

$\frac{7}{16}$" × $2\frac{3}{8}$" batten

1 × 6 baseboard

Plate rail supported by crown molding rings the dining and living rooms in this Craftsman house. Plate rail works as well for displaying family photographs as it does for ceramics.

Although the battens in Craftsman wainscot usually overlay flat panels, they can also be installed flush. The main problem with this approach, though, is that it leaves little room for the wood to expand and contract as humidity changes. That's why the batten next to the cane holder has bulged out slightly.

Mantel Details

If a room has a plate rail or similar horizontal trim, this design allows the overmantel shelf to rise a pleasing distance higher. However, this treatment may be too much for rooms where the existing fireplace surround is already higher than the wall trim. A simple wood mantel may work better.

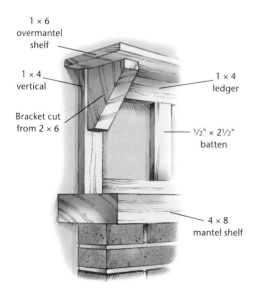

1 × 6 overmantel shelf

1 × 4 vertical

Bracket cut from 2 × 6

1 × 4 ledger

½" × 2½" batten

4 × 8 mantel shelf

The living and dining rooms of this house show a full array of Craftsman trim—exposed ceiling beams, built-in bookcases at the same height as the tall wainscot, and plate rail. Partial bookcases often divided dining and living spaces because one of the themes of this style was the rejection of overly fussy Victorian ways.

Country

Throughout rural America, there are homes with distinctive trimwork that wasn't designed by architects. Rather, country style reflects the tastes of individual owners and builders who use the materials and tools available to them to create vernacular styles.

A Wood Valance

A valance is a good example of a home-grown solution. This addition to window trimwork allows you to conceal the hardware of a roll-up blind or hide a fluorescent tube. Place it over the head casing of a window or door, or install it against the ceiling and run flat boards around the room at the same height.

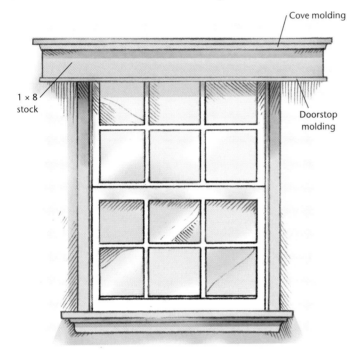

Cove molding

1 × 8 stock

Doorstop molding

VALANCE DETAILS

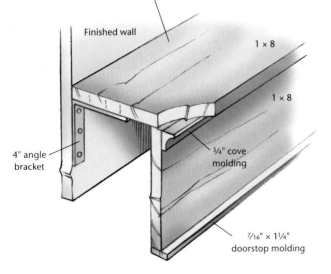

Make the top piece 3" longer than the front so cove molding can wrap around the ends; fill ends with short 1 × 8s.

Finished wall

1 × 8

1 × 8

4" angle bracket

¾" cove molding

⁷⁄₁₆" × 1¼" doorstop molding

Folk-style Valance

Use a jigsaw to cut a scalloped edge, then paint or stencil a design.

ABOVE: Peeled posts trim the front edges of a simple built-in bookcase to give it a rustic look. RIGHT: Split twigs, carefully mitered at the corners, convert a standard built-in to country one (see pages 236–237 for resources).

Country style celebrates thrift and handmade details, which means you can choose to use wood that contains some knots.

Art Deco & Modern

These streamlined styles, which dominated design between 1920 and 1950, caused trim-work to all but disappear. But working without trim requires careful workmanship, which is why even during this period, trimwork never completely went away.

Elements of the Style

Art Deco, which was a precursor to the early modern style, favors angular ornamentation applied to flat surfaces. Art Deco homes from the 1930s often had only the bare minimum of trim—perhaps just a thin quarter-round molding between the wall and the floor. But objects within the houses were heavily ornamented, and if you love this style, here's how to create trimwork in the same spirit.

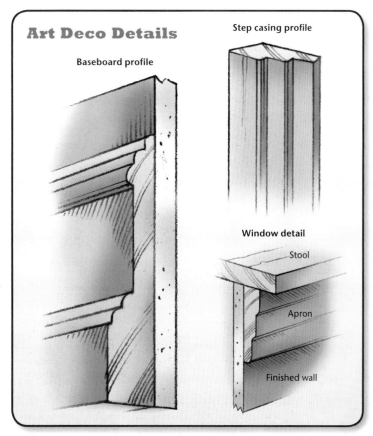

Art Deco Details

Baseboard profile

Step casing profile

Window detail

Stool

Apron

Finished wall

Modern style often emphasizes materials and their textures, rather than added-on ornamentation, which is why simple trim often looks best.

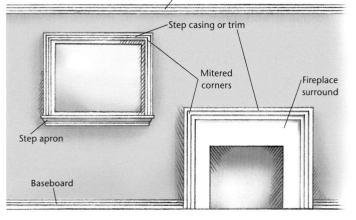

Crown molding

Step casing or trim

Mitered corners

Fireplace surround

Step apron

Baseboard

A stepped cap like the one above this tiled wall can be built with 2-bys or 1-bys.

Enhancing Basic Trim

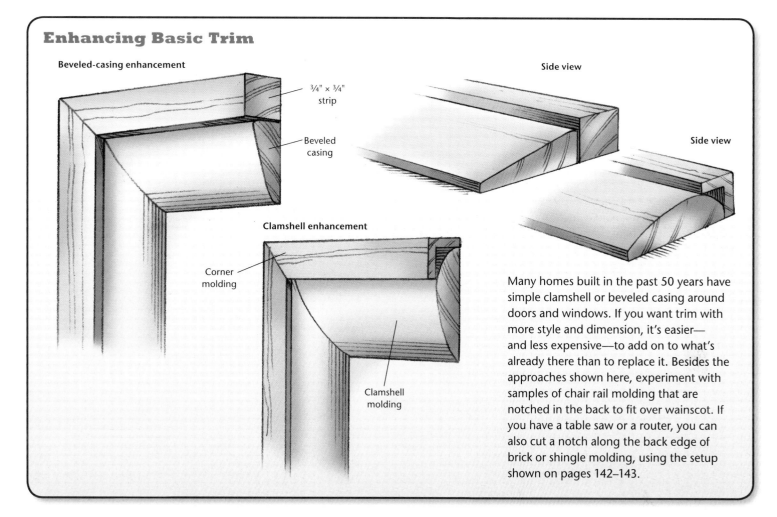

Beveled-casing enhancement

¾" × ¾" strip

Beveled casing

Side view

Side view

Clamshell enhancement

Corner molding

Clamshell molding

Many homes built in the past 50 years have simple clamshell or beveled casing around doors and windows. If you want trim with more style and dimension, it's easier—and less expensive—to add on to what's already there than to replace it. Besides the approaches shown here, experiment with samples of chair rail molding that are notched in the back to fit over wainscot. If you have a table saw or a router, you can also cut a notch along the back edge of brick or shingle molding, using the setup shown on pages 142–143.

Pilasters in an Archway

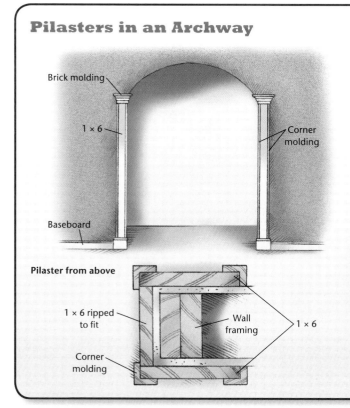

Brick molding

1 × 6

Corner molding

Baseboard

Pilaster from above

1 × 6 ripped to fit

Wall framing

1 × 6

Corner molding

Clearly modern but rooted in Neoclassical design, a wide arch links a mudroom with the main part of a house.

Choosing Materials

Most trimwork is created from molding made of solid wood, but there are many other materials to choose from. Besides hardwood and softwood molding, trim can be made of wood fibers and resin, various kinds of plastic, and composite materials.

Shopping Smart

The ingredients in a given piece of composite trim aren't always obvious, and labels tend to describe only generic attributes, such as "waterproof" or "prefinished." Before you commit to a major purchase, consider buying a test piece first to make sure you like working with it. Some plastics, for example, give off unpleasant odors and leave a row of partially melted slivers when you cut them on a miter saw.

The best choice for a specific job depends partly on practical issues—weight, resistance to moisture, your budget—and partly on the look you want. Some moldings are suitable for a clear finish or stain, while others must be painted.

Lumberyards and home centers sell a basic selection of trim. For more choices, contact a millwork company—ask whether they accept special orders. You can also purchase from a catalog or online (see Resources on page 236). And you can order molding custom-made to your design. On a large job, the extra cost might not be too much.

Resources on page 236

Green Option

If you plan to paint softwood trim, consider buying preprimed, finger-jointed molding, made from short pieces of wood glued together at interlocking ends. This kind of trim is considered a green option because it makes good use of smaller pieces of wood and reduces waste. The glue actually makes the sections stronger, and because the primer is factory-applied, it saves you a step. Cover with either latex or oil paint.

	Softwood	Hardwood	MDF
Material	Pine, fir, hemlock	Oak, maple, cherry, mahogany	Wood fibers and resin
Best Finishes	Clear, stain, paint	Clear, stain	Paint; usually sold preprimed
Range of Shapes	Wide array	Wide array; combine with plywood built-ins of same species	Often available in wider widths than solid wood trim
Where to Buy	Lumberyards, home centers, custom mills	Some home centers, plus specialty lumberyards and suppliers	Lumberyards, home centers
Weight	Moderate	Heavy	Moderate
Installation	Cope inside-corner joints; drive nails into studs	Requires pre-drilling before hand nailing	Like solid wood, but expect more dust from cutting and sanding
Cost	Moderate	Expensive	Economical

Wood

MDF

Design Tip

Medium-density fiberboard (MDF) trim is economical and widely available, so you might want to use it in most rooms. But MDF isn't water-resistant, so switch to softwood trim or a plastic or composite material for damp locations, such as bathroom baseboards. To maintain a unified look, choose molding profiles that are available in similar shapes in both MDF and the water-resistant material.

These baseboard moldings don't have the same profile. But the shapes are close enough so that you could use the bottom one, which is made of MDF, in a master bedroom and switch to the top one, solid hemlock, for an adjoining bathroom. You'd be the only person likely to notice the switch.

Polystyrene	Polyurethane	Flexible trim	Custom molding
	Corner block		
Dense plastic foam	Plastic and fillers	Various plastic composites, often polyurethane-based	Whatever wood you like (and can afford)
Often laminated with a wood design, or factory primed	Paint; sold with factory primer	Paint	Clear, stain, or paint
Limited; lengths are relatively short	Wide array, some quite intricate	Made to match standard casing profiles	The way to go if you need to match a discontinued profile
Home centers, online	Lumberyards, design centers	Lumberyards and home centers, often by special order	Millwork shops, cabinet companies
Light	Moderate	Varies by material	Depends on material
Use construction adhesive plus nails; caulk and paint to hide seams	Use blocks at corners or butt and miter joints; attach with polyurethane adhesive and nails	Nails, or glue and nails	Standard
Economical	Expensive	Moderate	Expensive

Details Make the Difference

When you're shopping for molding, the front shapes are what you notice most. But what's on the back matters, too. And there are other details that also affect how easy it will be for you to install the pieces, as well as what their effect will be once they're part of your house.

What to Look For

The following is a sampling of details to pay attention to when purchasing, handling, and installing trimwork. The time you spend up front thinking carefully about what you really want more than pays for itself later, when it may be too late, and expensive, to revise your plans.

Straight or Warped?

Some pieces of solid wood molding lie flat. Others, like the one on the left side of the ruler, cup or curve from top to bottom. Still others twist lengthwise. Pieces that aren't straight are especially troublesome where you want miter joints. To check, look at the ends; the curly grain on the left piece is a clue to a possible problem. Also peer down the piece lengthwise to see if it curves.

Crispy or Creamy?

These two molding designs look similar, but the right piece has crisp details, with sharp shadow lines separating and defining the curves and flat areas. The left sample's soft curves blur together, like peaks on whipped cream. In most cases, there's no right or wrong; choose what you prefer. If you want your trim to have a pre-1850s style, choose crisp details for more of a hand-planed look. Soft curves tend to have less impact, especially when trim and wall colors are the same.

Sticky Stuff

Mill Marks

Factories make molding by running boards past spinning knives. These knives leave undulating marks, like waves, across the surface. The marks are usually so shallow that you barely notice them, but sometimes they are rather pronounced. In most cases, you can't expect a finish alone to hide the marks; even if you paint, they'll affect the texture. If you must use a marred piece, sand away the marks, preferably before you install the trim. Start with sandpaper about 100-grit and progress to 150 and then 220.

Solid wood is a natural material. Even though molding is made from high-grade wood, you may still find small pockets of pitch or small knots. Inspect each piece before you begin cutting. Set aside problematic pieces; use their blemish-free sections where you need short pieces. Or use this trim in out-of-the-way places, such as closets; for a handrail (shown), orient the pitch pocket toward the wall.

Related Topics

Baseboards, 122–123
Fine-tuning baseboards, 126–127
Know when to fudge, 86–87
Lumber for trimwork, 46–47
Make it straight, level, plumb, 74–75
Table saws, 60–61

How the Pros Do It

"When we're trimming windows and doors with square stock [i.e., ordinary lumber, not wood milled as molding], we run one side of the back edge past a saw blade to shave off a little bit. That way, if a door jamb or window liner stands proud of the wall, or if the drywall sticks out a little bit, we can install the molding so it fits tightly to both surfaces without having to fuss with them."

Paul Venneman, Fairbank Construction

1 Cutting a recess

- Adjust a table saw's rip fence so the distance between it and the far side of the blade equals the thickness of the trim
- Attach a featherboard (see page 61) to push the trim to the fence; keep it completely in front of the blade
- Set the blade height to the width of recess you want; leave at least ½ inch uncut
- Place the best side of each piece toward the fence as you cut the recess

2 Using a recess

- Cut a short piece of trim that has the recess
- Test it against the surfaces where you will install the trim
- For casing, decide whether to place the uncut edge against the jamb (top) or wall (above)
- Go for the orientation that permits the trim to lay flat against the wall
- For baseboards, though, always place the uncut edge up

Relieved Back

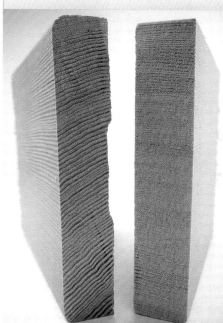

The left sample is a piece of molding with one rounded edge and a shallow recess on its back side. The right sample is ordinary lumber. The left sample is easier to use for casing or baseboard because of its relieved back. The recess helps the molding sit flat against two surfaces even if they don't line up precisely. On baseboards, for example, the gap bridges any bulges from drywall mud where seam tape ends. On casing, the design allows the molding to rest on the jamb and the wall.

Tapered or Symmetrical?

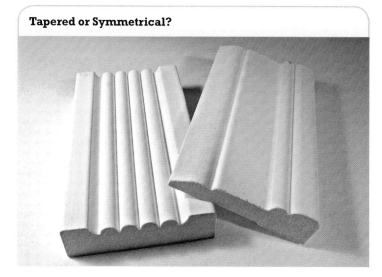

The casing on the left is symmetrical, with a repeating pattern of flutes across its face. Use this type of trimwork with corner blocks, head casings, and plinths, all of which require butt (square) joints. The casing on the right is tapered. Use this type of trimwork for miter joints.

Skin-deep Beauty

Some trim appears to be knot-free wood, but that's just its skin. Consider the two pieces of wood above. The front-facing surface of the piece of jamb stock on the left appears to be clear, tight-grain hemlock—wood that comes only from old-growth trees. But the back of the board on the right reveals what's underneath: short pieces of fast-grown knotty pine, finger-jointed together. The hemlock across the face of the jamb is very thin. The side laminates are a little thicker so you can sand or plane them to match the thickness of the wall. Laminating boards in this way stretches the use of knot-free wood, so this style of trim is considered good green option. Most of the time it makes sense. But, in some cases, you might be better off with solid wood.

Handle Tenderly

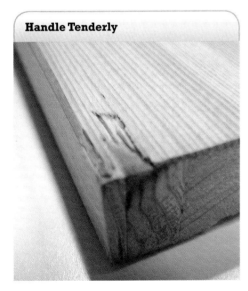

Especially before the piece is installed, the laminate can chip. The most vulnerable spots: the top and bottom edges. Repair with a stainable wood filler, or wait until the finish is on and then match the patch to that tone.

Use a Light Touch

Once installed, laminated trim looks like solid wood. It fooled this painter, who tried to scrape some dried glue off a spot where stain hadn't penetrated. The more he scraped, the worse it looked; he had scraped off the laminate.

Molding That Makes Your Project Easier

By using special corner blocks, you can eliminate the trickiest, most time-consuming part of installing trimwork. Some are designed to stand out and become key elements of a design, while others blend in well enough so that only you will be aware of the shortcut.

Blocks with turned designs are often called rosettes.

When to Use Solid Wood

At a home center or lumberyard, you might have to choose between jamb stock made of pine laminate (top board, below) or 1 by 6 clear pine (bottom board) that needs to be cut to size. The laminated board probably costs a few dollars less, but is it a better deal? There is no old-growth issue here, since the source wood for both boards is plantation-grown radiata pine. Using the precut jamb stock doesn't save that much time, either, provided you have access to a table saw. With a single rip cut and a little sanding, you can easily make a jamb that will be more durable than the laminated jamb since there's no surface layer to chip off.

CORNER BLOCKS FOR CASING

These blocks are used at the top corners of window and door casings or at all four corners of a picture-frame-style window. Choose flat, square blocks or pieces decorated with carved or turned designs. Select blocks at least as thick and wide as the casing. Make the blocks a little wider if they are thicker than the casing or if you are using plinths.

PLINTHS

Install plinths at the bottom of doorway trim. Choose flat, rectangular blocks or pieces decorated with carved designs or shaped edges. Make plinths thicker and taller than the baseboard, and thicker and wider than the casing.

CORNER BLOCKS FOR BASEBOARDS

For inside corners, use blocks with a square cross-section (see standing and bottom blocks). For inside corners, use blocks with a cutaway corner (see middle block). If blocks are double-ended (middle, bottom), trim one end to fit the baseboard height; you can get two corners from one block if baseboards are short. The outside corner pieces save you from making miter joints, while the inside corner pieces eliminate coping.

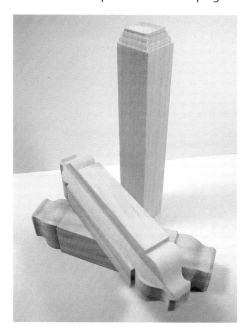

CORNER BLOCKS FOR CROWN MOLDING

Some corner blocks for crown molding (below, top left) extend below the crown and adds decorative flourish. The other corner blocks sit flush with the crown and blend in. The top two corners are hardwood; use these with molding made of hardwood, softwood, or MDF. The bottom corner is polyurethane; use only with polyurethane molding.

Built-up Molding

Crown molding, casing, baseboard, and other trimwork often appears to be made from a single kind of molding but is actually a combination of skinnier strips. Known as built-up molding, it allows you to create a custom look from stock parts. Using built-up molding also solves practical problems. Skinnier pieces are more flexible, so you can move the parts to follow surfaces that aren't flat. For example, if you're installing wainscot on a wall that isn't straight, you can move individual pieces of a cap assembly in and out to keep the molding tight to both the wall on top and the wainscot below. A one-piece cap would be stiffer, so you'd need to scribe and shape the molding—or squirt in caulk—to eliminate gaps.

A Colonial-style fireplace surround is made from built-up molding.

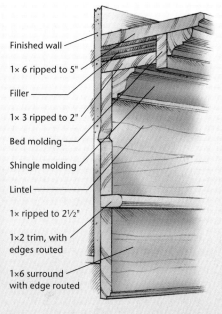

Finished wall
1× 6 ripped to 5"
Filler
1× 3 ripped to 2"
Bed molding
Shingle molding
Lintel
1× ripped to 2½"
1×2 trim, with edges routed
1×6 surround with edge routed

Making Wise Use of Wood

If your design calls for deep or large molding, building up the shape from smaller pieces makes better use of wood and reduces the chance that the molding might twist or cup because too much wood was removed from one side of the board. To make this casing profile from a single piece, you'd turn about one-third of the wood to sawdust. Making it from two smaller pieces greatly reduces the waste.

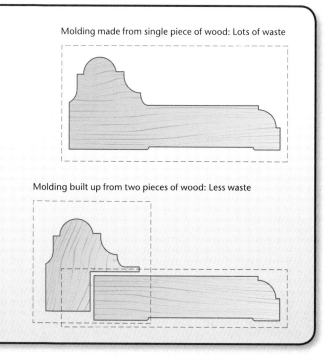

Molding made from single piece of wood: Lots of waste

Molding built up from two pieces of wood: Less waste

Lumber for Trimwork

Built-ins, wainscot, fireplace surrounds, and many other trimwork projects often call for use of solid wood, not just thin strips milled as molding. And some styles, notably Craftsman, are often created with lumber rather than molding per se.

About Softwood Lumber

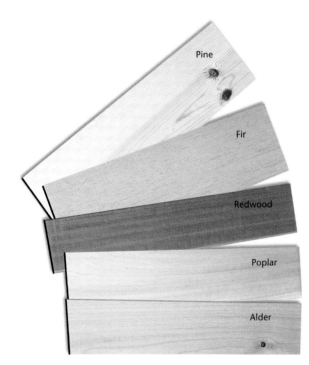

About Hardwood Lumber

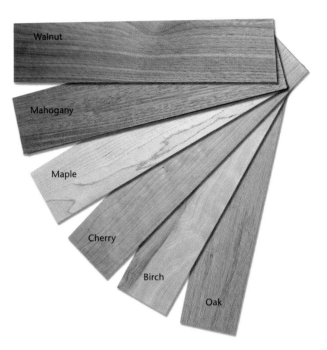

- Milled from conifer trees
- Most popular types for trimwork are pine and fir
- Smooth on all four sides
- Usually priced and sold by the linear foot at lumberyards, so you might ask for 40 linear feet of 1 by 10 boards
- Usually sold by the piece at home centers, so to get the same amount you might pick out five boards from a display of 1 by 10s that are each 8 feet long

- Milled from deciduous trees and a few broad-leaf evergreens
- Most popular types for trimwork are oak and mahogany
- May be smooth only on the front and back, but rough on edges
- Usually priced by the board foot, a volume measurement, at lumberyards, so you might ask for 4 board feet of 1-by-6 oak
- Usually priced by the piece at home centers, so to get 4 board feet, pick out an 8-foot-long 1 by 6 (which measures ¾ by 5½ inches; see sidebar on opposite page)

Design Considerations

If you want a natural finish on trimwork made from hardwood, you might choose a wood simply based on its appearance. However, there are also practical issues involved.

PAINTABILITY

Poplar is a particularly good choice for trimwork that you plan to paint. Knot-free boards are easy to find, relatively inexpensive, and easy to shape and sand because

the wood is quite soft for a hardwood. Poplar boards often have a greenish tinge that many people find unappealing, but paint covers it.

STABILITY

Maple tends to expand and contract across its width more than most other common hardwoods. If you use it, allow for this in your design. Avoid using wide boards for mitered trim, for example; choose narrow ones instead.

APPEARANCE

Birch, maple, and oak are the hardwoods most often used for the face (exterior) surfaces in hardwood plywood, as well as for iron-on veneer tape, which you can use to cover edges of plywood and particleboard. If you are planning a project that incorporates both solid and plywood pieces of these woods and you want to use a clear finish, line up all of the pieces before you buy them so you don't get stuck with unappealing contrasts and variations.

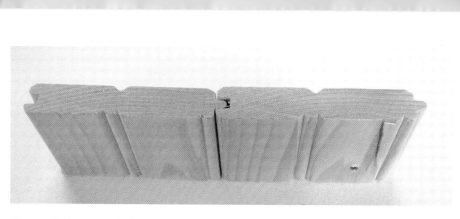

⊙ **Related Topics**

Baseboards, 122–123
Installing wainscot, 174–177
Power miter saws, 52–54
Sheet products, 48–49
Trimming a window, 102–107
Wainscot & wall paneling,
   20–21

Bead-board Options

Lumber that's been milled with interlocking edges is particularly useful for wainscot and trimwork that involves ceilings. The most popular kind is bead board, which has an ingenious design that diverts the eye from places where the individual boards expand and contract as humidity changes. Boards have a tongue on one edge and a groove along the other, plus a bead design down the middle of each board. A second bead goes along the top edge of the tongue side. On the groove side, the top edge is rounded. Installed, the bead board looks like thin boards separated by beads; any gaps disappear in the edges of the beads.

On the back, most bead board has a groove in the center and bevels along edges, so you can install that side face up for a slightly different look, if you want.

Many panel products made of plywood, MDF, and even plastic, mimic the look and are even easier to install.

The strong vertical lines in bead board disguise gaps where individual boards expand and contract.

Disappearing Wood

The measurements used to describe boards aren't their actual sizes. Rather, they refer to the size of the wood when it was freshly cut. Drying causes the boards to shrink, and more wood disappears when the rough fibers left over from sawing are shaved smooth in a planer. Labeled lengths do reflect actual board lengths, though.

The chart below lists nominal and actual sizes for softwood lumber. The same sizing applies to hardwoods if you are shopping at a home center. At a lumberyard, the nominal thickness of hardwood is usually expressed in quarters of an inch. So if you wanted a smooth, dry oak board ¾ inch thick, you'd ask for "four-four" wood, indicating it was 1 inch thick when milled. A "five-four" board was 1¼ inch thick originally but is 1 inch thick when you bring it home.

Lumber Sizes	
Sold As	*Actual Dimensions*
1 × 2	¾ × 1½
1 × 3	¾ × 2½
1 × 4	¾ × 3½
1 × 6	¾ × 5½
1 × 8	¾ × 7¼
1 × 10	¾ × 9¼
1 × 12	¾ × 11¼
2 × 2	1½ × 1½
2 × 4	1½ × 3½

Sheet Products

Plywood and particleboard offer advantages over solid wood in some trimwork projects, such as the wide, flat parts of fireplace surrounds. Sheet products come in large sizes, tend to remain flat, and usually cost less than the same amount of boards.

What You Need to Know

Depending on your project and how you are using sheet products, you may need to mask their edges with veneers, strips of solid wood, or molding. Then there's the outermost layer of the sheet itself, which, if it's plywood, has a distinct grain that runs in the long dimension of a sheet. Cut shelves and most other long pieces to follow this grain. This orientation usually looks better to the eye since it mimics the appearance of solid wood. Plus, it's the direction in which the plywood has the most strength and sag resistance, because more of its layers run that way. Particleboard, medium-density fiberboard (MDF), and hardboard don't have a grain, so you can cut pieces however you like in order to minimize waste.

Particleboard

- Made from slivers of wood bonded together with resin
- Suitable only for interior projects that don't get damp
- In trimwork, usually found only in built-ins or as a base for built-up moldings
- Weaker and more sag-prone than plywood
- Has a rougher consistency than MDF
- Edges crumble too much to be shaped with a router

Softwood Plywood

- Made from thin layers of pine or fir bonded together so the grain direction alternates
- Sold mostly for construction of buildings, but also useful for trimwork, especially built-ins
- Types are described by letters that primarily indicate the quality of the outside veneers
- A/B has an A-quality veneer, which is smooth and paintable, on one side, and a B-quality veneer, with patches, on the other
- CDX has C and D faces, which have larger knots and splits
- An X signals that the resin is waterproof, so the plywood is suitable for exterior use

Hardwood Plywood

- Made from thin layers of hardwood, at least on the face layers
- Except when specified as marine-grade, suitable for interior projects only
- Types vary depending on both the face layers and the core
- AA represents the highest-quality face veneer; E is the lowest
- The core is usually made of layers of hardwood veneer; the more layers, the flatter the sheet
- Particleboard and MDF cores help sheets stay even flatter but add weight; a ¾-inch-thick sheet with an MDF core weighs about 100 pounds, vs. 60 to 70 pounds for a veneer-core sheet

Medium-density Fiberboard

- Usually called MDF
- Except for special waterproof material, suitable only for interior projects that don't get damp
- Made from wood that has been broken down into individual fibers, plus resin
- Sheet materials are denser than standard particleboard, so they weigh more and dull tools faster
- More homogeneous as well, so paint sticks better and you can shape the edges with a router
- Very dusty when cut with a saw or sanded, so wear a respirator

Melamine

- A shorthand term for melamine-coated particleboard, referring to the plastic coating applied at the factory
- Popular for shelves and cabinet boxes
- Sold in sheets as well as pieces precut to shelving widths; sometimes predrilled for shelf-support pins
- The coating resists stains but isn't waterproof or durable enough for countertops

Tempered Hardboard

- A high-density type of particleboard made from highly compressed wood fibers
- Commonly available in two thicknesses, 1/8 and 1/4 inch
- Often used for bookcase and cabinet backs and for drawer bottoms; also makes a superb base for blackboard paint on doors, cabinet sides, or other elements of built-ins

Final Flourishes

Carved and pressed moldings and add-on trim are the jewelry of trimwork. Like pearls or costume jewelry with a black dress, they have the ability to transform flat trim into something elegant or folksy, depending on how they're used. A few guidelines:

Pick a style Ornate trim goes best with Victorian, Federal, or other classical styles that celebrated ornamentation. Simple details—a few carved stars, perhaps—work in country settings. But Craftsman-era styling was all about avoiding excessive decoration, so elaborate trim would look out of place with it.

Go for groups Thin pieces of elaborate trim look best in combination with simpler moldings. Alone, the narrow pieces don't have enough heft to make much impact, so they wind up looking like you wanted ornate trim but could splurge on only a bit of it.

Favor eye level If you want to add only a little ornate trim, consider using it close to eye level, where it will be most appreciated. A fireplace surround makes a great display place.

Simple bead molding and flat areas heighten the effect of narrow bands of egg-and-dart molding in this classical woodwork.

Getting It Done

In this chapter, we show you how to safely handle the essential power tools you will need to complete your trimwork project like a pro. The most useful of these is a power miter saw, which makes short work of complicated bevel cuts. Jigsaws, coping saws, and table saws are also covered, as are nail guns and a variety of levels and clamps. Finally, we help you set up an efficient work site.

Chapter Contents

Power Miter Saws
page 52

Making Curved Cuts
page 56

Circular Saws
page 58

Table Saws
page 60

Hammers & Nails
page 62

Other Tools You'll Need
page 64

Setting Up Shop
page 66

Power Miter Saws

Although generations of carpenters cut perfect trimwork joints with hand saws, pros today almost always use power miter saws. For novices, they're even more important, not because of the speed issue but because they go a long way toward ensuring great results.

What You Need to Know

For woodworkers who are new to power miter saws, there's definitely a learning curve, but it's shorter than the time it would take to learn how to make precision cuts by hand. Consider renting this tool if you don't own or want to invest in one.

As long as you follow a few basic safety rules, a power miter saw is relatively safe to use.

- Always wear safety glasses when operating the saw. If you are cutting more than a couple pieces, you also need ear protectors and a face mask
- Keep your hands well back from the blade at all times
- Press the work to the fence when you cut; don't cut freehand
- Don't let anyone stand behind the right side of the saw, where short cutoffs might fly out
- As you complete a cut, release the trigger, wait for the blade to stop, and then raise the saw to its upright position. Continue to hold the stock until the saw shuts off

Miter Saw Basics

- There are four types: standard, compound, sliding compound, and dual compound
- Depending on the model, blade diameter ranges from 8½ inches to 15 inches
- Use for crosswise or angled cuts on pieces up to about a foot wide
- Lock in any angle from 0 to 45 degrees, or a little more, right or left
- Leaves a smooth cut on the top surface
- Use a fine-tooth blade for solid wood or plywood and a carbide-tipped combination blade for MDF

How to Use a Miter Saw

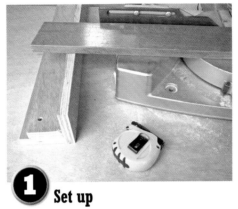

❶ Set up

- Adjust the saw's base to the angle or approximate angle you want to cut
- Set the molding or other trim on the saw's base
- If the piece is long, support the part that overhangs the saw's base (for details, see page 66)

❸ Make the cut

- Keep pressing the trim against the base and fence as you switch on the saw with your other hand
- Lower the spinning blade into the wood and make the cut
- Continue to hold the piece in position as you release the trigger and wait for the blade to stop
- Don't raise the blade until it has stopped, especially if the cutoff is short (so it doesn't get caught on the blade and fly across the room)

❷ Line up the blade

- Move the trim so the blade is just to the waste side of the cutoff mark
- Press the part you are cutting against the table and fence, usually with your left hand, left of the blade
- Without turning on the saw, lower the saw with your other hand so the blade's teeth touch the wood
- Check that the teeth are just to the waste side of the mark or cutoff line

A miter saw is often called a chopsaw because even a standard model, the simplest type, cuts straight down. It also pivots on a base to make angled cuts when the trim is standing up. A compound miter saw, pictured here, also tilts to one side, so you can make beveled cuts when trim is flat on the table. This saw also makes the beveled miter cuts you need for crown molding.

Related Topics

Baseboards, 122–127
Crown molding, 132–139
Mitered trim, 94–99, 112–113
Returned miters, 114–115

Beyond-the-basics Tips

Take the time to focus on some of the finer points of using a miter saw and it will reward you with accurate, splinter-free cuts.

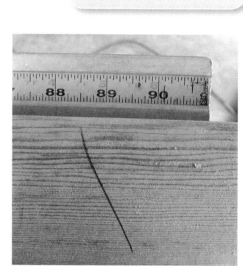

MAKE LONGER CUTS

- This trick lets you to cut trim pieces a little wider than your saw's capacity
- Place a scrap board on the saw table
- Set a trim piece on that
- Make the cut as usual
- Because the saw blade is circular, lifting the trim allows more of the blade to cut into it

MARKING A MITER CUT

- Unless you're trying to cut an odd angle that you've drawn, there's no need to mark the full miter line
- Just mark one tip of the cut; the short side works best because you can lower the blade to check where it will cut
- The long tip is too far back for the blade's teeth to touch
- The saw's setting will complete the angle for you

GUARD AGAINST MISTAKES

- If you're using symmetrical trim, such as this handrail, sketch a quick diagonal line showing how the angle tilts
- This guards against accidentally cutting the angle pointed the wrong way
- Put the sketch mark on the waste side of the cut mark

Using a Sliding Compound Miter Saw

A sliding compound miter saw makes beveled miter cuts, too, but they can be longer because the saw slides on rails. A dual compound miter saw works similarly, except that the saw tilts both ways, which eliminates mental gymnastics. With this saw, you can cut every angle with the trim positioned as it will be once it is installed.

For narrow trim, you can either lock the saw in position and cut straight down, in the standard way, or you can cut it with the saw moving toward the fence, as you would a wide piece of trim. For this, set up in the standard way, then, with the saw switched off and the blade raised, pull the saw toward you with the hand that isn't holding the trim against the fence. Switch on the saw, lower the blade all the way, and push the saw back to its starting point; continue to hold the trim

against the fence until you release the trigger and the blade stops. If you are familiar with using a radial-arm saw, note that this procedure is opposite to how you use that tool.

Shopping Tip

Every additional feature usually adds to the price and weight of a saw. For most projects, a 12-inch compound miter saw is a wise choice. It cuts trim up to 8 inches wide and is versatile enough for other projects around the house, such as building a deck with 4-by-6 supports. And it has fewer moving parts to get out of adjustment than more complex models.

Making Bevel Cuts

Standard miter saws make bevel cuts only one way: straight down, with the saw set at an angle to the fence. With other types of miter saws, you have a choice. You can cut a bevel straight down or place the trim flat on the saw's table and angle the saw.

1 **Cut bevels upright**

- Whenever possible, stand baseboard or other trim upright and cut bevels straight down
- This is usually more accurate than cutting a bevel with the trim flat on the saw's table, but you're limited to the height available under the saw
- Press trim against the fence as you cut

2 **Or tilt the saw**

- If the trim is too tall to cut upright, tilt the saw (not an option with a standard miter saw)
- Instead of relying on the angle gauge on the saw, use a bevel gauge
- Adjust the gauge to the slanted surface where the trim will go and transfer the angle directly (see steps on page 64)
- Or adjust the gauge to a set angle (see tip on page 77)

3 **Stretch the angle**

- To cut a sharper bevel than your saw is designed to cut when trim is flat, experiment first on a test piece
- Slip one or more shims under the test trim, away from the blade
- Press down and back on the piece to hold it to the fence and the table near the blade
- Make the cut and check it
- If the angle isn't right, move the shims closer or farther from the blade, or increase the height
- When the angle is correct, make the cut
- Be especially careful to keep holding the piece until the blade stops

Hand Saws

For small projects, or if you want to perfect your hand-woodworking skills, you can use nonmotorized tools. Hand tools require practice to master, so make test cuts on scrap material before you tackle your first project.

Backsaw

- Use to make straight or angled cuts with a miter box or block
- Has a hardened rib at the top to keep the blade from flexing
- Usually has Western-style teeth, which cut as you push

Frame-maker's Miter Saw

- Consists of a suspended saw built into a precision miter box
- Adjusts to a variety of angles
- Makes extremely accurate, smooth cuts
- Relatively expensive

Make Micro Adjustments

If the angle you cut is just a tad off, it's sometimes difficult to adjust the saw's angle to the exact setting you want, especially if it is close to one of the preset stops, such as 45 degrees.

1 Shim near the blade

- Instead of adjusting the gauge, slip thin shims between the trim and the fence
- Old playing cards or sample pieces of countertop laminate make great shims
- Place shims near the blade if you are trying to shave a little off the long tip of a miter to close a gap at the short side of that miter

2 Or shim farther back

- Place the wedges farther back along the fence if you are trying to remove a little from the short end of a miter
- This closes a gap at the long side of that miter

Miter Box

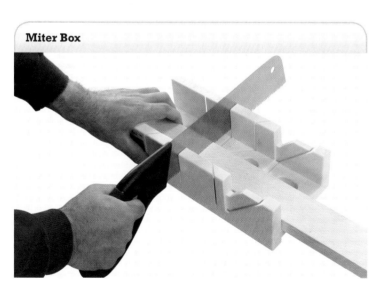

- Use with a fine-tooth saw to make straight or angled cuts
- Usually set for two angles: 90 and 45 degrees; shim between the side of the box and the trim to cut slightly different angles
- Slots guide the blade as you cut
- Hold trim to the front if the saw has Japanese-style teeth, which cut as you pull (as shown)
- Hold trim to the back if the saw cuts as you push
- Clamp the box to a workbench before you cut

Small Crosscut Saw

- Use to cut trim to rough lengths
- Also useful for cutting stock that's too thick or wide to cut in a miter box
- Can be used with a miter box, but isn't the best tool because the blade flexes
- The short length makes the saw easier to handle
- Short saws also tend to have smaller teeth, for smoother (but slower) cuts

Making Curved Cuts

Although most trimwork requires straight cuts, you need to know how to cut curves, too, if you want to cope molding at inside corners. You may also need curved cuts to make brackets or to scribe trim to follow the uneven contour of a wall.

Coping Saw

Used mostly to make coped joints at inside corners, a coping saw is also a good tool for other curved shapes, such as brackets.

HOW TO USE

- Orient saw so blade is vertical as you cut
- For a splinter-free cut, attach blade so teeth point toward the handle
- Teeth will cut as you pull down
- Designs vary, but turning the handle usually loosens or tightens tension on the blade
- Replace blades frequently

Jigsaw

Think of a jigsaw as the power equivalent of a coping saw. Designed for cutting curves, it can also make straight cuts. High-quality models offer adjustments that inexpensive saws often lack, such as a base plate that tilts so you can make bevel cuts or a blower to clear away sawdust (switch it off if you are cutting metal). Other useful features include adjustable blade speed and orbital action, or sideways motion. A saw with no sideways motion cuts a finer line, but a wider path results in a faster cut.

Using Sandpaper Efficiently

Sandpaper is another a great nibbling tool when you need to fine-tune a curved shape. Here's how to get the most out of a sheet of sandpaper.

1 **Fold and tear**

- Bring the short edges together and crease the sheet in half
- Place the fold over a sharp edge and tear off half
- Fold each half-piece in half again and tear apart
- You should wind up with four equal-size pieces

2 **Or make a jig**

- On a plywood scrap about 15 by 10 inches, draw two lines parallel to the scrap's long edge: one 5½ inches away, the other 1 inch away
- Draw a perpendicular line about 2 inches down from the top
- Loosely screw on a hacksaw blade so its teeth touch the 5½ inch line and its smooth side faces the edge you measured from; place the top screw about ½ inch above the perpendicular line

Related Topics

Building a bracket shelf, 146–147
Coping baseboard corners, 124–125
Installing crown molding, 134–135

HOW TO USE

- Orient the piece so you won't accidentally cut your work surface or saw through the cord
- Turn on the saw with its base planted on the piece
- Keep the blade's teeth away from the wood until the motor is running so the saw doesn't jerk
- Don't force the saw; advance it just enough so it keeps cutting steadily
- Even though a jigsaw cuts curves, don't try to cut crisp corners in one pass; make two cuts into the corner, one from each direction

Choosing Jigsaw Blades

Fit a jigsaw with a wide blade (left) for straight cuts. Use a skinny blade (right) for curved cuts. Standard blades have teeth that point up, so the top surface winds up rougher than the bottom.

For a smooth cut, mark the back and cut with that side up. If you are coping molding, you can't cut with the back side up; instead, master the technique of cutting with the saw upside down. Or use a down-cutting blade, which leaves a smooth edge on top (although it makes the saw bounce more as it cuts).

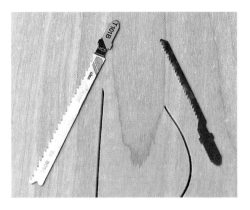

Rasps & Files

Though you can cut fairly accurate curves with a coping saw or a jigsaw, you'll still need to smooth or adjust the shapes with tools that take smaller bites.

FOUR-IN-HAND

- One side has curved and flat rasps
- The other has flat and curved double-cut files
- The rasps cut wood; the files are for metal

RATTAIL

- This rasp is skinny and round
- Use it to carve into tight curves

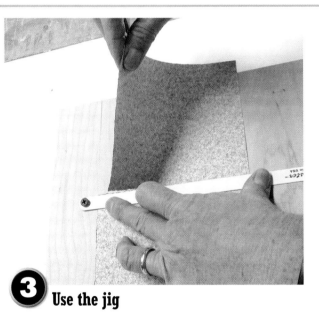

❸ Use the jig

- Slip sandpaper rough side up under the blade, with the short side against the edge and the long side along the perpendicular line
- Press down on the blade with one hand; with the other, lift up and tear off sandpaper beyond the blade
- Reorient each half-sheet to align with the lengthwise line and make the other tear

❹ Fold, tear, refold

- Fold one quarter-sheet in half one way, open, then refold the opposite way
- Open and tear along one short fold to the center
- With the back facing you, fold one small flap back onto an untorn flap, then fold the other untorn section down
- Tuck the remaining flap around to the other side, creating a stack so the grit sides don't face each other
- The final sandpaper package has enough heft so you can bend it to follow curves that need sanding
- When a sheet wears down, refold to expose a fresh one

Circular Saws

One of the most versatile power tools is a circular saw. It produces edges that are more reliably square than those cut by a jigsaw. It's also a safe option when you are cutting a big sheet of plywood into smaller pieces, perhaps to make panels for wainscot.

Safety First

There are a few safety issues to know about when using this tool, beyond the obvious advice to never put your hand in front of the blade and to always wear safety glasses. If you don't use a circular saw properly, the kerf, or blade-wide channel formed during cutting, can close up and bind the blade. Then the saw can suddenly jerk back, a situation known as kickback. Avoid problems like that with good work habits:

- Clamp pieces, especially small ones, so they don't wiggle as you cut them.
- Support thin material close to the cut line so the weight of the saw doesn't bend the wood and cause it to bind the blade.
- Let small pieces fall to the floor as you cut. Support large pieces so they don't tear off as you near the end of the cut.

- If you enlist a helper to keep cutoffs from falling, warn against lifting the material upward, which could also bind the blade.
- Check the electrical cord to be sure it can follow the saw to the end of the cut without encountering the blade or catching on the end of the sheet you are cutting.
- Adjust the blade so it cuts no more than ¼ inch deeper than the piece you are cutting.

Circular Saw Basics

There are two basic types of circular saw: worm drive (left), with the motor parallel to the blade, and sidewinder, with the motor perpendicular to the blade.

- Worm-drive saws are more powerful and give you a clearer look at the line you are cutting
- Sidewinders weigh less and have a more stable base
- Both types can be adjusted to make bevel cuts

Supporting Plywood

You should support a full sheet of plywood with four or five 2 by 4s set across two sawhorses.

- If you are cutting lengthwise, place one 2 by 4 under each side of the line where you will cut
- Use the others to support the rest of the panel
- Guide the saw against a straight-edge as shown
- If you are cutting crosswise, evenly space the 2 by 4s; keep them lengthwise
- As you cut, the blade will cut into the supports slightly, but they will still be plenty strong and can be reused as supports many times

Splinter-free Cuts

Circular saws leave a rough edge on the top, especially when cutting across wood grain. For a smooth surface, make crosscuts from the back, or use the following procedure.

① Score with knife

- Secure a straightedge along the line you want to cut
- Clamp it over the part you want to cut, not the waste part
- Incise the line with a sharp utility knife

② Make the cut

- If your straightedge is like the one on the opposite page, leave it where it is and make the cut
- If it does not have a factory edge to guide the saw's base, move it so the blade will cut just to the waste side of the scored line
- Use a fine-tooth saw blade for plywood and a carbide-tip combination blade for MDF

Cordless Circular Saws

A cordless circular saw can be a real time saver when you're cutting trim. It cuts as straight as a plug-in but doesn't tether you to a cord, so you can easily cart it from room to room as you work. The saws come in different sizes, with blades that range from 5⅜ inch to 7¼ inch, the standard size for plug-in circular saws. The smallest size is most useful for trimwork. The capacity is adequate for most molding, and it weighs considerably less than larger saws (around 5.7 pounds vs. almost 10 pounds for the largest model).

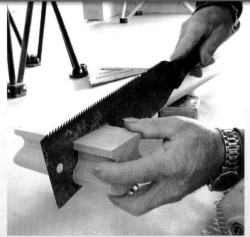

A small cordless saw is lightweight and easy to maneuver, so it makes accurate cuts even on trimwork where the base plate doesn't make much contact.

If a piece is too thick for the saw's blade, finish the cut with a handsaw. The kerf left by the circular saw guides the handsaw blade, just like the slot in a miter box does.

Making a Straightedge

This simple jig guides your circular saw along a straight line and automatically shows the offset needed for the saw's base plate, which saves lots of measuring.

❶ Make the guide strip

- With a carpenter's chalk line, mark a 3-inch-wide strip along a straight factory edge of the plywood
- With a circular saw, cut freehand along this line; it's okay if your saw wavers slightly
- Measure the distance between the edge of the saw's base (on the motor side) and the far side of the blade
- Add ½ inch more and snap a second line on the plywood
- Place the 3-inch strip you cut on the far side of the second line, with the factory edge facing the line
- Screw the strip in place

❷ Trim the edge

- Guiding the saw's base along the factory edge, trim the plywood
- This automatically trims the jig to reproduce the exact offset between the base plate and the inside of the blade

❸ Separate the jig

- Guiding the saw along the far side of the raised strip, separate the jig from the sheet of plywood
- To use the jig, clamp it to the part you want to use, not the waste section
- Align the guide so the cut you made in Step 2 just touches the line you want to keep
- Keep the saw's base against the factory edge as you cut

Table Saws

A table saw is good for ripping lumber and sheet material lengthwise, and it also makes precise crosscuts, especially on wide material like plywood. In trimwork, you can use it to rip boards down to size for jambs or other flat trim.

Safety First

A table saw is a powerful woodworking tool, so you must know what you are doing. To produce a clean cut on the top surface, the blade rotates toward you, pressing the wood against the table. This leaves the back of the blade rotating upward—the perfect position to send wood shooting toward you at lightning speed if it binds against the spinning blade. Safety rules are designed to prevent this.

- Never cut freehand: Use the rip fence to keep stock parallel to the blade or the miter gauge for perpendicular or angle cuts, but never use both at the same time
- Stand to the side, not behind the blade, when you operate the saw. If you are using the rip fence, you and it usually should be on opposite sides of the blade. If you are using the miter gauge, position yourself so you are on one side of the gauge and the blade is on the other
- If a board is bowed, do not attempt to rip a straight edge on it. Instead, attach a straightedge to it and guide that against the rip fence or the table edge
- Avoid crosscutting long boards. Use a handsaw, a jigsaw, a circular saw, or a miter saw instead
- On narrow rip cuts, replace the standard throat plate with a zero-clearance insert, which eliminates the usual gap alongside the blade. A wide opening could allow the strip you are cutting to drop down and catch against the blade
- Avoid wearing gloves or loose sleeves that could become caught and draw your hand into the blade. If you have long hair, tie it back. Wear safety goggles and ear protectors, plus a mask if you don't have a dust-collection system

Table Saw Basics

There are two basic types of table saws: stationary and portable. A stationary model (shown) can still be moved within a room if it's on a base with lockable casters. Lightweight saws usually run on standard 120-volt circuits, but more powerful models may require 240-volt circuits.

Making Angled Cuts

- Set the miter gauge to the desired angle
- If you are making a bevel cut, as shown, adjust the blade to the appropriate angle
- For added safety and accuracy, create a larger bearing surface by screwing a piece of wood to the front of the gauge, as was done here
- Set the trim piece on the saw and press the wood to the front of the gauge
- With the motor off, move the wood up to the blade; the blade should be just on the waste side of your cutting mark
- Keep both parts aligned as you back them away from the blade
- With your other hand, switch on the saw
- Move that hand to the gauge to help keep it and the wood pressed together as you make the cut; continue gripping the wood and gauge until the stock completely clears the blade
- Do not move the cut-off piece (waste) until the blade stops

Making Crosscuts

Improve safety and accuracy by replacing a standard miter gauge with a crosscut sled.

- Attach front and back uprights to a plywood or MDF base
- On the base's back, glue and screw hardwood runners sized to slide snugly in the saw's miter gauge slots
- Place the runners so they keep the front upright perfectly perpendicular to the blade; the jig's accuracy depends on this
- Mark where the saw blade will exit the sled so you don't accidentally put your hand there; consider attaching a scrap block there as a reminder
- Run the sled through the saw
- The kerf, or opening cut by the blade, shows precisely where to align stock for subsequent cuts

What's a Featherboard?

When you are making rip cuts in thin stock, keep the piece firmly pressed against the rip fence with a featherboard—a guide piece with a series of cuts that resemble the vanes of a feather. Besides helping to ensure a straight cut, a featherboard helps prevent kickback. You can buy one or make your own.

1 Making a featherboard

- Get a piece of ¾-inch-thick plywood or straight-grained wood that's about 18 inches long and wide enough so you can clamp it and have a 5-inch-wide feather strip against the stock
- Cut a 40-degree angle along that 5-inch strip
- Draw a line at the same angle about 4 inches in from the end
- Using a table saw's rip fence as a guide, make a series of cuts up to the line so that you leave wooden fingers about ¼ inch wide, separated by gaps about ⅛ inch wide.
- Keep the long edge against the fence as you cut; putting the short side there isn't safe

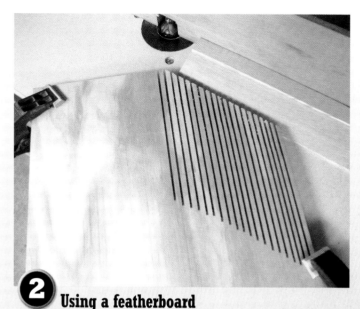

2 Using a featherboard

- Clamp the featherboard to the table so the tips press against the stock but still allow you to move the board forward without forcing it
- If your saw's table has ribs underneath, slip a piece of wood between them so you have a solid surface to clamp against
- If you will be cutting through the stock, the featherboard must be completely in front of the blade
- If you are cutting a groove, the feathers can apply pressure where the blade begins to cut, but they cannot touch the stock beyond the first half of the blade, or there could be kickback

Making Lengthwise Cuts & Grooves

- Set the fence to the width you want; measure from the inside edge of the blade
- If the blade is close to the rip fence, attach an auxiliary wooden fence to the metal one, as shown above
- Raise the blade so it's half a tooth higher than the piece you are cutting; for a groove, as shown here, adjust the dado set to the right height
- If you are cutting a narrow strip, get a push stick that fits between the blade and fence

- After you turn on the saw, move the piece past the blade while you also keep the wood pressed against the fence; if you are cutting all the way through, hold onto the piece between the fence and the blade (use a push stick if the piece is narrow until it clears the blade)
- Hold onto the piece between the blade and the fence until it clears the blade
- Let the cut piece on the other side of the blade fall away naturally

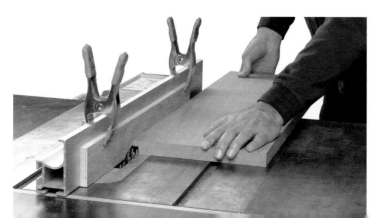

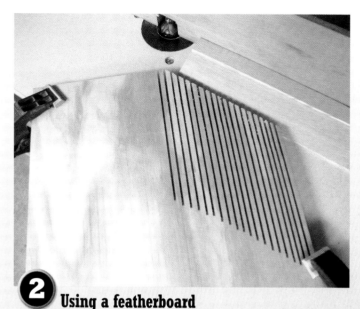

A dado set allows a table saw to cut grooves, rabbets, dadoes, and tenons for strong joints.

Hammers & Nails

Fastening choices for trimwork are a study in contrasts. Some people prefer a trusty claw hammer and a handful of nails. Others go for an arsenal of nail guns accompanied by orderly stacks of nails and brads.

Using Nail Guns

With a nail gun (also called a power nailer), you can secure trim quickly, in one step, and you don't risk knocking parts out of alignment. Pros often have several nail guns since different models are designed to drive different-size nails, staples, or even headless pins that leave miniscule holes that don't need to be puttied.

As a safety measure, many power nailers don't fire until you press the tip against a surface. If the surface is slippery, the tip may move out of position and the nail might not wind up precisely where you want it. That's one reason why it makes sense to predrill and hand-hammer nails that are close to an edge, where there is little leeway for error. Using thinner, shorter power-driven nails near edges also minimizes the risk.

Because of the way nail-gun tips are designed, it's sometimes hard to see exactly where a nail will exit. Drive test nails in a scrap piece first to get a sense of where your gun will shoot its nails.

Fastening by Hand

When you're installing trim, hand-hammering tricky details like mitered corners can be frustrating. You can bend a nail, split the wood, knock parts out of alignment, and dent the trim. But with a few extra steps, you can get great results every time.

① Predrill

- Drill a pilot hole where you want each nail, especially close to an edge
- Make the hole the same width as the finish nail in hardwood, a little narrower in softwood
- If you lack a small drill bit, secure a finish nail in the drill and use that

② Drive the nail

- Tap the finish nail into the hole
- Stop hammering when the head is about 1/8 inch out

③ Seat the head

- Choose a nail set matched to the size of the nail head; its tip should fit into the dimple on the nail head
- Brace your hand against the trim to help keep the nail set steady
- Hammer the nail set to drive the nail head about 1/8 inch below the surface

A Trio of Power Nailers

Different nailers excel at different tasks. The gun on the far left drove 15-gauge nails through the door casing on the side toward the corner, where the nails went through drywall and into studs. The smaller gun to its right drove 18-gauge brads into the casing edge near the jamb and into the short baseboard section, where the thicker nails might have split the trim. A pin nailer (above, right) is perfect for holding small trim parts in place while glue dries. On prefinished parts, like these, the holes are so small that you don't need to patch them.

What Nail to Use?

Whether you drive a nail with a hammer or a gun, its holding power depends on its length, thickness and head size. But the fatter a nail, the more likely it is to split the wood. Here are a few things to keep in mind:

Length matters Select a nail that allows one-half to two-thirds of its length to be in wood behind the trim piece. Whatever drywall might be there doesn't count.

Terminology Nails for hand hammering are listed by "penny" size, which used to refer to the weight of 100 nails but now refers to a set length and thickness. The smallest finishing nail is a 2-penny, also called a 2d; it's 1 inch long. The biggest, a 40d, is 5 inches long. For trimwork, nails 3d to 8d nails (1¼ to 2½ inches long) usually suffice. The higher the gauge number, the skinnier the nail.

About brads Wire brads, which look like miniature finishing nails, are great for holding return miters and other small parts while glue dries. Standard brads aren't as useful because they have larger heads.

Shopping Tip

Any given power nailer will only drive one diameter of nail, so if you only want to purchase one power nailer for your trimwork project, consider getting one that shoots 16-gauge nails. The nails are sturdy enough for any trim task, and the gun is relatively lightweight and easy to maneuver.

18-gauge Brads

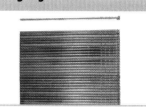

- Great for fastening wood trim to wood, such as casing resting on a jamb
- Suitable for fastening trim to walls where the trim isn't likely to be knocked loose
- Brads have heads, but they're small and easy to putty over
- Lengths available: ½ inch to 2⅛ inches

Hammer-driven Nails

- Sturdy and traditional
- Sold by the pound or in boxes
- Bright-finish nails (shown) are smooth; galvanized nails are rougher
- Shown are 3d, 4d, 6d, and 8d finishing nails, 1¼ to 2½ inches long
- At the bottom are two 20-gauge, ¾ inch-long brads
- The wire brad is the most useful kind for trim; the standard brad has a larger head

15-gauge Finish Nails

- The sturdiest option for fastening trim to studs that are behind drywall
- Nails usually come attached at an angle, which helps the big nail guns that fire this size fit into tight corners
- Nails are round in cross-section and have heads
- Shafts are scored to add gripping power
- Lengths available: 1 to 2½ inches

16-gauge Nails

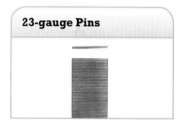

- Also suitable for fastening trim to walls
- Nail guns that fire these are smaller and lighter than the 15-gauge models
- Nails are rectangular in cross-section, which helps them hold about as well as fatter 15-gauge nails do
- Nails have heads
- Lengths available: ¾ inch to 2½ inches

23-gauge Pins

- Great for holding thin trim parts while glue dries
- Use for return miters on molding and when attaching decorative molding to plainer molding
- Not suitable for attaching trim to walls
- Available without heads or with slight heads
- Headless types leave tiny holes that disappear after one coat of paint; or leave them as is if you're using prefinished trim with a clear coat
- Lengths available: ⅜ inch to 2 inches

How the Pros Do It

"I always use galvanized nails, even inside, because bright-finish nails can rust just from the humidity of a shower or pots of water boiling on a stove. The rust eventually works through to the finish and stains it, even if you've plugged the holes."
Dewey Goodrich, Blumenthal Construction

Other Tools You'll Need

To install trim, you'll use many of the same tools that you turn to for basic tasks around the house. But if you're shopping for new tools with trimwork in mind, consider some of these special tools to help improve accuracy and make your job easier.

Choosing a Square

Framing squares, which have arms up to 2 feet long, are great when you're framing a roof or walls. But for trimwork, you're usually better off with a combination square, an angle square, or both. A sliding bevel comes in handy, too.

COMBINATION SQUARE
- Depending on orientation, marks and tests 90- or 45-degree angles
- Has a built-in spirit level so you can mark level and plumb lines (a right angle from a level line is automatically plumb)
- Blade adjusts and can be removed to use as a flat ruler
- Ruler increments start at the end of the blade; if there is more than one scale, you can install the ruler so the most useful scale is handiest
- Use the adjustable feature when you are marking or testing corners
- Also use it to establish reveals (see pages 82–83) or to mark a set distance from the edge of numerous boards

ANGLE SQUARE
- Compact and sturdy; nothing to adjust or get knocked out of alignment
- Marks and tests 90- and 45-degree angles
- Great for checking inside and outside corners
- Ruler increments read from the inside edge of the shoulder
- Numbers along diagonal lines help mark rafters; ignore these for trimwork
- Some models have a notch at the 3½-inch mark; it guides a pencil as you slide the square along a board to mark the width of a 2-by-4

SLIDING T-BEVEL
- Allows you to copy angles that aren't just 90 or 45 degrees
- Just loosen the nut, move the blade to the angle you want to match, and retighten the nut
- No need to calculate degrees in the angle; just transfer the angle directly

Transferring an Angle to a Miter Saw

A sliding bevel can be used to transfer angles directly to a piece of wood you need to cut or to a power saw that will make the cut.

For an angled crosswise cut
- Set the bevel's handle against the saw's fence
- Adjust the mechanism that turns the saw so its blade looks parallel with the bevel's blade
- With the saw off, lower the saw so you can check that the two blades are parallel
- Gauge by either the outside edges of the teeth or the flat part of the blade, not some of each

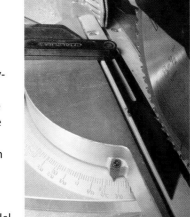

For a beveled crosswise cut
- This procedure works only with a miter saw that makes compound cuts, not a standard miter saw
- Set the bevel's handle against the saw's base
- Adjust the tilt mechanism until the saw blade is parallel to the bevel's blade
- Make sure the bevel blade is against the main part of the saw's blade, not a tooth
- When the saw angle matches, the line of light between the two blades should disappear or be evenly thin

Leveling & Plumbing Tools

A variety of simple, time-tested tools can help you install trimwork that's horizontally level and vertically plumb.

SPIRIT LEVEL

- The actual working parts are the vials, each with a bubble of air floating in liquid
- The housing around the vials allows you to check much longer distances—provided the vials are adjusted properly
- To check, set the level on a surface and note the reading, then turn the level end-over-end and side-over-side and take new readings each time
- All of the readings should be the same
- If not, adjust the vial if it has a screw-out case, or get a new level
- It helps to have levels in several lengths (see page 75)

PLUMB BOB

- This ancient tool is basically just a string with a pointed weight at one end
- Use it to locate a point on the floor directly under a point on the ceiling, such as the center of a column
- Also use it to mark a vertical line on a tall wall or to check whether a door jamb bows in or out

CHALK LINE

- Use it to mark straight lines on walls, ceilings, or floors
- Also helpful when marking large sheets of plywood
- For more tips, see page 74

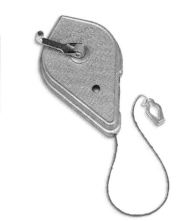

Helping-hand Tools

C clamp

Bar clamp

Spring clamp

HAMMERS

- 12- or 16-ounce models are plenty heavy for trimwork; this is not framing
- Lighter hammers are usually easier to control
- For trimwork, curved claws are better than straight ones; the curve helps pull nails when you make a mistake
- The face should be smooth, not waffled; this minimizes damage to trim if you miss the nail

CLAMPS

- Use them to hold material when you cut, shape, nail, or glue
- Choose clamps with rubber pads that prevent denting trim, or slip a small wood scrap between the clamp and trim
- Clamp types vary by how easy they are to install and remove, and how wide they open
- For quick, one-hand installation, use spring clamps if they open wide enough
- Bar clamps are almost as quick to install and open much wider, but they sometimes come loose because of vibrations from power tools
- C clamps are more time-consuming to attach and loosen, but they grip securely

CAT'S PAW

- Also called a pry bar
- Use to remove trim so that you can reuse or reposition it
- The best type for trimwork has a thin, flat blade at one end
- At the other end, the curved claws are sharp enough to reach under and pull out nail heads
- For more tips, see page 85

Setting Up Shop

If your trimwork project is part of a major renovation, set up your tools in the room where you are working. For a small job in a furnished room, it makes more sense to minimize mess there and do the sawing and sanding on a nearby deck or in the garage.

A Place for Your Saw

If you are cutting trim by hand, you need to clamp the miter box to a sturdy counter-top or workbench that's at a convenient height. More likely, though, you'll be cutting most pieces with a miter saw. You can put it on the floor or a nearby deck if you are cutting just a few pieces. But for larger jobs, raise the saw on a stand. Purchase a ready-made model or make an inexpensive, lightweight one from a hollow-core door plus a few plywood scraps.

① Set up

- Place a 24-inch-wide hollow-core door on two sawhorses that are relatively close together
- Set the saw on the door between the sawhorses; keep it close to the door's front edge to minimize sagging

② Make L brackets

- Measure the height from the door to the top of the saw's table
- Rip four 24-inch-long pieces of plywood to that width; also make two strips that are narrower by the thickness of the plywood
- For each bracket, screw two wider pieces together to form an L when viewed from the end; counterbore first so the screw heads seat completely
- Screw one narrower strip to the inside face of the taller side of each bracket

③ Use as a support

- When you're cutting to a mark or measuring, set brackets with the thick side down
- Move as needed to support long trim so it stays flat on the table near the blade
- Also support trim on the waste side so the cutoff doesn't drop at an angle and catch on the blade

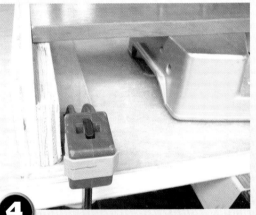

④ Make multiples quickly

- When you need to cut several pieces to the same length, tip one bracket so the thick side points up and the bottom of the L faces the saw
- Move the bracket so trim resting on it is the appropriate distance from the saw when the end of the trim presses against the tallest part of the L
- Clamp the bracket there; also clamp or screw the saw in place so vibrations don't throw off your measurement
- No need to measure for each piece—simply butt it against the stop and cut

---

How the Pros Do It

"I resisted wearing safety glasses for years because they always seemed to get scratched up. But my pre-scription glasses kept getting scratches. Now I buy the kind of safety glasses that fit over other glasses. I buy them by the box, so they don't cost very much, and I put on a new pair as soon as I see the first scratch. I see so clearly that I completely forget they're there. And my $500 glasses don't get a scratch."

John Backland, Carley Construction

Work-smart Tips

To mark and fit pieces precisely, you need to be able see your work in detail. Avoid shadows by using a light you can easily reposition; clip-on lights or ones on a stand work well. Halogen bulbs (shown here) allow details to show crisply. Compact fluorescent bulbs make details look a little less crisp, but the bulbs are cooler and therefore safer, and they use less energy.

Here are a few other work-smart tips:

EXTEND YOUR VIEW

- Put yourself at eye level when marking trim; viewing work at an angle leads to errors
- Have a low stepstool handy, as well as a ladder

PROVIDE TEMPORARY SUPPORTS

- Two sawhorses provide a little extra workspace for tasks such as sanding
- Types that fold flat can be stored when not in use

Creating an Efficient, Safe Workspace

1 Think about workflow

- Consider how you will move trim from your storage area to your saw
- Try to set up tools so trim goes past all machines in the same direction, as this pro crew did with its table saw, jointer (the machine just behind the table saw), and miter saw
- Because the trim always moves parallel to the wall on the right, boards are stored in the same direction, against the wall that's just out of sight on the left
- If the room has good natural light, orient tools to take advantage of it
- Give your miter saw the prime spot, since you'll use it most for trimwork
- Add a dust collection system, if possible; the hoses here connect to a shop vac

2 Store trim flat

- To keep trim from warping, store it horizontally, not propped against a wall
- Don't set piles directly on a concrete floor; moisture might wick up
- Place the trim on wooden blocks; consider adding stickers (thin strips) between layers to boost air circulation
- Use enough blocks and stickers so trim doesn't sag
- Keep trim at indoor temperatures and humidity for several days before you install it
- Don't install damp wood or MDF trim; it will shrink as it dries, causing your tight joints to open up

3 Manage the scraps

- Make a habit of storing scraps where you won't stumble on them
- One quick solution: kick them under the miter saw table
- Periodically pick up the scraps and sort them
- Keep unfinished, natural wood separate to burn in a fireplace or recycle into mulch

3

Ten Rules of the Trim Carpenter

In this chapter, we share 10 of the most common practices of professional woodworkers. These include knowing when to use a tape measure vs. when to simply mark up a template; ensuring that a project is level and plumb; transferring angles accurately; using shims to get tight fits; staying within one's skill zone; working in a way that makes it easy to correct mistakes; and even knowing when it's best to settle for cosmetic fixes.

Chapter Contents

**Rule 1:
Mind Your Measurements**
page 70

**Rule 2:
Minimize Math**
page 72

**Rule 3:
Make It Straight, Level, Plumb**
page 74

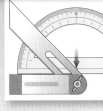

**Rule 4:
Check Every Angle**
page 76

**Rule 5:
Make It Fit**
page 78

**Rule 6:
Use Back Bevels**
page 80

Rule 7:
Know Your
Skills
page 81

Rule 8:
Use Reveals
page 82

Rule 9:
Give Yourself a
Second Chance
page 84

Rule 10:
Know When
to Fudge
page 86

Rule 1: Mind Your Measurements

Some trim carpenters measure everything; others take readings directly whenever possible (see Rule 2, pages 72–73). Even if you're in the second camp, you'll still need to use a ruler sometimes.

Finer Points of Using a Tape Measure

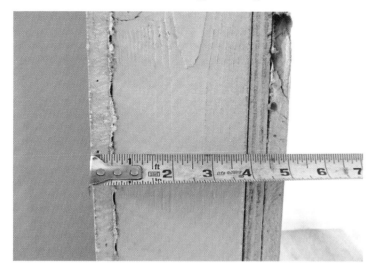

Taking an outside measurement

- Hook the tape over an edge and pull the tape toward you
- This causes the tip to extend so you can easily take the reading
- Calibrations begin on the tape itself and don't include the tab's thickness

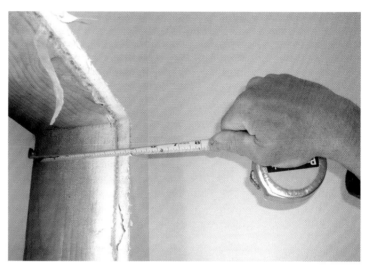

Taking an inside measurement

- To measure a point that's boxed in, push against the end of the tape as you take the reading
- This causes the tab at the end to slide in, so your measurement doesn't include its thickness (usually 1/16 inch)

Measuring in the middle

- Line up your beginning point with an inch mark (2 in this example)
- Measure over from there
- Subtract the first number from the second; the result is the length you are measuring
- Often called "burning an inch," because carpenters frequently begin at the 1-inch mark

How the Pros Do It

"When I have a lot of simple cuts to make, such as when I am making blanks for window trim, I save steps by doing all the measuring first. I write down exact lengths for the head and jamb pieces but allow extra length for sills (stools). I take my list with me to the saw, and cut everything in one trip."

Billy Lounsbury,
Lounsbury Carpentry

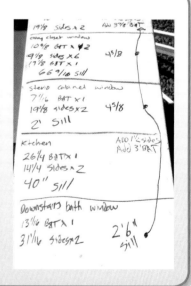

Measuring & Marking Tips

Use the long ends

- Measure mitered pieces from long tip to long tip whenever possible
- This allows you to hook the tab over the end, making the measurement easy
- See page 97 for tips on measuring along the short side

Touch-and-read

- Note how the tape curves across its width to keep it rigid
- But the curvature leaves a gap between the tape and whatever you are measuring
- For an accurate reading, tip the tape so an edge touches the work's surface

Use the edge

- It's not the best straightedge, but it works in a pinch
- Tip the tape so the edge is close to the surface as you draw the line

Marking a midpoint

- Measure down from the end and draw a horizontal line at the distance you want
- Measure crosswise and divide the reading in half
- To divide fractions, just double the bottom number (half of 3/8 is 3/16, for example)
- Draw a vertical line; the X marks the spot

How to Measure a Long Wall

If you are designing wainscot or built-ins, you may need to measure multiple elements on a wall. If you measure three features individually and are off just 1/8 inch each time, you could think that the last feature is nearly half an inch too wide or too skinny. But if you follow the approach shown here and make the same mistakes, you'll always be within 1/8 inch of the correct distance.

❶ Establish a reference point

- Use a carpenter's level to determine whether your starting point, such as a wall or door trim, is plumb
- If the feature slants, make a vertical mark that is plumb
- Measure up at a convenient distance and make a mark

❷ Take first measurement

- From the reference point, measure over to the next significant feature
- Here, that's the outside edge of the window casing
- Note this dimension on a piece of paper

❸ Find the next point

- Measure over from the initial starting point to the next significant feature
- Here, that's the far side of the window casing
- Use the same starting point for each measurement along that wall

Rule 2: Minimize Math

It's easy to waste time or make mistakes if you rely solely on a ruler for keeping track of trim lengths. All those little lines for $1/16$ and $1/32$ of an inch tend to blur after a while, so you wind up re-measuring—or wishing you had. Luckily, there are easier ways.

Mark Parts Directly

Instead of measuring, you can hold stock in position and mark it to show where you need to cut or drill.

Mark a miter in place

- Use this technique for outside miters on base-boards or crowns
- Hold trim piece in position
- Trace against the wall onto the back of the trim
- The line represents the short point of the miter
- See page 126 for ways to deal with corners that aren't square or walls that aren't plumb

Use hardware as a template

- Hold hardware, such as a sliding door rail, in place
- Mark the center point of each fastener
- Do not trace the perimeter of each hole
- Drill pilot holes with or without the hardware in position, whichever is easier

The Advantages of Templates

If one end of a long piece of trim needs to fit in a recessed area and you can't mark it directly, make a short template.

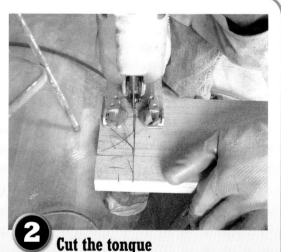

1 Mark the template

- For the tongue on this pocket door jamb (see pages 200–205), draw short vertical lines at both sides of the opening
- Then turn the scrap sideways, insert it in the opening, and mark the tongue depth

2 Cut the tongue

- Make an X to show what you want to save (or cut away—just be consistent)
- Using a jigsaw or a handsaw to cut out each shoulder in two passes, one vertical, one sideways
- Test the fit, then use the template to mark the actual trim piece

How to Use a Story Pole

A story pole is a strip of wood that shows the widths or heights of all the features in a straight line. You can use it to transfer dimensions from a plan to a wall, or to a part you need to cut.

1 A vertical story pole

- Mark the height of fixed features such as a window frame
- Mark the height of trim details in the position you will install them
- Include any reveals (see pages 82–83)
- Label the parts on the pole

2 Transfer measurements

- Place the story pole on or next to the trim piece you need to cut
- Find the appropriate line on the story pole
- Transfer the mark to the piece you are cutting
- Here, the bottom of the bead is the place to cut the top edge of the side casing

Using a Story Pole as a Design Aid

If you are designing a complicated project, such as a built-in with numerous components, vertical and horizontal story poles help with both the design and construction phases. Without story poles, it's easy to forget details, such as the space needed for drawer slides. Here's how to make a horizontal story pole for a bathroom vanity. Use a story pole at least 2 inches shorter than the built-in's width, to allow for filler strips on each end of the cabinet.

1 Create a basic plan

- Start with a picture or sketch of what you want to build
- Determine how many cabinet boxes it will require
- In this example there are five boxes: three narrow ones between two wider ones
- Determine the width of any fixed parts (such as ready-made drawers)

2 Mark the plan on the pole

- At each end, mark off at least 1 inch for a scribe strip, then mark the thickness of one layer of cabinet material
- Mark one drawer width, centered on the pole's midpoint
- Past each mark, draw in the drawer glide
- Move out on each side: two thicknesses of cabinet material, another drawer glide, a drawer, a second drawer slide, and one box thickness
- The remaining space equals the width of the end cabinets

Rule 3: Make It Straight, Level, Plumb

When you install trim, your job is to make everything look straight, level, and plumb, even if the surfaces underlying the trim are not. It's far easier if those underlying surfaces are close to those ideals before you begin the actual trimwork.

Smoothing the Surface

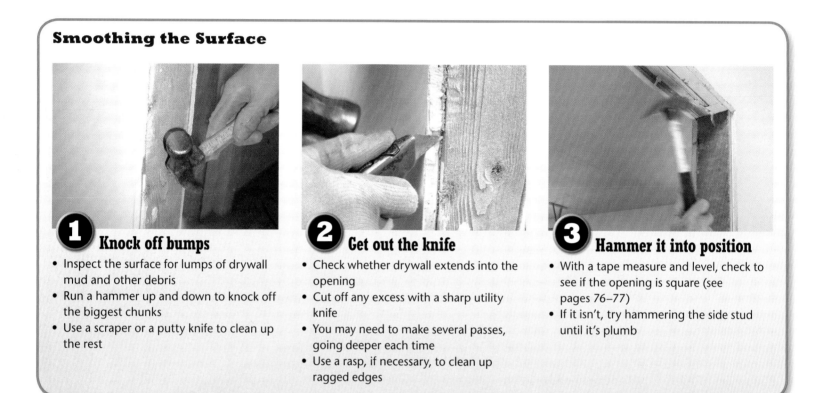

1 Knock off bumps

- Inspect the surface for lumps of drywall mud and other debris
- Run a hammer up and down to knock off the biggest chunks
- Use a scraper or a putty knife to clean up the rest

2 Get out the knife

- Check whether drywall extends into the opening
- Cut off any excess with a sharp utility knife
- You may need to make several passes, going deeper each time
- Use a rasp, if necessary, to clean up ragged edges

3 Hammer it into position

- With a tape measure and level, check to see if the opening is square (see pages 76–77)
- If it isn't, try hammering the side stud until it's plumb

How to Keep Things Straight

Snap a line

- To install wall frames or wainscot, make a reference line with chalk
- Mark the height on one wall; use a level to make marks to a far corner
- At the corner, hook the chalk line's end tab over a nail, or have someone hold it
- Extend the line to another corner and pull it taut
- Lift the string near its center, then let go

Look at the light

- To check if a door or window jamb bows out, hold a straightedge against the face of the jamb
- Stand where you can see light between the pieces
- If the beam is uneven, the jamb is not straight
- Shim where the beam of light is widest so the trim moves outward

The teeter-totter test

- Another way to check if a jamb is straight is to rock a straightedge back and forth against the surface
- If it rocks, the trim is bulging at a pivot point
- A long level is designed not to warp, so it makes a good straightedge

How to Tell If Trim Is Level

On a narrow surface

- To check whether a shelf slants in or out, a short level works best
- This model has a diagonal vial, so it can also check 45-degree angles
- If you must use a long level, hold it tight to the surface

On a wide surface

- To check whether a shelf tilts from right to left, use a long level
- A level like this seems long enough, but it could gives a misleading reading since it really only checks the middle of the shelf's span

When to go higher-tech

- If you need to line up features on different walls, consider buying or renting a builder's level, transit, or laser level
- With these, you can set a tripod in one spot and pivot the leveling tool to take readings on each wall

How to Tell If a Feature Is Plumb

Read the bubble

- Hold a spirit level tightly against the surface you are checking
- Position your face so you can look straight ahead at the bubble
- Marks on the vial should appear as single lines or equally wide ovals
- The surface is plumb if bubbles in the end vials are centered within the marks
- Read either end vial; the bubbles should be in the same position

Using a Plumb Bob

To check whether an opening (or any other feature) is plumb, suspend the bob in a doorway. Wait for the string to stop moving, then measure across from the string to the jambs in several places. If the measurements are equal, the jambs are plumb. Many chalk lines are designed to double as a plumb bob, or you can use an eye bolt tied to a string.

Rule 4: Check Every Angle

Trim carpentry is a lot easier if you stick with 90- and 45-degree angles. But for you to be able to do that with the trim, you need openings or walls that are square.

How to Tell If an Opening Is Square

Test two corners

- Hold a combination square in one corner
- If the square fits snugly, the corner is square
- Check another corner
- If both are square and the sides are equally long, the opening has 90-degree angles

Improving accuracy

- A framing square works even better
- Because the arms are longer, it checks a wider area

Measure the diagonals

- Measure from the lower corner on one side to the upper corner on the other
- Do the same, but for the opposite corners
- If the measurements are equal, the opening is square
- The tape won't fit precisely into the corners, so place the tab the same way each time

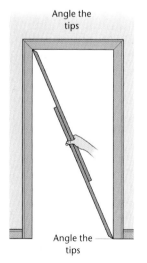

Angle the tips

Angle the tips

Check with sticks

- Find two wooden strips that are each a little more than half the diagonal width of the opening
- Cut diagonally across one end of each piece to make an angled tip
- Fit the pieces diagonally across the opening
- Grip them tightly and move them into the opposite diagonal
- If the fit is just as snug, the opening is square
- You can also use this technique to check whether drawers and cabinets are square

Dust Off Your Geometry

From the corner you are checking, measure out 3 feet along one wall or side. From the same corner, measure out 4 feet along the other side. If the diagonal distance between the two end points is 5 feet, the corner is square. If 3, 4, and 5 feet are not suitable for your situation, multiply the numbers by a set number to get dimensions that are useful. For example: multiply by 3 and switch to inches: 9, 12, and 15 inches. Or multiply by 4 to get 12, 16, and 20 inches.

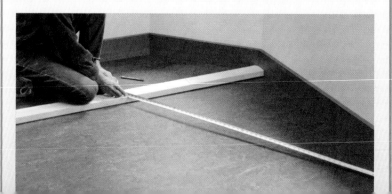

Other Square Details

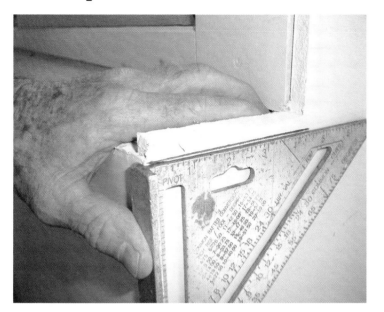

Outside corners

- Slip the shoulder of an angle square or a combination square over one side of a corner
- To mark a square corner, trace against the other arm

How to Find Odd Angles

Sometimes there's no way to avoid dealing with an angle that isn't square. To copy the angle so you can cut trim appropriately, use a sliding T-bevel. Fit the handle against one side and the blade against the other. Tighten the nut. Then you can transfer the angle directly, for example, by placing the bevel on a table saw and adjusting the blade to tilt at the same angle. Or you can use the bevel with a protractor, as shown, to measure the angle in degrees. Then you can adjust the saw's cutting angle to that reading.

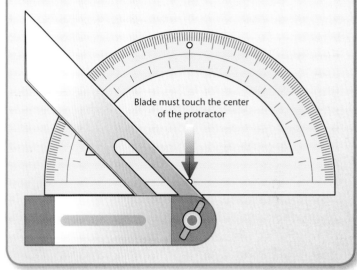

Blade must touch the center of the protractor

Checking a trim board

- Don't assume that trim boards have square ends; check each piece with a square
- Note how the shoulder of an angle square (or combination square) extends around the edge
- Use this feature if you've marked the length on an edge and want to extend a cutting line across the face of the board, or vice versa

Getting a square cut

- To cut perpendicular to a surface, the blade of a handheld saw must be at right angles to the base plate
- In most cases, orient the saw so most of the plate is on the piece you want to keep
- For an angled backcut, the base can be on the waste side, as shown; viewing the line is easiest this way
- Clamp on a straightedge when accuracy matters

Rule 5: Make It Fit

Trim carpentry is all about making things look like they fit exactly in a space, even if they really don't. Shims and scribes help trim carpenters work magic.

How to Shim

Shims are thin strips of materials that you insert under or behind a piece of trim to raise it or bring it forward. They're essential aids in making things look straight, level, plumb, and square.

Types of shims

- Shims come in tapered and straight styles
- Buy tapered shims in little bundles, or cut your own from leftover shingles
- Make straight shims from thin scraps of wood or plywood, or shop at masonry supply companies for horseshoe-shape shims
- With horseshoe shims, the color indicates the thickness

When you can reach both sides

- Select two tapered shims; they are always used in pairs
- Slip in the second shim, thin end first
- Push and pull until they're tight and together create the thickness you want

When you can reach only one side

- Insert the thick end of one tapered shim
- Slip in the second shim's thin end
- If the gap is so wide that the first shim would fall out, insert them together
- Leave enough of a thick end sticking out to allow for adjustment

Fasten the shims

- Nail or screw where fasteners will pass through shims
- At a hinge on a prehung door, replace one of the short screws with one that's long enough to pass through the shim and into a stud

Trim in place

- Score one shim along the drywall edge
- Snap off the projecting end
- Repeat for the other shim

Clean up slivers

- If rough edges stick out, tap them down with a hammer
- If there is too much wood to tap down, saw off the excess, using a saw with a fine-tooth blade
- If the blade flexes, steady it with one hand as you push and pull on the handle with the other

Using straight shims

- Save thin scraps of different thicknesses
- Sandwich several layers together if you need a thickness you don't have
- Because the thickness isn't dependent on the depth these shims are set, you can trim them to length before you nail them in place

How the Pros Do It

"When you're working with prefinished material, or are taking off just a tiny amount, it can be hard to see a scribe line. I mark the edge that I need to trim. When the marks are gone, the fit will probably be fine."

John Tyler, Carley Construction

How to Scribe

Scribing involves marking a piece with a line that follows the contour of a wall or other surface, and then shaping the marked piece so it fits precisely. An inexpensive compass—the type of tool you used as a kid to draw circles—works well as a scriber. These steps show how to scribe an alcove shelf in a closet, but you can adapt them to a variety of situations.

1 Cut oversize and scribe

- Measure the opening's width in several places
- Cut the shelf 1¼ to 2 inches longer than the longest dimension
- Put the board in place but tip up one end
- Adjust a compass to the biggest gap along the edge slanting down, or about ½ inch if the gap is narrow
- Holding the scriber upright, with the tip against the wall, trace along the wall to mark the shelf

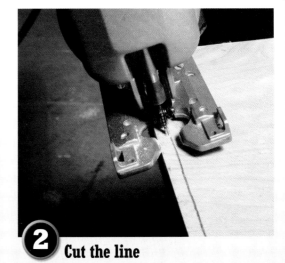

2 Cut the line

- Trim the shelf to the scribed line
- Use a jigsaw or a belt sander
- Make a square cut at the front
- If you want a back bevel (see page 80), gradually tip the saw or sander toward the outside of the line

Rule 6: Use Back Bevels

A back bevel is a slanted edge that's square in the front or at the top but undercut toward the back or underneath, where it doesn't show. The slanted edge is easy to pare with a knife or sand down if the initial fit isn't perfect.

How to Cut a Back Bevel

If you are cutting trim with a miter saw, slip a shim $1/16$ inch at its thickest under the trim to elevate the end slightly. Leave the saw blade at 90 degrees to the table. When you make the cut, you'll wind up with a small back bevel, which is usually all you want.

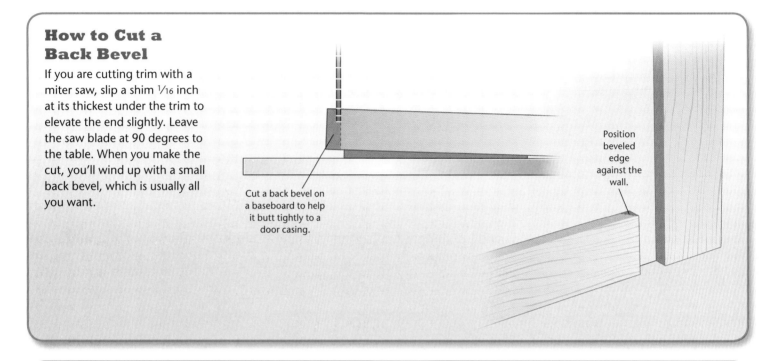

Cut a back bevel on a baseboard to help it butt tightly to a door casing.

Position beveled edge against the wall.

Using a Belt Sander to Make a Back Bevel

1 Trim to the line

- First remove most of the excess material with the sander flat against the edge
- Leave the scribe line so it can be seen in the next Step

2 Create the bevel

- Tip the sander so it's contacting the back of the edge
- Do not dig past the scribe line on the front surface

Rule 7: Know Your Skills

Simple projects done well are better than complicated ones done poorly. Worse are projects that never get finished because you realized mid-job that you have taken on more than you should have. Here are a couple of tips to keep you out of trouble.

Opt for Butt Joints

Simple butt joints are a lot more forgiving than miters. Yet they can look just as classy, especially if you embellish the design by choosing materials of different thicknesses and varying the way the pieces meet. The trim design shown for this built-in bookcase would look good even if some of the parts weren't cut as precisely as these are.

Up top

- Add variety by varying the thickness of trim pieces
- The head casing in this example is thicker than the side piece and extends past it

At the bottom

- The side casing extends past the bottom trim
- This allows the sides to fit, even if one is slightly longer than the other

Hammers vs. Nail Guns

Hand-tool skills usually take more time to master than those required for power tools. Yet for novices and pros alike, each type excels in certain situations. Professional trim carpenters usually use nail guns to secure trim. But the gun's tip design makes it hard to pinpoint where a nail will go, and at what angle. Hand-hammering, on the other hand, makes it more likely that trim will be knocked out of alignment before it's secured, and there's a risk of denting the trim with each swing of the hammer. A combination approach works best.

Predrill close to an edge

- A slanted nail can split the wood
- Use a thin bit, suitable for No. 6 finish nails
- If you don't have a thin bit, use a nail in the drill instead

Pick up speed

- Farther from an edge, save time by using a nail gun
- Practice on scrap first so you learn to pinpoint where the nail will land

Use a nail set

- Drive a finish nail through each hole
- Stop when the head is slightly above the surface
- After all of the pieces are secure, use a nail set to tap heads slightly below the surface
- Choose a nail set with a tip that's the right size for the nail

When you need a one-step fix

- Use a nail gun when there is no good way to hold parts while you predrill or nail
- Nail guns are also handy when the nails are merely fortifying a connection
- Here, two handrail sections are glued and bolted; the nails keep them from twisting while the glue dries

Rule 8: Use Reveals

Reveals are the small offsets that often separate one piece of trim from another. Reveals are both handsome and forgiving: When a joint is supposed to be perfect you notice if it's even a little off, but if there's a gap your eye isn't as discriminating.

Predesigned for Reveals

Some wood window frames are made of two layers. The inside layer is the same type of wood as the sash. That part will be the reveal—the wood that will remain in view once the window is trimmed—plus a little extra. The part that's sure to be covered by trim is made of less expensive wood. Building windows this way makes best use of a scarce resources (in this case, vertical-grain fir).

Design On the Fly

1 Block out the reveal

- When you're working out trim details, include reveals whenever possible
- With this basement shelf, the reveal is the shelf overhang
- Including the overhang creates a pleasing stool-and-apron look

2 Reap the rewards

- Thanks to the reveal, you don't need to scribe the shelf to match the wall's thickness
- If the overhang wavers slightly in width, no one will notice
- Trim will cover the back of this shelf, so any gaps there will be hidden
- If that edge were exposed, you would still need to scribe there

How to Mark Reveals

With the shelf overhang at left the reveal happens automatically if you have left enough depth across the entire width of the shelf, so there's really no need to mark the reveal. In other situations, though, you need a guide.

Using a combination square

- Adjust the blade of a combination square to the width of the reveal, often ¼ inch
- At each corner, place the square's shoulder against the inside edge of the window frame
- Hold a pencil against the end of the blade and make a light mark
- If you need a guide line all along the frame, hold the pencil to the blade as you slide the square along each edge

How to Make a Reveal Jig

1 Begin with the blade

- Install a zero-clearance (tight-fitting) plate on a table saw
- Adjust a combination square so the blade projects by the reveal depth (here it's ¼ inch)
- Raise the saw blade a little higher than ¼ inch and set the square over it
- Watch the light under the square's blade as you gradually lower the saw's blade
- When no light remains, the saw is set

2 Set the rip fence

- Move the saw's rip fence to cut the same reveal depth
- Measure from the fence to the far side of the blade

3 Cut the reveal

- Use a big scrap piece, perhaps 6 by 8 inches
- Place it flat on the table
- Run each side along the fence and blade to cut a groove

4 Cut off the waste

- Tip the board on edge, with the groove facing the blade
- Hold the back of the board tight against the fence as you slide each side past the blade
- Stand with the fence between you and the blade as you do this

5 Use it at corners

- With channels at the edges of all four sides, your jig can show the reveals at both sides of a corner
- It can also be used as a depth gauge along long straight sections
- Instead of marking the reveal, you can place trim alongside and position it as you work

Rule 9: Give Yourself a Second Chance

It might seem sensible to tackle a step, finish it, and then move on without ever looking back. But in the real world of trimwork, it's a lot smarter to work in ways that allow you to go back and fix problems that may only become evident later.

Make the Trickiest Cuts First

The numbers on the illustration at right show a typical order for installing crown molding in a room with a bay window. However, consider cutting the piece for the door wall first. It is longest and has coped joints on both ends, the trickiest situation. If you cut it first and mess up, you still have two options:

- Trim the piece and use the parts on other walls
- Keep the good end and make a scarf joint to splice to a second piece

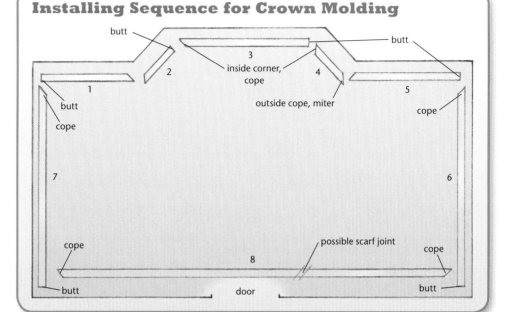

Installing Sequence for Crown Molding

butt

butt

3

2 inside corner, cope 4

1 5

butt

cope

outside cope, miter

cope

7 6

cope cope

possible scarf joint

8

butt door butt

Test First, Nail Later

Use this method when you're installing tricky joints, such as miters on trim that will have a clear finish, where you can't plug gaps with caulk.

1 Position the first piece

- Cut the first piece to the length and angle you think you need
- Hold it in place with clamps
- If the situation precludes clamps, drive one or two nails part way so they're easy to remove

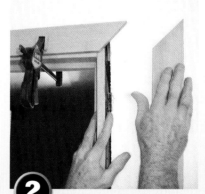

2 Test the next piece

- Measure the remaining space and cut the next piece to fit
- Position it, and check the fit; here, a shim was sticking out too far
- If you see a gap in the miter, now's the time to find and fix that, too
- When the fit's right, nail the pieces in place

Pro-level Tip

In general, when you're installing crown, chair rail, or baseboard, it usually makes sense to start by nailing the first piece to the wall opposite the door. Then, when you cope the mating pieces on the side walls, the joints wind up oriented to look best as you walk into the room.

How to Start Over

There's an art to removing trim without damaging it or the underlying surface. The steps are the same whether you've just installed a piece incorrectly or are removing trim that you want to reuse.

1 Start small

- Slip or hammer a wide putty knife into the connection you want to loosen near a nail
- Move the blade back and forth to open up a gap
- Take care not to gouge the wood
- If paint hides the nails, locate them by sliding the knife in the joint until it hits them

2 Pry apart

- At a nail, insert a pry bar in the gap
- Place a scrap of wood or a wide putty knife behind the bar to protect the wall
- Pry outward until the nails loosen or the molding slips away from them

3 Work your way down

- If you have two bars, work in pairs
- Gradually ease out the trim to reduce the chance of splitting it

4 Remove nails

- Once the trim is free, remove nails from the back
- Grip each nail, pry back, and pull out the nail a little bit at a time until it's out
- Pliers with curved blades (wire cutters or end-cutting nippers) work best
- Do not hammer nails out the front; that could split the wood

Plugging Small Holes

When you're hanging a door or installing hardware, screw holes sometimes wind up in the wrong place. Here's an easy fix.

1 Cut and glue slivers

- Use a sharp utility knife to slice a thin strip from the corner of a scrap board
- Dribble wood glue (white or yellow) into each hole
- Insert one or more slivers into each hole
- Make sure glue coats the slivers, and fill the holes completely

2 Trim them flush

- With the utility knife, cut off the excess slivers
- Aim to make the slivers flush or a little above the surface
- Wipe off excess glue with a damp cloth
- Wait for glue to set

3 Sand smooth

- If the patch will be visible, sand smooth
- No need to sand if the patch will be hidden, perhaps by a hinge
- If you are installing new screws in the same area, pre-drill first

Cope First

- Select molding that is longer than you need
- Cut the cope
- Test the fit against a scrap piece
- Fine-tune the shape until you're satisfied
- Then trim the piece to length

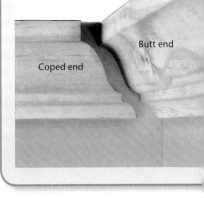

Butt end

Coped end

Rule 10: Know When to Fudge

Sometimes it's not possible to line up pieces of trim precisely. A bit of creative fudging can make them look like they are. The key is to line up the most dominant elements and fill in gaps as needed.

Go for the Big Picture

This example shows a room where trim on the doorway (on the left) needs to look like it lines up with trim around the closet, even though the openings are at slightly different heights.

1 Establish a level reference line

- Here, the reference line is the top of the reveal where the doorway trim will go
- Tack up a scrap piece so one edge is along the line
- Attach the strip with a single nail; drive it where trim will later cover the hole
- Check that the scrap is level

2 Transfer the height

- Mark the reference edge to show the height for the adjoining closet
- Pivot the scrap strip up out of the way, or remove it

3 Fill in the difference

- Add a reveal or other trim to make features look lined up
- For this sliding door, a deep trim strip across the top did the trick
- The trim strip also covers the sliding door hardware

Design Around Problems

When there's no way to get all trim details to line up or be symmetrical, try changing your design. To avoid a hodge-podge look, keep some of the trim elements aligned to signal that there is an underlying logic behind your design. In the room depicted in this illustration, it wouldn't be possible to install equal-size wall frames, but the trim in this room still looks balanced and well-planned because the sides of the middle frame line up with the window casing above and the two frames on either side are symmetrical.

Narrow space has no frame

Frame aligns with casing

Outlet set on block

Split the Difference, or Not?

Sometimes you're faced with conflicting priorities: you want level trim, but you also want it to look parallel to a surface that's slanted. You have several options:

Split the difference This means spreading out or tapering each piece so that none is off by more than a tiny bit. For example, if you're installing wainscot between walls that aren't plumb, you can skew individual boards slightly to make up the difference.

Taper the biggest piece This approach let's you make up the difference in one place. If a 9-inch-wide board gradually narrows to 8¾ inches, it will be far less noticeable than narrowing a 2-inch-wide piece by the same amount.

If you do taper a piece, you may need to adjust the angles on mating pieces to something other than 90- or 45-degree angles. On this fireplace surround, for example, if the top piece tapers, the top edge of the side pieces must also slant or they won't be plumb.

Here, the plan calls for a 6-inch stone reveal around the fire box, topped by a surround about 9 inches high, and a mantle. If the bottom edge of the stone isn't level, you could taper the surround or split the difference and taper it and the surround each by a little bit. Either way, you'd want the surround level on top so things don't roll off the mantle.

Dealing with Slanted Surfaces

If a floor or ceiling slopes, it's often difficult to decide whether to make baseboards or crown level, or to install them so they have the same slant. Here are two strategies to consider:

Chase the shadow

- This crown molding isn't level; the bubble is slightly off center
- Yet the shadow line between the trim and ceiling is evenly wide
- In cases like this, where molding is clear or prefinished, it's usually best to install the trim to preserve that even shadow line

Erase the shadow

- If you will paint the trim, you can caulk any gaps
- This makes the shadow line disappear
- This permits you to install level trim even if the room slants

Trimwork for Windows & Doors

I n this chapter, we show you how to finish off your home's doors and windows with handsome bands of mitered trim. Both picture-frame windows and windows with classic aprons and stools are covered, plus we share lots of tips to help you trouble-shoot fit problems. Trimwork for pass-throughs is also covered, as is the use of plinths and corner blocks. Finally, we teach you how to cut a tricky mitered return.

Chapter Contents

Pass-throughs
page 90

Trimming a Pass-through
page 92

Mitered Trim for Doors
page 94

Trouble-shooting Mitered Trim
page 98

Plinths & Corner Blocks
page 100

Trimming a Window
page 102

88

Traditional Window Casing
page 108

Picture-frame Windows
page 112

Creating Mitered Returns
page 114

page 98

Pass-throughs

In the open floor plans so popular today, homes often have rooms connected by pass-throughs rather than doors. From simple mitered or butt-joint casings to elaborate compositions of pedestals, columns, and entablatures, trim can turn pass-throughs into architectural features that make you want to stop and notice the details.

Designed in a classical style, this pass-through features strong verticals divided into panels that have the same proportions as the posts on the far staircase.

Thick columns and flexible molding on the arch decorate a deep pass-through and add to its architectural punch. The arch also serves as a handsome frame for the stairway and landing in the room beyond.

Creating an Arched Pass-through

Arches are usually framed in when a house is built, but they can also be added later. Remove drywall above your future arch on both sides of the wall. From ¼-inch-thick plywood, cut two replacement pieces with a curve at the bottom. Screw them to the wall, and add short 2 by 4s between the curved edges. Top the plywood with ¼- or ⅜-inch-thick drywall, to make the arch flush with the existing wall. If you want to cover the curve itself with drywall, use flexible drywall (see Resources, page 236) or score the back of ½-inch-thick sheets every ½ to 1 inch, depending on the curve. If you want wood trim on the curve, use bending plywood (see Resources, page 236).

A wide pass-through—more than just what's needed to cover the framing between the rooms—increases the apparent distance between spaces. It's a useful trick when the front door is just a few paces from the living room.

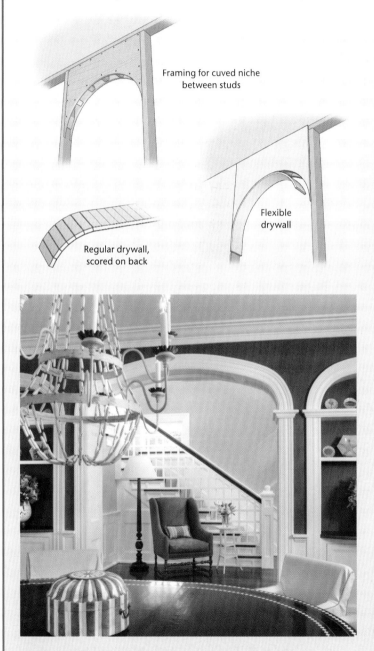

Framing for cuved niche between studs

Flexible drywall

Regular drywall, scored on back

Arches for niches and for pass-throughs are built in similar ways.

Trimming a Pass-through

This is an ideal beginner project. It's also the first step in a number of other projects, such as hanging bypass doors (pages 198–199). Do it right, and your family and friends just may end up lingering in these now-welcoming pass-through spaces.

1 Measure wall thickness

- Check several places, on sides and top
- Standard interior wall is 4½ inches thick
- Some openings also show a plywood layer, added for sheer bracing
- Rip trim to wall's maximum thickness plus ¹⁄₁₆ inch

2 Cut header and mark location

- Measure the distance across top of opening
- Cut piece to length
- Hold header in place and mark lower edge on both sides of opening

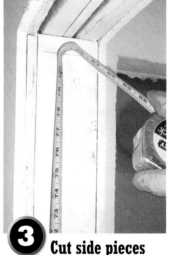

3 Cut side pieces

- Set header aside
- Measure from floor up to line on each side
- Cut side trim pieces to fit

How the Pros Do It

Even when putty is tinted to match the wood, nail holes inevitably still show on trim that has a clear finish. On these jobs, I use a speed square to mark where to drive nails so pairs line up.

Larry Bell, Blumenthal Construction

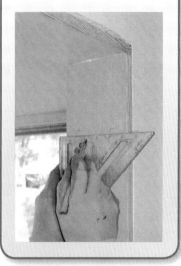

4 Sand exposed edges

- Smooth the front and both long edges of each piece
- Start with 100 grit, finish with 180 grit
- Lightly round over corners along front face
- Do not round over corners along back face

5 Test the fit

- Set one vertical piece and the horizontal piece in opening
- Slip the other vertical piece into place
- If the fit is too tight, trim pieces as needed
- Mark trim to show orientation of boards

6 Check for square and plumb

- Use a level on vertical pieces
- Check top corners with a speed square
- The distances from each top corner to each opposite bottom corner should be equal

Stuff to Buy

LUMBER Casing, shim stock
BASIC SUPPLIES Wood glue,
2½"-long nails, 100- and
180-grit sandpaper

Time Commitment

Three hours

Tools You'll Need

Level
Nail gun
Power miter saw
Rotary sander
Speed square
Tape measure

Related Topics

Choosing a style, 26–27
Hammers & nails, 62–63
Make it straight, level, plumb,
74–75
Trimming a door, 94–99

7 Adjust if needed

- If trim is not plumb and square, shim as needed
- Insert shims, narrow ends first, in pairs, one from each side
- Wait to trim the shims until trim is nailed on

8 Attach shims

- Mark the wall to show where the shims are
- Also mark shims for depth
- Remove trim boards
- Nail through shims into framing

9 Nail frame

- Reassemble trim on the floor or other flat space
- Spread glue on the top edge of each side piece
- Nail the frame with three 2½-inch nails at corners
- Use a power nailer, or predrill and hammer in finish nails

10 Install frame

- Carefully move the assembled frame back into the opening
- Line up sides so they are flush with drywall

11 Nail trim in place

- Check with a level to make sure trim is plumb
- Use a speed square to make sure trim stays flush with drywall
- Nail on trim with pairs of 2½-inch finish nails
- Remove excess glue with a damp rag; use a chisel if the glue has set

12 Install face trim

- Add mitered trim, as shown on pages 94–99
- Or choose another design

The finished pass-through is trimmed in the same manner as several doorways leading to a series of rooms.

Mitered Trim for Doors

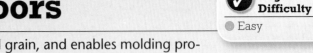

Mitered trim creates attractively crisp angles, hides end grain, and enables molding profiles to turn corners without interruption. No wonder this type of trim has endured through many stylistic periods, even though it is tricky to install.

When mitered trim is made from single pieces of molding, it's important to choose narrow stock, especially if you're using solid wood rather than MDF. Otherwise, gaps are likely to open up at the joints as humidity fluctuates.

To get the look of wide mitered molding without the risk of joints opening up, build up mitered trim from separate pieces and miter each layer. One common element of built-up mitered trim is a back band, a thick piece around the perimeter.

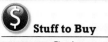
LUMBER Casing
BASIC SUPPLIES White wood glue, rags, 2½" 15-gauge nails, 1¼" finishing nails

🕐 **Time Commitment**

Three hours

🛠 **Tools You'll Need**

Clamps
Drill
Level
Nail set
Power miter saw
Power nailer
Speed square
Tape measure

◎ **Related Topics**

Choosing a style, 26–27
Hammers & nails, 62–63
Make it straight, level, plumb, 74–75
Trimming a pass-through, 90–93

Installing Mitered Door Trim

To give themselves leeway to adjust mitered trim for a perfect fit, some trim carpenters install side casings first, then fit the top piece. Others reverse the order. The procedure shown here combines the benefits of both approaches. Best of all, you don't need to nail anything until you're sure all the pieces fit.

 Measure between jambs

- Add ½ inch to the total distance (assuming you want a ¼-inch reveal)
- That total is the length of the top molding's short edge

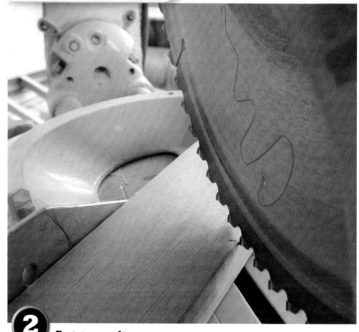

2 **Cut top miters**

- Cut one end at a 45-degree angle
- From the short end, measure the distance found in Step 1 (see How the Pros Do It on page 98)
- Cut the second miter so it angles in the opposite direction

Miter Joints & Humidity

Wood expands and contracts mostly across its width as humidity changes. Because a miter joint cuts diagonally across the grain, these changes cause a gap at the heel (short point) in dry weather and a gap at the toe (long point) in humid weather. The wider the molding, the more you'll notice these changes.

Miters open here in dry weather

Miters open here in humid weather

Wood shrinks across the grain

Humidity has little affect on length

3 **Clamp top molding**

- Set piece ¼ inch above edge of door frame
- Line up mitered ends ¼ inch back from side jambs
- Don't nail anything yet

4 Measure side

- Measure from floor to top edge of molding
- Subtract for finished flooring if it is not yet in place

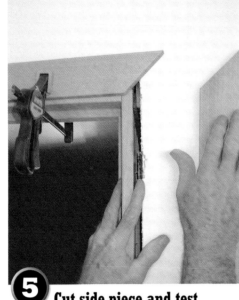

5 Cut side piece and test

- Cut top end at 45 degrees
- Cut bottom end at 90 degrees
- Make the piece a shade too long

6 Cut other side

- Repeat Steps 4 and 5
- Hold both side pieces upright, ¼ inch beyond jambs
- Move top or sides until both miters are tight

7 Nail top piece

- Move the side pieces; leave the top piece clamped
- Use power nailer, or predrill as in Step 8
- Drive 15-gauge, 2½-inch-long nails about ½ inch down from the top edge into framing
- Place one nail at the center and one near each end

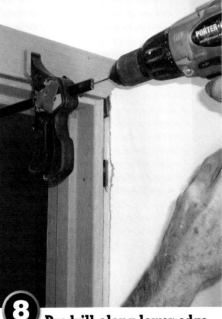

8 Predrill along lower edge

- Drill three pilot holes ½ inch up from bottom edge
- Line up these holes with nails along the top edge
- Use a 1¼"-long nail as a bit if you lack a small drill bit

9 Nail lower edge

- Drive 1¼"-long nails through the holes
- Use a nail set to tap heads ¹⁄₁₆ inch below surface
- Avoid power nailing here; the molding might crack

10 **Glue miter**

- Squirt glue onto mitered end of one side piece
- Use a generous amount
- Use white, not yellow, carpenter's glue for a longer working time

11 **Position miter**

- Position the side piece and adjust it so the miter is tight
- Don't worry yet about aligning the full length of the piece
- Leave excess glue for now

12 **Nail side piece**

- Use same procedure as for top piece
- Power nail along the outside edge; align as you go
- Predrill and hand-hammer on the inside edge
- Use four pairs of nails for a standard-height door

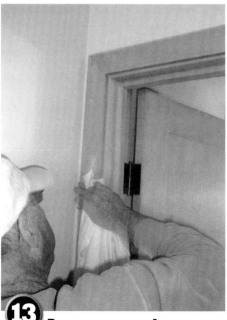

13 **Remove excess glue**

- Immediately after nailing, wipe off excess glue with a damp cloth
- If you plan to apply stain or a clear finish, be sure to remove all glue residue
- See sanding tip on page 112

How the Pros Do It

"Measuring from the short edge of a miter is tricky because a tape's end tab slips off. I place the mitered piece against a scrap board with a square end. Then I measure from that when I mark the mitered piece."
Bob Stanton, Stanton Specialties

"I 'burn an inch' by placing the tape's 1-inch mark at the short edge of the miter. Then I measure down the correct distance and add 1 inch."
Larry Bell, Blumenthal Construction

Trouble-shooting Mitered Trim

Sometimes mitered trim fits perfectly and you can breeze through a job. Other times, one piece sticks out more than the other, or gaps show up where they shouldn't. Here are a few tips for fine-tuning the fit.

Squaring Uneven Surfaces

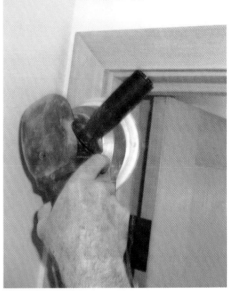

TRIM A SHIM

- Check whether a shim behind the jamb protrudes too far forward
- If so, trim the stub with a utility knife or a fine-tooth saw, as shown
- If the saw blade flexes, steady it as your other hand moves the tool up and down

CHECK FOR A BULGE

- Move a flat board across the drywall in the trim area
- If the board teeters, the drywall bulges at the pivot point
- Grind off the excess with a rasp
- Or tap the bulge flush, taking care not to crack the drywall
- Hammer only where the trim will hide any dents

SAND THE JOINT SMOOTH

- If the trim is flat and unfinished, sand the joint until both sides are flush
- Sand in the direction of the wood grain if you are sanding by hand
- Or use a random-orbit finish sander; it lets you sand on top of the joint without leaving noticeable cross-grain scratches
- Keep the sander in motion
- Even out the surface by also sanding away from the corner in both directions

---

How the Pros Do It

"If the pieces fit before you nailed but not after, a nail that went in at an angle could be the problem. Try tapping on the side of the molding to nudge the piece back into position. If the wall is painted, protect the finish with scrap paper."

Larry Bell,
Blumenthal
Construction

SHIM FROM THE BACK

- Use this fix if the molding has curves that make sanding difficult or if it's prefinished
- Insert a shim under the lower piece, just far enough to bring the pieces level
- Undercut slightly as you trim the shim with sharp utility knife
- Run a bead of caulk along the back of the trim (see page 111)

Angles for Out-of-square Corners

Miters are maddening enough when you're dealing with 90-degree corners. But what if you're trying to miter trim for other shapes? Each miter cut needs to be half of the total angle. A sheet of paper and a sliding bevel eliminate math and a protractor.

- Set the bevel to the total angle that the two trim pieces need to make
- Transfer this to the paper and cut it to the shape

- Fold the paper in half, with the corner-to-be at the tip
- Adjust your miter saw to cut at the angle of the fold when the two long edges are against the fence

Solving Other Problems

WHEN MITERED TIPS DON'T MEET

- Trim the piece that has its long tip sticking out
- Cut off only a pencil line's width
- Recheck and trim again, if needed

WHEN NAILING WRECKS ALIGNMENT

- As soon as you notice a problem, stop hammering into the face
- Adjust the pieces, using your hands or a slim pry bar
- Drive a nail in from the side to secure the miter
- Resume nailing into face of trim

WHEN MOLDING BOWS

- First nail molding near the mitered joint plus several lower nails
- Then bend the lower section into line
- Use a clamp if hand pressure isn't enough
- Remove clamp only once all nails are in place

Plinths & Corner Blocks

Plinths and corner blocks make great accents for door and window trim. Because they use butt joints, they are easy to install. Fluted, reeded, and flat moldings are the most popular types of accompanying casing, but you may prefer symmetrical casing with curves.

Elements of the Style

If you want to create a Neoclassical or Victorian look with plinths and corner blocks, it's important to pay attention to which parts stand proud, a trim carpenter's term for which parts stick out farther than others.

From Above

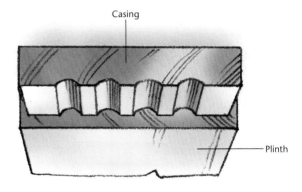

Casing

Plinth

Plinth

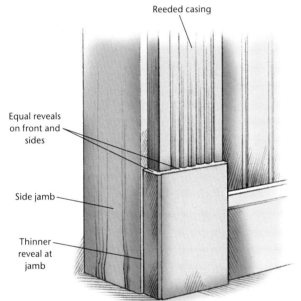

Reeded casing

Equal reveals on front and sides

Side jamb

Thinner reveal at jamb

Side View

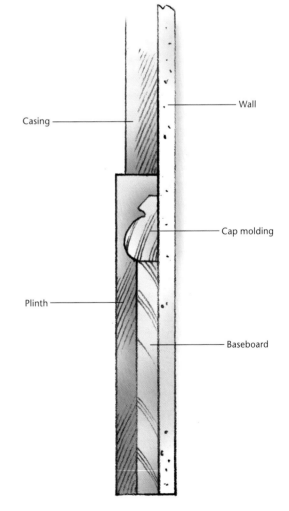

Wall

Casing

Cap molding

Plinth

Baseboard

Corner Block

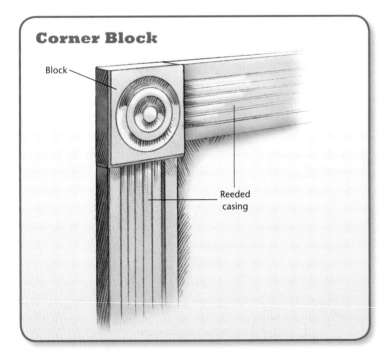

Block

Reeded casing

 **Stuff to Buy**
LUMBER Molding, plinths, corner blocks
BASIC SUPPLIES Finish nails, sandpaper

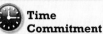 **Time Commitment**
A few hours

 **Tools You'll Need**
Clamps
Nail gun
Power miter saw
Rasp
Tape measure

 Related Topics
Power miter saws, 52–55
Mitering crown, 136–137
Use reveals, 82–83

How To Do It

1 **Install side casing**

- Make a reveal block, as shown on pages 82–83
- Use it to mark equal offsets on the side and head jambs
- Also mark the bottom jamb if you are installing blocks on all corners
- Measure to the marks and cut the side casing pieces
- Use the corner block to align the casing; nail it in place

2 **Tack corners with nail gun**

- Attach the corner blocks with a single nail in each
- Center the blocks so the reveals on both sides of the casing are equal

3 **Fit the head casing**

- Measure between the blocks and cut the head casing to fit
- Position the piece against the reveal lines and check the fit with the corner blocks
- If you see gaps, try twisting the blocks, fudging on the reveal or shaving a little off one or both ends of the casing

4 **Attach the head casing**

- When the fit is perfect, nail the head casing
- Then finish nailing the blocks

Make Your Own Blocks

Modern styles don't necessarily follow the proportion guidelines of the past, so some manufactures today make plinth and corner blocks that are just as wide as casing designed to go with them. To get the traditional reveals, you might need to make your own corner blocks and plinths. This approach also allows you to create a distinctive style for your home, and it saves money.

Clockwise from top:
- Three-line pattern for a plinth; bottom edge is not rounded
- 45-degree bevel on all edges
- Shallow holes drilled in a pattern
- 1/8-inch-deep lines cut on a table saw

Safety Advice

Corner blocks and plinths are relatively small, so if you are shaping them with a compound miter saw, you need a fence that fits close to the blade. Use an L-shape jig (page 137), and adjust the saw to cut at 45 degrees.

Trimming a Window

Covering the exposed framing and drywall around a new window is the first step to trimming it. Here we show you how to cut the pieces, on page 105 we help you fine-tune the stool, and on 106–107 we show you how to install everything.

Time Saver

Some windows come with jambs already installed, so they just need casing (the trim that goes on the wall around the window). If that's what you have, or if you are just changing the trim around existing windows, skip this section and move right to Traditional Window Casing, pages 108–111, or Picture-frame Windows, pages 112–113. However, if your windows have a gap that leaves rough framing exposed, follow the steps shown here to create a jamb and a stool.

Cutting the Parts

1 Determine dimensions

- Leave enough space for a latch if it's a casement window, like this one
- Measure the width between the inside edges of the sash frame and add the offsets, the thickness of two jambs, and about 1/2 inch for shims
- This is the length of the head jamb
- Measure the height inside the sash frames and add the offsets plus 1/2 inch; then subtract the thickness of the stool and head jamb
- This is the length of the side jambs

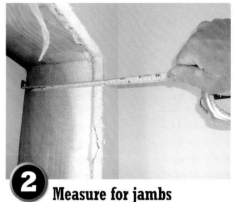

2 Measure for jambs

- Measure for jamb depth from the wall to the window frame along the top and sides
- Measure every foot or so
- Average the measurements to determine the width of the jambs

3 Measure for stool's depth

- Place a scrap of the apron trim along the bottom of the window well
- If you want a compound apron (as shown), hold both pieces in place
- Measure the distance from the window frame to the outermost apron edge
- Add the distance you want the stool to overhang the apron (typically 1/2 to 3/4 inch)

4 Measure for stool's length

- Measure the width of the window plus the casing on both sides
- Add a few extra inches on each side
- You now have the dimensions for a blank; you will cut the stool to its final length later

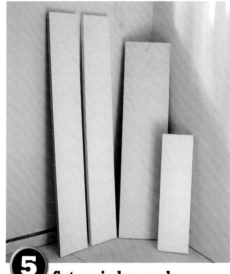

5 Cut a window pack

- Cut top and side jambs to the lengths and width found in Step 2
- Cut a stool blank to the dimensions found in Steps 3 and 4
- Orient cut edges toward the window

 Stuff to Buy	Time Commitment	Tools You'll Need	Related Topics
LUMBER Casing **BASIC SUPPLIES** 1½"-long staples, 1½"-long finish nails, carpenter's pencil, sandpaper	Three to four hours	Circular saw Drill Nail set Power miter saw Power nailer/stapler Speed square Tape measure Utility knife	Choosing a style, 26–27 Hammers & nails, 62–63 Installing mitered door trim, 94–99 Make it straight, level, plumb, 74–75

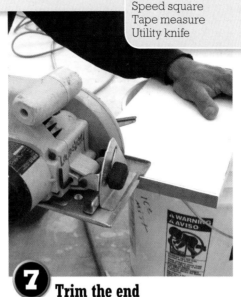

6 Scribe one end

- If the stool dead-ends at a wall, check the fit
- If you see a gap, mark the wall's contour on the stool
- To use a carpenter's pencil as a scriber, hold a flat side to the wall

7 Trim the end

- Cut the stool along the line with a small circular saw
- If the fit is close, remove tiny amounts of material with a rasp or power sander

8 Mark window location

- Push the stool tight against the wall in front of the window opening
- Use a speed square to mark the inside edges of the window frame on the stool

9 Mark the setback

- On each side, make a second mark to show the amount of window frame you want to leave exposed (1⅞ inches here)

10 Mark horns

- From the marks made in Step 9, extend lines as long as the depth of the window framing
- Use a square so the lines are perpendicular to the back edge
- Hold a scrap of trim or other straight-edge where the two lines end
- At each end, trace against the straight-edge to the end of the stool

How the Pros Do It

"I have a little trick that saves me from having to struggle to hold the stool steady while I mark it. I temporarily tack on two scraps of wood. Then I just set the stool in place."

Billy Lounsbury,
Lounsbury Carpentry

The project on these pages focuses on installing jambs and a stool around a single window. Adding a cornice above a window and wainscot below, as shown in this sitting area off a kitchen, are logical extensions of these techniques.

Fine-tuning the Stool

Even when you can use caulk to fill small gaps in trim, the stool still needs to fit perfectly. The steps needed to accomplish that include cutting the horns and scribing them to the wall.

1 Cut horns

- Cut out the square section at each end of the stool
- If you use a small circular saw, stop before the corners and finish with a handsaw or a jigsaw
- Stay just outside of the lines, so you can still see them

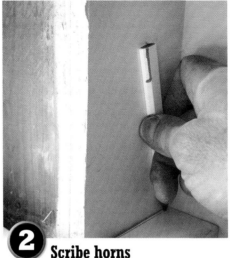

2 Scribe horns

- Set stool in place
- Check how stool fits against the window and against the drywall on both sides
- If needed, scribe horns to the wall to improve the fit there
- Scribing will let you slide the stool closer to the window

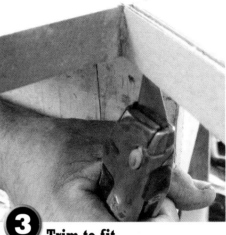

3 Trim to fit

- Cut along scribe lines with a small circular saw, a jigsaw, or a handsaw
- If you use a circular saw, stop just shy of the corner and finish the cut with a utility knife

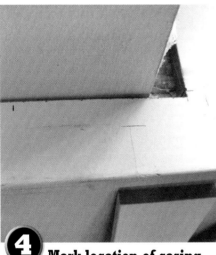

4 Mark location of casing

- Place the stool in position, centered or tight against a side wall
- Find the marks showing the window frame setback (Step 8 on page 103)
- On each side, measure back by the reveal you want to allow (typically ¼ inch)
- Measure back by the width of the casing and make another mark

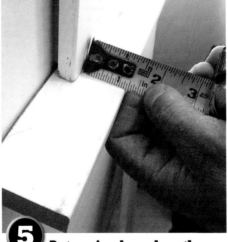

5 Determine horn length

- Set a scrap of casing between the marks you made in Step 1
- Measure out to the edge of the stool
- Mark an equal distance from the edge of the casing toward the end of the stool
- Cut the stool to that mark

6 Cut and shape

- Cut horns to length
- Sand ends
- If you are using trim with edges rounded at the factory, create matching edges where cut sides will be exposed with a router, rasp, or sandpaper

"There's a quick way to make sure you leave an even amount of window frame exposed on all sides. Cut a scrap piece to the width you want. Use it as a gauge to check the alignment as you shim and nail."

Billy Lounsbury, Lounsbury Carpentry

Installing the Pieces

Although it's possible to nail the stool and window liner pieces on separately, it's easier to fasten them together into an independent frame first. You can then slide the unit into place.

The look and feel of the trim on this window match the bed's platform, wood floor, and exposed beams.

1 Assemble the frame

- On a flat area such as the floor, arrange the jambs and stool
- Set the front edges against the floor
- Place the sides against the stool at the marks made in Step 8 on page 103
- Fit the top piece over the sides

2 Attach liners to stool

- Drive heavy-duty staples through the stool and top into the sides
- Use 1½-inch-long staples with ⁷⁄₁₆-inch crowns
- Alternatively, you can use screws or finish nails, but predrill pilot holes first

3 Set frame in place

- Slide the frame into position carefully so you don't twist it
- Leave about an equal amount of the window's frame exposed on both sides

4 Shim the stool

- Wedge pairs of shims under the stool until it is level
- Raise the stool until the exposed edge of the window frame equals what you see on the sides and top
- For each pair of shims, slide in the fat end of the first one as far as it will go
- Then slide in the thin end of the other shim as far as needed

5 Nail the stool

- Drive two 2½-inch-long nails through the stool over each pair of shims
- Set one nail close to the window
- Other nail should go closer to the front but must still hit the stud below the stool

6 Shim the sides

- Insert shims so jambs reveal the proper width of window framing
- Place shims near the top and bottom of the jambs
- Nail through the jambs into the shims

7 Plumb the jambs

- Place a straightedge against one of the jambs
- Look at light shining through to learn where to add shims to make it straight
- After you add the shims, nail through them to secure the jamb
- Repeat this procedure on the other side of the window

8 Shim the top

- If the window is wide, add one or more pairs of shims at the top
- Nail through these shims, too

9 Finishing up

- With a sharp utility knife, score shims below the stool, then snap them off
- If slivers of wood still project beyond the drywall, trim them with the knife
- Add an apron below the stool to hide the shims and gap
- Add casing around the window to hide gaps between the jambs and the wall

Traditional Window Casing

Traditional window trim calls for casing on the top and sides, plus a stool and apron at the bottom. Within that general definition, there are many variations. On the following pages, we complete the project that we began on page 102.

You can embellish basic casing by adding crown molding and a narrow shelf at the top.

To give the stool a decorative edge, shape it with a router or attach narrow molding. You can omit an apron if the stool rests on tile or a cabinet.

Creating Craftsman-style Window Casing

Craftsman-style window casing calls for simple butt joints at the corners, as well as a few beyond-the-basics flourishes. For example, this project features a cabinet head plus a two-piece apron.

Create a cabinet head to give the top casing a different look from pieces on the sides.

Stuff to Buy

LUMBER Casing
BASIC SUPPLIES 15-gauge
2½" nails, 18-gauge 1½"
nails, latex caulk

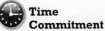 **Time Commitment**

Half a day

 Tools You'll Need

Brad nailer
Drill
Nail set
Power miter saw
Power nailer
Putty knife
Tape measure
Utility knife

 **Related Topics**

Choosing a style, 26–27
Hammers & nails, 62–63
Make it straight, level, plumb, 74–75
Trimming a window, 102–107

① Mark reveals

- Use a piece of scrap to mark how much of the jamb edges will remain visible
- See page 83 to learn how to make a gauge that speeds this step

② Cut side casings

- Measure up from the stool to the reveal marked on the top jamb
- The distance should be the same on both sides
- Cut casing pieces to that length

③ Nail sides

- Hold casing along the reveal line
- Drive 15-gauge, 2½-inch nails near the outside edge into framing
- Prevent splits by nailing the inside edge with thinner (18-gauge) nails 1½ inches long, or predrill and hammer finish nails

④ Cut the fillet

- To start the cabinet head, set a thin band of molding, known as a fillet, over the side casings
- Measure how far the fillet projects in front and allow that overlap at each end
- Cut the molding to length
- With a router or a rasp, shape the ends to match the front edge

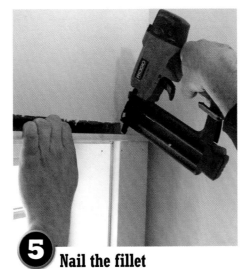

⑤ Nail the fillet

- Nail down through the molding into the side casings
- Use thin 18-gauge nails in a brad nailer
- Or predrill and hammer finish nails
- Use a single nail at least 1 inch from each end

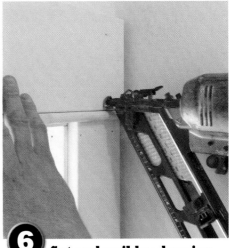

⑥ Cut and nail head casing

- Measure the distance between the outside edges of the side casings
- Cut the head casing to this length
- Set the piece in place and line up its ends with the side casings
- Drive 15-gauge, 2½-inch nails through the head casing into studs

7 Secure the fillet

- Nail up through the fillet into the head casing
- Use 18-gauge nails, or predrill and hammer finish nails

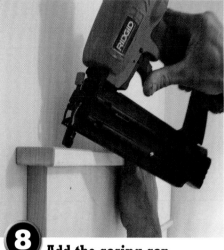

8 Add the casing cap

- This piece should be thicker and wider than the fillet
- The length should equal the total stool length, including horns
- Or, the length can be what's needed for the casing cap to overhang equally on the ends and front
- Round the ends to match the front edge, then nail in place

9 Make the apron

- Cut the main part of the apron to the same length as the head casing
- For a two-piece design like this one, cut the strip that goes directly below the stool a little longer so it's recessed equally on the ends and across the front
- Hold the pieces in position and draw a line showing where to connect them

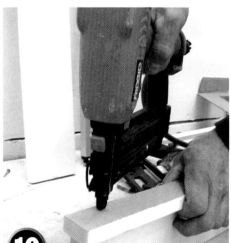

10 Assemble the apron

- Shape ends of the apron pieces to match the front edges
- On the floor, align the top apron piece over the bottom piece
- Line up the marks you made in Step 9
- Nail through the top piece into the lower one

11 Attach the apron

- Line up the apron with the side casings
- Press the apron assembly up so it's tight against the stool
- Attach the apron to the wall with 15-gauge nails, driven into studs

The finished window has a classic, Craftsman look thanks to the butt joints and horizontal lines in the trimwork that pick up on similar lines on the window itself.

When Things Go Wrong

When you're trimming a window, everything may seem to be going along perfectly. Then you stand back and notice a problem, such as casing that doesn't sit squarely on the stool. There may be a gap at the back that you didn't notice, but not to worry—there's an easy fix.

1 Pry out casing

- Slip the thin blade of a putty knife behind the casing
- Push a wooden shim between the tool and the wall, then pull the handle toward you
- As a gap opens between the trim and the wall, push the shim's tip into the space
- Repeat near every nail where the casing needs to be adjusted

2 Drive shims

- Hammer on the ends of the shims enough to bring the casing forward
- As you hammer, pull out on the fat end of each shim so you don't mar the wall
- Stop hammering when the casing surface is square with the outside edge of the stool

3 Trim shims

- Score each shim close to the casing with a utility knife
- Pull out on the fat end of the shim to break the wood along the line
- Use the knife to slice off remaining splinters

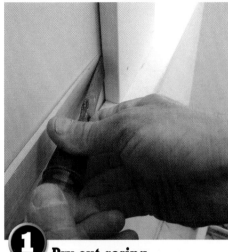

4 Caulk the gap

- Use a paintable, latex-type caulk
- Cut the tube's tip so only a small amount can flow through
- Caulk from the top to the bottom of each trim section in one pass

5 Smooth the bead

- Though purists may frown, a finger works well

6 Check for large gaps

- Inspect the seam the next day
- If caulk has shrunk and left a low spot, apply a second layer

Picture-frame Windows

Framed like a painting with simple mitered joints at each corner, this window becomes a work of art. There is no stool with this style of trim: just four strips of molding, each cut on both ends with angles at, or close to, 45 degrees.

Windows trimmed with molding to resemble a picture frame draw the eye to the scene outside.

How the Pros Do It

"When I'm working with flat trim that isn't prefinished, I don't bother with wiping off the excess glue. Instead, I sand it away. The sawdust mixes with the glue and plugs any tiny gaps in the miter joint. You have to do this before the glue hardens, though."

Larry Bell, Blumenthal Construction

1 Level jambs to wall

- If drywall extends slightly past window jambs, remove excess with a utility knife
- For situations in which drywall is actually in front of the jambs, nail wood strips to the jambs to extend them
- If the jambs extends past the drywall, shave wood with a block plane

2 Check opening

- Measure diagonally across the opening in both directions
- If measurements are equal, miters can all be 45 degrees
- If measurements aren't equal, two corners will need custom angles

3 Measure width and cut

- Measure distance between jambs at the top and bottom of the window
- Add ½ inch (assuming you want a standard ¼-inch reveal, or setback, between the jamb and the casing)
- Using that total as the length between the short sides of the miters, cut the top and bottom pieces with 45-degree angles on both ends
- Also cut two scrap pieces with 45-degree angles in opposite directions

Stuff to Buy

LUMBER Casing
BASIC SUPPLIES White wood
glue, 15-gauge 2½" nails,
1¼" finish nails

Time Commitment

Three hours

Tools You'll Need

Drill
Hammer
Nail set
Power miter saw
Power nailer
Tape measure
Utility knife

Related Topics

Choosing a style, 26–27
Installing mitered door trim,
94–99
Make it straight, level, plumb,
74–75
Trimming a window, 102–107

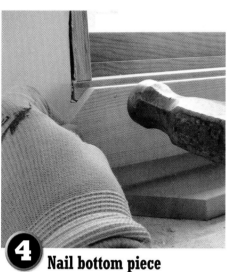

④ Nail bottom piece

- Align the bottom piece so it's centered and ¼ inch below the jamb edge
- Predrill and hammer, or use a power nailer
- Use 15-gauge, 2½-inch-long nails ½ inch up from lower edge
- Also nail ⅜ inch down from the top edge using 1¼-inch-long finish nails, which are less likely to split the jamb

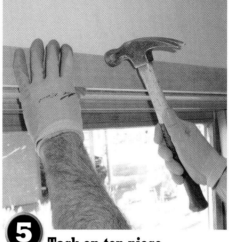

⑤ Tack on top piece

- Hold the top trim in place, ¼ inch above the edge of the head jamb
- Drive one finish nail in the center, ½ inch down from top edge
- Hammer it only part way so you can remove it in Step 9

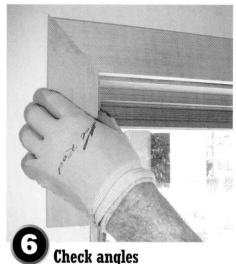

⑥ Check angles

- At each corner, hold a mitered scrap piece in place
- If miters are tight, keep your miter saw set for 45 degrees
- If gaps show at corners, adjust saw as needed (see page 55)

⑦ Measure and cut sides

- Hook a tape measure over an outside corner at the top
- Measure down to outside corner below
- Cut side piece so its long edge matches measurement
- Test the fit

⑧ Glue and nail

- Spread glue on bottom mitered edge of side jamb
- Slip piece into place and align so that both miters are tight
- Partially drive several nails ½ inch from outside edge
- Repeat for other side

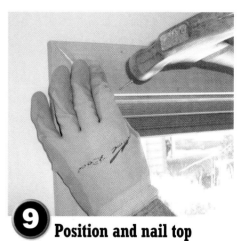

⑨ Position and nail top

- Remove top trim piece and spread glue on miters
- Replace piece, making sure nail goes into the same hole
- Nail in place and finish nailing sides
- Wipe off excess glue with a damp cloth

Creating Mitered Returns

When window or door casing has a crown that isn't flat, or when an apron has an interesting profile, you have to detail the ends so the trim doesn't look chopped off. Mitered returns allow you to wrap the trim around the ends, creating a finished look.

Cutting Upright in a Jig

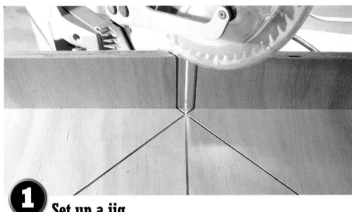

1 Set up a jig

- Very short cutoffs tend to become airborne projectiles
- Prevent this by building an L-shape jig (see page 137)
- Attach the jig by screwing from the back through slots in the saw's fence
- Adjust the miter saw so it cuts only a very shallow line in the base of the jig
- If the molding fits upright, make three cuts as shown—at 90 degrees, and at 45 degrees to the right and left

2 Make a marking block

- An inch or so from the end of the trim, make a straight cut
- Set the cutoff on its side on the stock, next to the end you just cut
- Line up the top and bottom edges
- At the thickest end of the cutoff, mark the molding to show where you will cut the first mitered return
- Draw a short diagonal line to keep track of which way to angle the cut

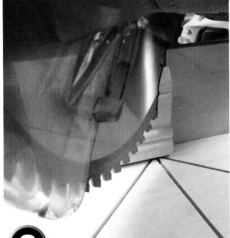

3 Cut the miter

- Adjust the miter saw to cut at 45 degrees in the direction you just marked
- Place the trim board so the kerf on the jig is just to the waste side of the cut mark
- Make the cut
- Save the small cutoff

4 Cut an opposite miter

- Adjust the blade to cut at 45 degrees in the opposite direction
- At the same end of the stock, cut just inside of where you made the first bevel
- Discard the triangular cutoff

5 Measure and cut to length

- From the long tip you just cut, mark the front length of the trim
- If you are installing head casing for a window, the length may be equal to the stool's length
- If so, just place the head casing on the stool and mark it

 **Stuff to Buy**
LUMBER Molding, plywood
BASIC SUPPLIES Sandpaper,
wood glue, painter's tape

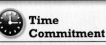 **Time Commitment**
An hour or so

 **Tools You'll Need**
Power miter saw
Rasp
Tape measure
Utility knife

Related Topics
Mitering crown, 136–137
Power miter saws, 52–55

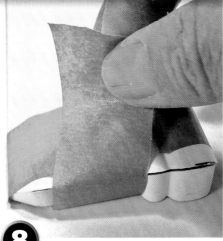

6 Cut the remaining miter

- Reset the saw to cut 45 degrees in the opposite direction
- Cut close to the end you cut in Step 5; discard the cutoff

7 Make a straight cut

- With the molding upright or flat, cut off the mitered end
- Line up the cut using the kerf on the jig; it should be along the waste side of the bevel

8 Glue and tape

- One end at a time, spread wood glue on the returns and the main molding
- Press the pieces together and align them
- Wipe off excess glue
- Secure with painter's tape until the glue dries
- Don't use nails; they might split the molding

Shaping Returns

Instead of cutting mitered returns, it's also possible to shape molding so its profile continues around the ends. If you're using lightweight MDF molding, it's actually quite simple because this material cuts and sands easily.

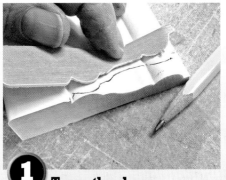

1 Trace the shape

- Cut a very thin slice from one end of a piece of molding
- Use it as a template to trace the shape on the end of the stock
- Bend it down as needed so you get a fairly accurate line

2 Cut along the line

- With a coping saw, cut out the shape
- Try to keep the saw vertical; don't undercut, as you would for a coped joint
- Stay just outside the line
- If the blade binds, ease it backward and make a relief cut from the end

3 Smooth the shape

- With a sharp utility blade, clean up any straight lines on the profile
- Make them lead straight back, not at an angle
- Then tidy up the curved areas with a rasp or sandpaper

5

Installing Running Trim

In this chapter, we focus on the horizontal bands of trim that run around your home—from the wide baseboards down by the floor to the eye-catching ribbons of crown up near the ceiling. Mitering the corners of these types of running trim is covered in detail, as are techniques such as coping an inside corner, fastening crown to masonry, and cutting your own custom trim profiles out of regular stock.

Chapter Contents

Baseboard, Chair Rail, Crown
page 118

Working with Horizontal Trim
page 120

Baseboards
page 122

Coping Inside Corners
page 124

Other Baseboard Techniques
page 126

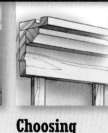
Choosing Horizontal Trim
page 128

Choosing Crown Molding
page 130

Preparing for Crown Molding
page 132

Installing Crown Molding
page 134

Mitering Crown
page 136

Built-up Crown
page 138

Making Your Own Molding
page 140

Baseboard, Chair Rail, Crown

Like ribbon on a package, horizontal trim makes a room look tidy and complete. All rooms deserve at least a thin baseboard to cover what's otherwise an ugly junction of the wall and flooring. But in elegant rooms, baseboards are just the beginning.

Bands of horizontal trim give this room a modern Craftsman look that's also rooted in Japanese style. Craftsman designers borrowed many ideas from Japanese traditions, including an emphasis on finely crafted but otherwise unadorned woodwork.

Bands of flat, mostly straight trim make a dramatic statement in this living room and continue the horizontal theme set by the alternating bands of white and taupe on the fireplace surround at the far left.

In modern décor, the difference between an elegantly spare interior and a room that seems flat and lifeless can literally be a fine line. In this living room, it's a band of horizontal chair rail. The rail is repeated in the room beyond, adding texture and creating an interesting shadow-box effect.

Chair or picture-rail molding divide a wall into distinct sections, so they allow you to create multiple-color paint schemes. You can stick with one color for the molding, the lower portion of the wall, and the baseboard, or choose a three-color paint scheme, as was done in this room.

Adding Practical Features to Horizontal Trim

With the addition of hooks or pegs, horizontal trim becomes a storage system. Mounting the hangers to the trim eliminates the need to align the fittings over studs or fasten them to drywall anchors. The top trim in this room lines up with the top of the door; the lower rail lines up with the crosspiece near the center of the door.

Pegs on horizontal trim can support far more than coats and bags. In traditional Shaker communities, even chairs went up when it was time to clean, and this strategy for keeping the floor clear works just as well today.

A bracket shelf (see pages 146–147) works well as an element of horizontal trim, especially over windows or doors. If you live where earthquakes are a possibility, use special putty, straps, or hook-and-loop fasteners to anchor display pieces that are heavy or fragile.

Working with Horizontal Trim

Chair rail, plate rail, and picture rail make ideal beginner projects. At the other end of the spectrum is crown molding. If you're new to trimwork, start with an easy project before you tackle a job that requires you to be up on a ladder as you deal with two surfaces.

Joinery for Horizontal Trim

You'll use four kinds of joints on horizontal trim: butt, scarf, coped, and mitered. You need to know what they are in order to plan your installation. See the rest of this chapter for details about how to cut them.

Butt Joint	Scarf Joint	Miter Joint	Coped Joint

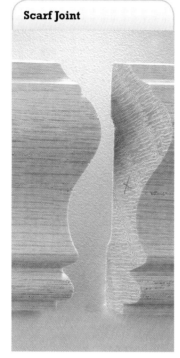

Butt Joint
- On each piece, make a straight cut perpendicular to the length of the molding unless you need to scribe the second piece to accommodate a slanted wall
- Use when molding dead-ends into a wall or another flat surface, including flat trim
- Also suitable for end-to-end connections in plastic molding
- Do not use to splice wood or MDF molding; you'll see a gap if the wood shrinks

Scarf Joint
- Make 30-degree bevel cuts in opposite directions on the ends of two pieces of molding
- Use when splicing wood or MDF molding to get a longer piece
- From the front, this joint looks like a butt joint; on the edges, you see the bevels
- Always locate this joint over a stud, except for narrow baseboard (which is nailed only to the bottom plate of wall framing)
- Orient bevels so the top piece points away from you as you walk into a room
- The joint stays tight even if the molding shrinks

Miter Joint
- Make bevel cuts of 45 degrees on two trim pieces so they meet to form a crisp corner; on out-of-square corners, adjust angle as necessary
- For outside corners, cut so the short end is against the wall and the long tip faces out
- Also suitable for inside corners on some plastic molding; cut so the long tip is at the back, aimed into the corner
- Not recommended for inside corners on wood or MDF molding because you'll see a gap if the material shrinks

Coped Joint
- Make a straight cut on the first piece and butt it into the corner
- Shape the end of the second piece so it fits tightly against the side of its mating piece
- Use for inside corners when trimwork is wood or MDF molding
- Though time-consuming, this joint easily accommodates corners that aren't perfectly square; the joint stays tight even if the molding shrinks

Planning an Installation

With horizontal trim, it makes a big difference which pieces you install first. The correct order saves time and hassle, and helps minimize waste. It also ensures that your trimwork will look best from the angle that's most important to you. Sketch the room and work out several scenarios until you settle on a plan that gives you as many advantages as possible. Here are some general rules of thumb:

- Try to avoid having a complex cut (a cope or a miter) on both ends of a single piece. This way, you can leave the molding a little long as you cut the tricky joint. If it doesn't turn out as you like, just try again an inch or so further in. Once you're satisfied, trim the piece to length.
- Coped joints look best from the end or at an angle, not when you are directly across from them. To ensure that trim looks great when people enter a room, put the first piece, with the butt cuts, on the wall opposite the door. Cope the trim that goes on either side.
- In a room with many twists and turns, try to cut the longest pieces first. If you mess up, you can use that molding to make shorter pieces.

CUTTING SEQUENCE

As you work out a cutting sequence, try to maximize the advantages and minimize the disadvantages of the order you choose. This is the most common cutting sequence for a basic, rectangular room. It puts coped joints in the direction that looks best as you enter, but it results in having copes on both ends of Piece 4—not ideal but acceptable. If you cut a messy cope joint on one end, use the good end and splice on a new piece (with a scarf joint) for the end you need to redo.

Efficiency Tip

If you're right-handed, it's easier to work counter-clockwise as you install horizontal trim. If you're left-handed, try to work clockwise. With either strategy, you can install each piece by using your unfavored hand to support the free end while the good hand drives the fasteners.

Cutting Sequence

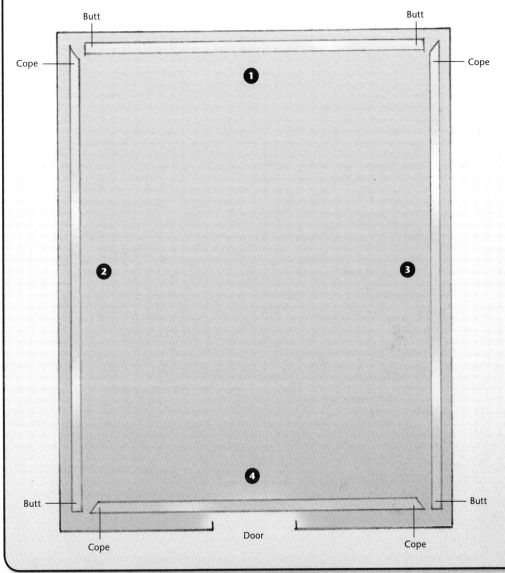

Trim details on built-ins often call for the same strategies that work for horizontal molding. For example, the cove molding under the divider on this cabinet is mitered on the outside corner but coped on the inside corner, which is hidden from view.

Baseboards

Baseboards are usually the last trim pieces to go into a room. That lets you fit them to door and window casing and against a finished floor. If flooring will be installed later, place spacers of the appropriate height under the baseboard pieces as you work.

Baseboard Evolution

Baseboard styles have changed over the years as materials and building methods have changed. An older baseboard often has three parts: a thick baseboard, plus a separate cap and shoe. The thinner pieces are flexible enough to follow wavy walls or floorboards, hiding gaps and plugging drafts. A modern baseboard often has the cap shape milled into the top; the baseboard itself is thin enough to follow slight irregularities in a wall. Streamlined baseboard skips the cap shape entirely. Though it's often called clamshell trim today, it was originally known as sanitary base, a reference to the way the shape sheds dust.

Your Choices

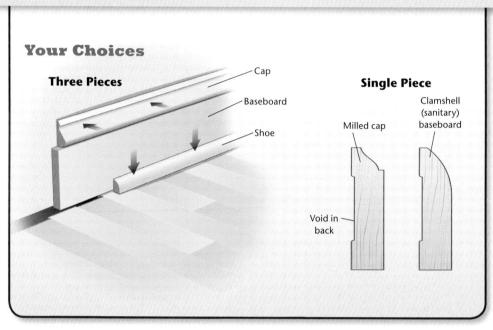

Three Pieces
Cap
Baseboard
Shoe

Single Piece
Milled cap
Clamshell (sanitary) baseboard
Void in back

Installing Flat Baseboard

With flat baseboard you don't need to cope joints. But the same cutting sequence for coped joints (see pages 120–121) makes sense because butt joints on inside corners look best from the same angle that coped joints do.

1 Evaluate surfaces

- As with any trim project, start by checking whether the wall and floor are straight
- If drywall bulges out in a corner, hammer it in; pound against a thin piece of wood so the drywall doesn't crack
- Also locate and mark studs; use a stud sensor or tap on the wall

2 Position first piece

- Measure the width of the first wall
- Cut a baseboard to that length
- Put it in position
- If you need to tap the baseboard to seat it against the floor, hammer on scrap wood so you don't dent the baseboard

3 Nail the baseboard

- Attach the baseboard to studs at the corners
- Put one nail near the top, into the stud, and the other near the bottom, into the wall's base plate
- Use 15- or 18-gauge nails in a power fastener, or hand-hammer 2- to 2½-inch nails, depending on the baseboard's thickness
- At each stud, drive two more nails through the baseboard

 **Stuff to Buy**
LUMBER Baseboard molding
BASIC SUPPLIES Nails, wood glue

 **Time Commitment**
Depends on extent of project

 Tools You'll Need
Hammer
Power miter saw

 **Related Topics**
Other baseboard techniques, 126–127
Power miter saws, 52–55
Working with horizontal trim, 120–121

④ Fit the mate

- Make a square cut on a trim piece that's a little longer than you need
- If you see a gap where the baseboards meet, re-cut the end at a slightly different angle

⑤ Outside corners

- After you cut the non-mitered end, hold the piece in position
- Press it tightly to the wall and back into the first corner
- At the end you plan to miter, trace against the wall to mark the back face of the baseboard

⑥ Make a miter cut

- Depending on your saw and the baseboard height, decide whether to cut the baseboard upright or flat
- Adjust the saw to cut a 45-degree bevel
- Make the cut, then place the piece in position
- Check that the inside edge of the bevel lines up exactly with the corner or reaches a tad beyond
- If it's too short, either cut a new piece or drive a shim behind the mating baseboard on the other end and plug the gap there with caulk

⑦ Nail the miter

- If the piece for the other side of the corner is short and you have extra material, cut a matching miter in the same way
- Otherwise, cut and fit a test piece first
- Spread wood glue on both beveled surfaces
- Snug the baseboard into position
- Nail in place, starting with two nails into framing behind the drywall corner
- Immediately wipe or sand off any glue residue

⑧ Doorway detail

- Use this procedure to ensure a tight fit to door casing or a plinth
- Cut and install the other end of the baseboard first
- Then put the piece in position, but out from the wall by the thickness of the casing
- Mark where it intersects with the casing
- Cut just outside of the mark
- Or use a preacher which automatically adjusts for trim or a plinth that isn't plumb

How the Pros Do It

"Instead of marking every stud, I just measure from an electrical outlet if I know a house has studs on 16-inch centers. Outlets usually have a stud on one side or the other, so I tap on the wall to find the location. I measure over ¾ inch from the side of the outlet to get to the center of the stud. Then I stretch out my tape and nail."

*Dewey Goodrich,
Blumenthal Construction*

Coping Baseboard Corners

Installing baseboard with surface details calls for a different procedure on inside corners. The quickest option is to cut inside miters on both pieces. However, if the room is not square, coped joints are actually easier and will look better if a gap opens at the corner.

1 Miter the end

- Start with trim that's longer than you need by at least the thickness of the baseboard
- Adjust a miter saw to cut a 45-degree bevel with the baseboard flat or standing, depending on the type of miter saw and the height of the baseboard
- Cut the bevel on the end that you want to cope
- Orient the bevel so its longest tip will be against the wall

2 Make a partial butt cut

- Most baseboard is primarily flat, with a small curved area on top
- Only the top part needs to be coped; the flat section can have a butt cut
- After you bevel the end, adjust the miter saw to cut straight down
- With the long part of bevel flat on the saw table, carefully cut off the bevel, but only as far as the curved section
- You will need to cut the last bit by hand

3 Mark the cope

- Rub the side of a pencil lead along the curved portion of the molding
- This makes the profile easier to see

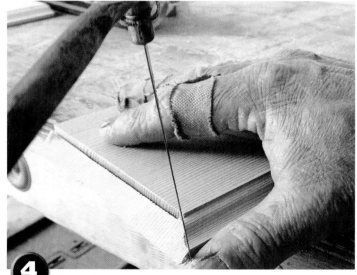

4 Start the cope

- Clamp or press the baseboard against a firm surface, with the area to cope facing you
- With one hand, hold a coping saw tilted just slightly forward of vertical
- With the thumb of your other hand steadying the back of the blade, make a few shallow strokes to begin cutting at the edge of the molding
- From the top edge of the baseboard, these strokes should result in what looks like a butt cut

Tools You'll Need
Coping saw
Power miter saw
Rasp

Related Topics
Give yourself a second chance, 84–85
Other baseboard techniques, 126–127
Power miter saws, 52–55

⑤ Twist and turn

- Continue cutting just outside of the line
- Back-cut the edge, so the angle between the edge and the front is a little more than 90 degrees
- This helps ensure that the joint will be tight at the front, where it matters

⑥ Clean up the edges

- Test how the baseboard fits against its mating piece
- If you see gaps, shave off high spots
- A rattail rasp (shown) gets into tight curves
- You might also need sandpaper, an oval rasp, or even a utility knife

How the Pros Do It

"To test whether a cope fits, just hold the piece you are cutting against a scrap of the same material."

John Backland, Carley Construction

Coping with Tight Turns

If a piece of molding has sharp curves that a coping saw blade can't negotiate easily, don't try to force it or you won't wind up with a crisp edge. Ease the blade out of the molding by pulling it backward through the opening you just cut. You might need to move the blade up and down as you do this so it doesn't bind. From the waste side, make a relief cut straight through to the part where the blade wouldn't turn. Then resume cutting.

Other Baseboard Techniques

Coping the inside corners (pages 124–125) is just one of many tricks and techniques you may need to know when installing baseboards. Here are a few of the most common situations you are likely to encounter, along with simple solutions.

Mitering Outside Corners

Save time and frustration by cutting test pieces for outside mitered corners. Start with a scrap about 2 feet long, and cut a 45-degree bevel on one end. Mark which side goes up if the orientation isn't obvious. Install a real length of baseboard on one side of the corner first; make certain the inside edge of the bevel reaches all the way to the corner. Then place the test piece on the other side, and check how the joint fits.

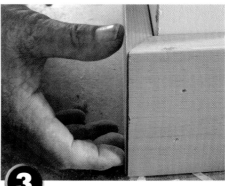

3 **If you see an overlap**

- Once you cut the actual piece, you may see a uniform overlap on the end
- This means the piece is a little too long
- Trim a tiny amount at the same angle

1 **If you see a uniform gap**

- If the gap is at the front, pivot out the back end of the scrap piece
- If the gap doesn't close, check for debris
- If the gap closes, you need to remove material from the back of the bevel
- Return the test piece to the wall
- Next to the corner, mark a distance that corresponds to the width of the gap at the front of the bevel
- If the gap is at the back, you need to remove material from the front

2 **Trim to the line**

- Adjust the miter saw angle so the blade will shave up to the mark but just skim the bevel's tip
- If your saw can't cut an angle that steep, use shims to change the position
- Place the shims under the baseboard if it's flat on the saw's base or behind the baseboard if it's vertical (see page 55)
- Cut the test piece, check the fit, then use the same saw setting and shim placement to cut the actual piece

4 **If the gap isn't equally wide**

- Check with a square to determine whether the bevel on the first piece was cut straight up and down
- If that angle is off, cut the test piece again so the bevel runs at an angle across its face
- Or, if you don't have a saw that cuts compound angles, shim under the baseboard to make it tilt on the end, then cut it vertically
- If the bevel on the first piece is fine, the problem may be that the drywall does not reach all the way to the floor
- Drive screws into the base plate just far enough so the heads project as far as the drywall above them
- If this fixes the problem, note the screw locations so you don't nail the baseboard into the same spots

Wrapping Registers

If you are using Colonial baseboard or another style of one-piece baseboard with a shaped top, rip an edge strip from scrap material to make molding that you can miter around the register. If you are using shoe molding, stop it in front of the register. Miter the ends and glue on a return miter (see pages 114–115), or just bevel it.

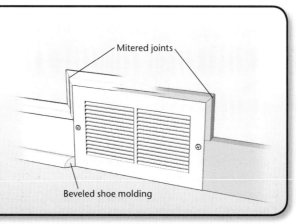

Mitered joints

Beveled shoe molding

Related Topics
Baseboards, 122–123
Mitered trim for doors, 94–97
Power miter saws, 52–55

Avoiding the Splits

Next to a doorway, you may have room for only a slender piece of baseboard. Don't nail it; that's too likely to split the wood. This nail-free approach works well.

1 Make the piece
- Install the short piece before installing the long side
- Measure the gap
- Cut the baseboard to fit

2 Tap in place
- Slip the piece into position
- Tap on a scrap piece to seat it to the floor
- If the fit isn't snug, cut a new piece that's a bit wider

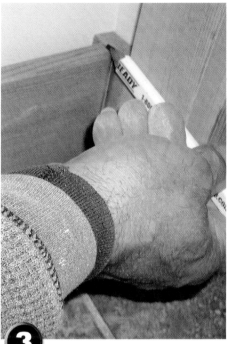

3 Fit the next piece
- If the short baseboard piece isn't vertical, you may see a gap
- Correct this by scribing along the end of the second piece; trim to the line

Make a Preacher

This homemade gauge helps you accurately mark baseboard where it dead-ends into door casing. Instead of going by a single mark on the top edge, as shown on page 123, you get a full line across the baseboard, and it's automatically adjusted to account for any tilt in the casing or plinth.

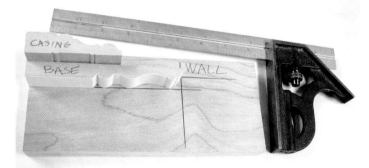

1 Making the gauge
- Choose a rectangular scrap of wood or plywood about 3 inches taller than the baseboard and about 5 inches wide
- Mark one long edge as "wall"
- Measure across by the thickness of the door casing or plinth and draw a parallel line
- Using that as one side and one of the 5-inch edges as another, draw a rectangle that matches the baseboard's height and thickness
- Cut along those lines

2 Using it
- Position the baseboard along the wall
- Hook the jig over it as shown
- Snug the preacher to the casing
- Trace against the preacher on the side facing the casing

Choosing Horizontal Trim

When a room already has door trim, window casing, and baseboard, it's a good candidate for another kind of horizontal trim, such as chair rail, picture rail, or plate rail. There is no fixed height for these types of trim; placement depends on how the elements line up.

Design Considerations

Bands of horizontal trim help make especially tall rooms seem more human-scale. They also help unify an interior space, especially if the same theme is repeated from room to room. This kind of trim tends to be flat rather than ornate. It works especially well in houses with modern styling or details that evoke a Craftsman feel.

Determine placement by the highest opening in the room so that the bands can circle each room unobstructed. If some windows or doors are lower, plug the gap between the head casing and the band with a slightly recessed filler strip. Don't make a zig-zag band or it will look like a mistake.

Chair Rails

This kind of horizontal trim was invented to keep the backs of chairs from denting plaster walls. If you have the same need today, measure where your chairs hit when they are tipped back, and install the trim accordingly. Otherwise, consider going with the most common height, 36 inches. You can use chair rail or plate rail on its own, or make it the top piece of a wainscot project. Install single-piece chair rail so its widest part is oriented toward the top, as shown at top, right.

For a more substantial chair rail, use several pieces of trim (right). First install a piece about 4 inches wide flat against the wall. Above that, nail on a narrower cap, maybe 2 inches wide. Consider supporting the cap underneath with cove, quarter-round, or bed molding.

Single-piece Chair Rail

Built-up Chair Rail

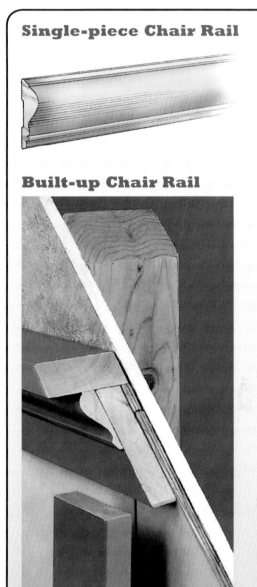

PAIRING THICK WITH THIN

If door or window casing is thicker than chair rail (left), just dead-end the rail into the casing with a butt cut. But if the chair rail is thicker than the casing (far left), it should wrap over the casing a little way. Notch the end of the rail to get a good fit.

Plate Rails

Plate rail is similar to chair rail, but the cap projects more and it has a groove that cradles plates or other display items so they don't topple if someone slams a door. Choose a simple, relatively streamlined design (below) if you want the molding low, like standard chair rail. More substantial plate rails (bottom) are often found higher up on the wall. In Craftsman houses, plate rails are often about 60 inches up from the floor.

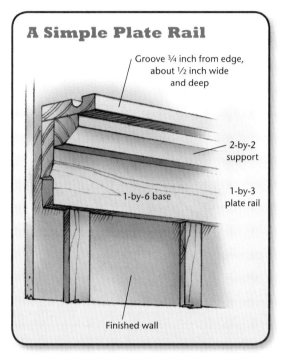

A Simple Plate Rail

Groove ¾ inch from edge, about ½ inch wide and deep

2-by-2 support

1-by-6 base

1-by-3 plate rail

Finished wall

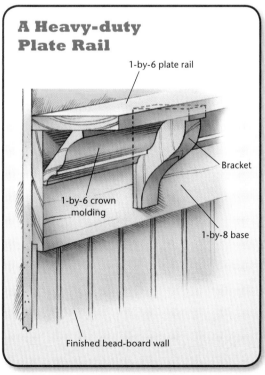

A Heavy-duty Plate Rail

1-by-6 plate rail

Bracket

1-by-6 crown molding

1-by-8 base

Finished bead-board wall

Picture Rails

Picture rail came about so that people could hang framed paintings without nailing into plaster walls. Today, most walls are drywall, which isn't as likely to crack if you hammer in a nail, but picture rail endures because it adds style and still serves a practical purpose.

In Victorian interiors with high ceilings, picture rail is often about a foot below the crown molding, and the band in between is often decorated. Some Craftsman houses have picture molding directly below the crown molding, with just enough of a gap to insert the hangers. This makes the picture rail look like an extension of the crown. But many other Craftsman houses don't have crown molding. In those, as well as in homes of other architectural styles, the picture rail often runs along the top of the door and window head casing, or it butts into the head casing about halfway down.

Related Topics

Baseboards, 122–127
Bead-board wainscot, 172–178
Crown molding, 130–139

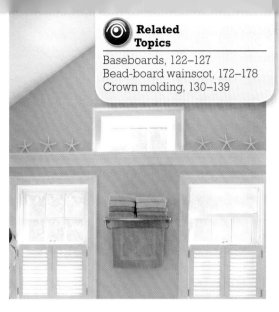

A plate rail can be used to display many types of collections, not just ceramic plates.

Picture rail has a recess at the back along the top edge. You can purchase special metal hangers that clip over the edge and secure wires or cords attached to picture frames.

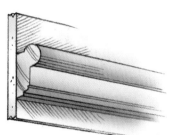

In this girl's room, picture rail butts into the side of the window head casing. Though no longer used to hang pictures, it still serves a useful design role because it and the walls above are painted white. That border keeps the room's predominant lilac-and-orange color scheme from being overbearing.

Choosing Crown Molding

Crown molding gets its name from its position at the corner of a ceiling and a wall, but the royal symbolism is also appropriate. Nothing polishes off a room and elevates its sense of style quite like a band of crown molding.

Elegant yet simple, the one-piece crown molding in this room harmonizes well with the baseboard trim. Both feature soft, elliptical curves. The crown molding is the same style featured in the installation on pages 132–137.

Built up from several layers and painted in almost as many colors, the crown in this house is relatively elaborate. Yet it's still somewhat subdued, thanks to the pastel shades and its emphasis on simple shapes.

Going Ornate

Far at the other end of the scale from simple crown, this sculptural treatment works well in formal rooms with high ceilings. It would overwhelm a smaller space and look out of character with many decorating styles. But if you want drama, it certainly delivers. Details like these are often made of plastic these days but they were traditionally made from plaster or wood.

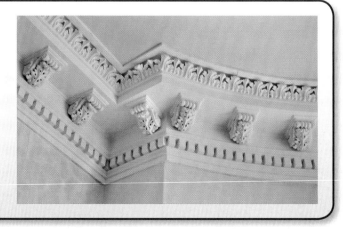

Shopping Tip

When you shop for crown molding, you might wonder which edge goes down. The answer is easy: it's the edge with the most detail.

A high ceiling can give a bedroom an airy feeling, but it can also leave a space seeming too open and cold. Crown molding can help achieve a better balance in situations like this, where walls are lower on two sides. Wrapping the crown around the high end walls visually lowers them and creates a cozier atmosphere.

A simple bookcase evolved into an elegant built-in with the addition of crown molding. If the room already has crown, you might want to choose a smaller or less ornate version for a cabinet top. In other rooms, such as this one where there is no crown, you can go the opposite way. The cabinet crown is a beefier version of the trimwork over the window's head casing.

Linking window treatments to crown molding can make short walls seem taller because it creates the illusion that the windows reach all the way to the ceiling. Here, a two-part crown rings a room with uninterrupted molding, yet still accommodates a curtain rod.

Preparing for Crown Molding

Crown molding requires special preparation because of the way ceilings are framed. Some ceilings do not have framing where you need it, so you need to add blocking. The shape of the blocking needs to match the angle that the crown tilts into the room.

Installing Blocking

1 Establish a level line

- Position a scrap of molding against a wall and ceiling
- Mark the void behind the molding on the drywall and ceiling, then draw a short line ¼ inch below the molding
- Mark other places on the wall that are level with the line, then snap a chalk line to connect the marks
- Measure up from the line to the ceiling to determine where the ceiling sags most
- Use that measurement to adjust the gap between the chalk line and the bottom edge of the crown

2 Locate joists and studs

- Joists typically run the same direction as rafters, perpendicular to the roof peak, 16 inches apart on center
- If you hit an empty space, test an inch or so to either side
- When you hit wood, make holes on both sides to determine the joist's center
- Once you're sure of the spacing, mark remaining increments here and on the opposite side of the room

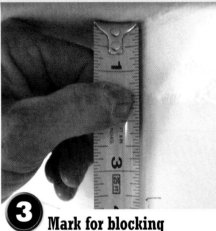

3 Mark for blocking

- Over walls perpendicular to joists, you need to add triangular blocking to secure nails aimed at the ceiling
- To determine the size of the blocking, measure the distances from the corner of the wall and ceiling to the lines you made in Step 1 to mark the void behind the crown
- Don't worry if the corner is not perfectly square

4 Make blocking

- Cut a square edge on a scrap piece of 2 by 4 or similar stock that's at least 1½ inches thick
- Draw a line connecting the marks and a second line about ⅛ inch inside and parallel to that
- Cut along the second line with a circular saw

5 Attach blocking

- Squirt construction adhesive on the blocking edge that fits against the wall
- Place the blocking between the ceiling and the wall, over one of the studs you marked
- To hold the piece while the adhesive cures, shoot one or two nails horizontally through the blocking into the stud; use nails at least 2 inches long

Temporary Corner Braces

Give yourself an extra hand by tacking temporary support strips across the corners in a room where you plan to install crown molding. Cut the braces with 45-degree ends, and nail them a little lower than the crown molding's bottom edge.

 **Stuff to Buy**	**Time Commitment**	**Tools You'll Need**	**Related Topics**
LUMBER Crown molding, 2 x 4s, 1 x 4s **BASIC SUPPLIES** Nails, construction adhesive	A day to a weekend	Chalk line Circular saw Hammer Level Nail gun Power miter saw Tape measure	Choosing materials, 40–41 Installing crown molding, 134–135 Mitering crown molding, 136–137 Power miter saws, 52–55

Fastening Crown to Masonry

Although you can use masonry anchors to fix crown molding to brick or block, that approach requires drilling fairly large holes, which then need to be patched. It's easier to attach support boards and then nail the crown to them. You can't just glue on the crown because only a thin edge of it would be against the brick. But you can glue a wide and light piece of framing.

1 Cut and glue

- Extend a level line across the masonry
- Cut 1 by 4s or other flat boards to follow the line; miter the outside corners, butt the inside ones
- Test the fit and establish a way to clamp or brace each piece
- Spread a generous amount of construction adhesive on the back of one piece
- Put it in place without smearing the adhesive
- Set the bottom edge 1/8 inch lower than you want the crown's bottom edge to be

2 Set braces

- Attach bracing to hold the trim while the adhesive dries
- A two-piece brace that rests on the floor or mantel keeps the support board from sliding down
- Add diagonal braces between the trim and the ceiling
- Drive one nail at each end of each brace

3 Nail and set clamps

- On outside corners, miter the ends of the support boards
- Spread construction adhesive on the back and wood glue on the miters
- Use clamps or braces, plus nails, to hold the joints while glue cures; nail only through the miter, not into the masonry
- The horizontal stick on the right is wedged against a nearby wall so it pushes the board against the brick

4 Install molding

- Wait until the next day to remove the clamps and braces
- Cut and install crown molding as shown on pages 134–137
- Leave the bottom 1/8 inch of the trim board exposed; creating this reveal is much easier than trying to get the pieces to line up precisely

Installing Crown Molding

Once you finish the preparation steps on pages 132–133, map out a plan for yourself to minimize the places where you need to cut two tricky joints—a cope or a miter—on the same piece. Start installation on the longest wall opposite the main door.

① Cut and install the first piece

- Measure the distance between the two walls where you will start
- Assuming both ends butt against walls, make straight cuts
- Nail the piece horizontally near the bottom edge, into each of the studs you marked

② Nail into ceiling or blocking

- Higher up on the molding, drive a nail at an angle into the ceiling joist
- Or, if you installed triangular blocking along the wall, nail at an angle into it
- Nailing should pull the crown tight against the ceiling
- If the ceiling dips considerably, some gaps may remain; plug those later with caulk

③ Cut for an inside corner

- Choose a second piece at least 6 inches longer than you'll need
- To cope this joint, first cut an inside miter
- Cut the molding so the long tip is at the back

④ Cope the curve

- Use a coping saw (pages 124–125)
- Or cut with a jigsaw held upside down so the rough edge is on the back
- Use a long jigsaw blade so it clears the molding
- Clamp or hold the molding to a stiff work surface, and keep the teeth away from the molding when you switch on the motor
- Begin cutting in the middle of the molding, not on the top or bottom edge
- Tilt the saw so it angles in slightly on the back

⑤ Cut at different angles

- Move your body and the saw as needed to follow the molding's shape
- If you get into a tight spot, turn off the saw and extract the blade
- Remove some of the waste material by making a separate cut in from the outside edge

⑥ Switch to a coping saw

- To cut the delicate edges, use a hand coping saw
- Also use the saw's tiny teeth to clean up sharp corners

Stuff to Buy

LUMBER Crown molding
BASIC SUPPLIES Nails,
  sandpaper, wood glue

Time Commitment

A day or weekend per room

Tools You'll Need

Coping saw
Jigsaw
Nail gun
Power miter saw
Spring clamp
Utility knife

Related Topics

Coping inside corners, 124–125
Other baseboard techniques,
  126–127
Mitering crown, 136–137
Preparing for crown molding,
  132–133

7 Fine-tune the fit

- Place the coped edge against the side of a scrap of the molding, with the molding cocked to the angle of the crown
- If you see gaps, there are high spots you need to remove
- Fine-tune with sandpaper, a rasp, or a sharp utility knife
- As a final check, snug the coped end against its installed mate
- Wait to install the coped molding until you have shaped the other end

8 Miter an outside corner

- First shape the other end of the molding
- Position the crown at the correct distance up from your guideline; push the other end against its mating surface
- Trace against the outside corner of the wall to mark the short end of the crown on the molding's back lower edge

9 Miter and test

- Using the same procedure and settings as in Step 3, cut the miter
- This time, though, the long tip will point away from the wall
- Hold a test piece against the opposite wall to check the miter's fit
- Close a gap by adapting the strategies shown for baseboard miters on pages 126–127

10 Finish installing the first piece

- If the piece has a miter or cope on the other end, spread wood glue on it
- Position the molding
- Nail in place, using the same procedure described in Steps 1 and 2

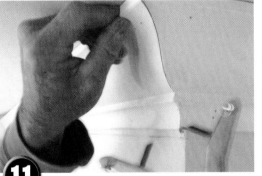

11 Install the second piece

- Cut the mating miter according to what you learned from the test piece in Step 9
- Spread wood glue on the mitered ends (and also on the far end, if it is not a butt cut)
- Position the molding
- Drive a single nail horizontally through the lower part of the molding, into a stud
- Secure a spring clamp, if available, to pull the miter closed
- Or shoot a couple of thin nails sideways at the top to hold the joint while the glue dries
- Wipe off any excess glue

12 Continue fastening

- With the corner secure, nail the molding to the other studs and blocking
- Continue on around the room, using the same procedure
- If you need to splice sections, locate the joint over a stud and cut the end at 30 degrees
- Install that piece, then measure the remaining distance and cut the matching piece
- If you need to cope both ends on the last wall, measure the length from the inside lower edges of the crown on the side walls, not from the walls themselves

Mitering Crown

Miter cuts on crown molding are more involved than those for other horizontal trim because most crown sits at an angle. To adjust for this, hold the trim at an angle (by hand or with a jig) as you cut, or place it on a miter saw's base and angle the saw and the table.

Make Samples

Unless you own a saw that cuts compound bevels right and left, you have to cut crown either upside down and backwards, or at an angle that isn't intuitive. Avoid confusion, and mistakes, by spending a few minutes making four sample blocks, each with a miter oriented a different way.

If you are cutting trim while holding it at an angle, the arrow reminds you to point the wall edge up.

Hold the pieces as if they were on a wall and label them.

Cool Tool

Instead of using a sliding bevel and a protractor to determine the molding's angle, you can instead use a miter saw protractor, which has arms that act as a bevel gauge and a dial that shows the angle.

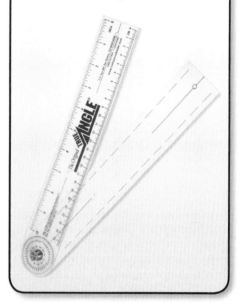

Mitering with the Crown Flat

This method allows you to cut wider crown molding, but it's possible only with a saw that cuts compound angles. The tilt of the blade and the angle on the base vary with the style of the molding. You could work out the angles through a formula, but the math is dizzying. Use the chart at right instead. Always cut test pieces to check and fine-tune angles before you cut long pieces of crown.

FIND THE MOLDING'S ANGLE

- Adjust a sliding bevel to the angle between the bottom of the crown (the wall edge) and the flat back of the molding
- Align the bevel with a protractor as shown on page 77
- Use the chart at right to determine settings for your saw

DEGREE SETTINGS WHEN CROWN IS MITERED FLAT

Most crown molding is angled at either 38 or 45 degrees. The adjustment mechanisms on miter saws usually have catches that are set for these. You may also encounter molding with the other angles in this table.

Molding angle	Miter angle on table	Bevel or tilt of the blade
30	27	38
35	30.5	38
38	31.5	34
40	33	33
45	35	30
52	38	26

Option 1: Mitering Crown at an Angle

This is the simplest way to cut miters on crown molding, and it's the only option if you have a basic miter saw. The crown needs to be skinny enough for your saw to cut it in that position.

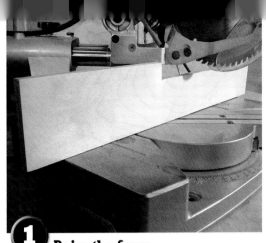

1 Raise the fence

- Cut a scrap of crown molding
- Hold it right side up at an angle, with the ceiling edge against the table and the wall edge against the fence
- If the fence is too low for the molding, make a taller fence from plywood; you may need to notch near the blade, as shown
- Secure the plywood by screwing from the back through slots in the saw's fence

2 Draw a guideline

- Position a baseboard scrap so the ceiling edge is against the table and the wall edge is against the fence
- Mark the height in several places
- Use a straightedge to connect the marks
- Hold molding against this line as you cut it

Option 2: Making a Crown Jig

Gravity works in your favor with this jig. Instead of holding the molding at an angle against a line on the fence, you just nestle it against a stop on the jig's base.

1 Make an L bracket

- Cut a strip of ½ inch plywood about 24 inches long and as wide as the height under your saw
- Cut a second piece at least 1 inch wider than the distance the crown will project on the ceiling
- Place the first piece against the fence and mark where the blade hits when adjusted to the maximum angle left and right
- Nail the pieces together, but don't put any nails within the marked area
- Attach the jig by screwing through slots in the saw's fence

2 Cut diagonals

- Adjust the depth of the cut so the blade just cuts into the surface of the jig
- Cut a 45-degree angle one way, then the other
- Make a third cut up the middle
- Use the cuts as guidelines when you need to cut to precise lengths

3 Complete jig

- Place a short piece of crown face up on the jig; treat the back of the jig as the wall and the base as the ceiling
- Trace along the crown on the base
- Attach a thin strip of wood on the side of the line toward you; again keep nails away from where the blade will cut
- The strip on the base will now line up the ceiling edge
- Press the wall edge of the crown against the back of the jig as you cut

Built-up Crown

If you want a look that's showier than one-piece crown molding, consider adding additional layers. For a less flashy, more tailored look, you can move in the opposite direction and install molding that's more like upside-down baseboard.

Multilayer Crown Molding

Built-up molding made from separate pieces of wood is a good alternative to wide crown molding because the individual layers are easier to maneuver. Plus, you can use layers of mostly flat material, such as baseboard, to provide the backing you need for sprung crown molding.

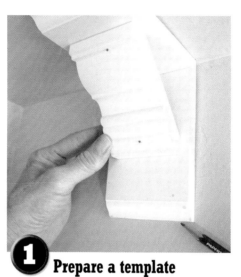

1 Prepare a template

- Assemble a sample section
- Extend the ceiling piece to the corner, and fit the wall piece underneath
- Make the sprung molding edge with the most detail point down
- Using the template, establish a level line and mark studs, but make one chalk line on the ceiling and one on the wall

2 Prepare a ceiling piece

- Cut the first ceiling piece to length; miter the ends unless the crown dead-ends
- If the piece is above a wall perpendicular to ceiling joists, drill for molly or toggle bolts since no framing is overhead
- Select bolts appropriate for the thickness of the ceiling plus the molding

3 Attach to the ceiling

- Tack a temporary support strip across each corner about an inch down from the ceiling
- If joists are overhead, screw the molding directly into them
- If not, drill through a bolt hole into the ceiling with the bit you used in Step 2
- Tap in a molly bolt; make sure the teeth bite into the molding
- With a drill or screwdriver, turn the bolt clockwise; above the ceiling, the sleeve's metal legs will expand
- Repeat at the remaining holes

4 Attach horizontal pieces

- Treat this layer as if it were baseboard, but upside down
- Miter and cope corners
- Snug the top of the molding to the ceiling piece if the ceiling is flat, otherwise, follow the chalk line for the lower edge
- Nail or screw the molding to studs where the sprung molding will cover the fasteners

5 Add sprung molding

- Cut and attach these pieces as if you were installing single-piece crown (see pages 132–133)
- Miter outside corners and cope inside corners
- Skip the triangular blocking; just nail into the ceiling pieces

Crown from Flat Boards

To avoid the hassles of dealing with sprung crown molding, use molding with a flat back. Installing this kind of crown is as easy as putting in baseboard—except that you're up on a ladder and working against the ceiling. Suitable materials include brick mold and casing that has a thick edge on one side. Install it with the thickest portion against the ceiling. Or install several layers of boards that become progressively narrower. Miter all outside corners, just as you'd do for baseboard. On inside corners, cope joints if the molding has a surface shape; if you are using flat boards, butt them into the corner in alternating directions.

Two-piece Crown

The project on the opposite page calls for three-piece crown molding. Two-piece crown is even easier. For this type, fasten the first layer to the wall, just as if you were installing baseboard, but upside down. On walls that are in line with ceiling joists, use triangular blocking as shown on page 132.

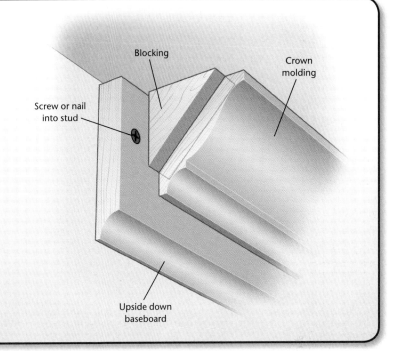

Blocking

Crown molding

Screw or nail into stud

Upside down baseboard

Two Types of Stacks

By stacking boards horizontally at the top of walls or along edges of a ceiling, you can create a crown in a Craftsman (bottom) or Art Deco (below) style. You could also adapt this concept and use baseboard with a shaped edge for one or more of the layers. Attaching the layers to the walls is easier because there are always studs—you don't need to worry about using toggle bolts, as you do on a ceiling.

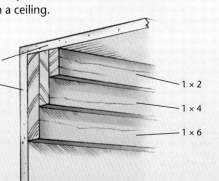

Ceiling

Wall

1 × 2   1 × 4   1 × 6

Ceiling

Wall

1 × 2

1 × 4

1 × 6

Backlit Crown Molding

By installing crown molding a few inches below the ceiling, you can leave space for strip or rope lights, which add drama to a room and emphasize the trimwork. Backlit crown works especially well on walls topped by sloping ceilings. The light bounces off the ceiling at an angle, providing soft light for a large area of the room.

Lighting for backlit crown is available in standard and low-voltage versions. For standard 120-volt systems, you will probably need to install an outlet behind the crown or have it hard-wired. Low-voltage systems connect to a transformer, which is too big to hide behind the crown. See if you can tuck it into a closet on the other side of the wall.

Installing the backlit molding uses the same basic procedure as that shown on pages 132–135, except that the reference line is lower and you need triangular blocking on all walls. Instead of fastening the blocking to the walls directly, you can fasten the blocking to a piece of baseboard with the shaped edge pointed down. This allows you to preassemble all the pieces and install each section as a unit.

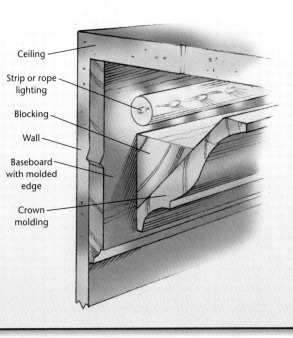

Ceiling

Strip or rope lighting

Blocking

Wall

Baseboard with molded edge

Crown molding

Making Your Own Molding

With so many molding profiles available, why make your own? Perhaps you want to match existing molding, or your house is in a period style and you relish authentic detail. Especially for small projects, making your own molding costs far less than a custom order.

Design Inspiration

The molding featured in this project is based on drawings from "Radford's Portfolio of Details of Building Construction," a book about interior trim details published in 1911. Shaping this Craftsman picture rail called for both a table saw and a router. Every custom job is a little different, so you'll need to adapt the sequence shown here, using some of the general principles discussed. The setup steps may seem elaborate, but once they're done, milling the molding goes quickly.

1 Plan the job

- Make a life-size drawing of the shape you want on paper or the edge of a piece of stock
- Draw in the cuts you need
- Simplify the shape, if necessary
- Plan a sequence of cuts that gives you enough bearing surface each time

2 Set up for angle cut

- This step makes the angled face on the front of the picture rail
- Set a bevel gauge on your sketch and adjust it to match the angle shown
- Set the table saw's tilt to match that angle
- Raise the blade to set the angle, then lower the blade below the throat plate

3 Change the throat plate

- It's not safe to run a narrow edge past a blade with a wide gap on the throat plate
- Switch to a zero-clearance throat plate, which has an opening just as wide as the blade
- Anchor the plate with the rip fence, and raise the spinning blade at the angle you set
- Orient the fence so the waste strip falls away on the outside of the blade, not on the fence side

4 Set up featherboard

- See page 61 to make a featherboard
- If you are removing a strip, keep the featherboard entirely in front of the blade
- If you are cutting a groove or other shape but not changing the top surface, the featherboard can be as far forward as the blade's midpoint
- Use a push stick to keep your hands away from the blade

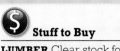

Stuff to Buy

LUMBER Clear stock for molding, plywood for featherboard
BASIC SUPPLIES Sandpaper

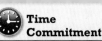

Time Commitment

A few hours to a weekend

Tools You'll Need

Bevel square
Router table
Table saw
Tape measure

Related Topics

Lumber for trimwork, 46–47
Mind your measurements, 70–71
Table saws, 60–61

5 Make additional cuts

- Cut one line to divide the slanted and straight sections on the front
- For the groove at the back, make the cut shown, then orient the stock on edge and make a deeper cut
- The waste strip on the last cut must fall on the outside of the blade, not toward the fence
- Use an adjustable square to check the height of each cut
- Use a push stick, especially when you can't see the blade

6 Set up a router table

- Don't attempt to cut narrow molding with a router guided only by a self-piloting bit
- Instead, mount the router under a table and guide the stock against a fence
- If you are using a bit with a self-piloting wheel, recess it behind the fence

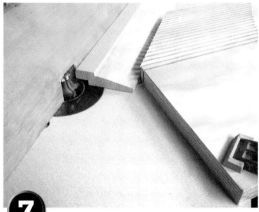

7 Attach featherboard and cut

- Clamp a featherboard to the router table to keep the stock against the fence
- This helps ensure a consistent shape and protects against kickback
- You might need a second featherboard (attached to the fence) to press the stock against the table
- A push stick was sufficient for this project

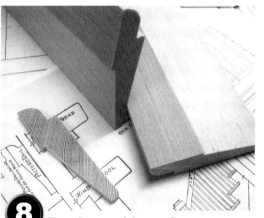

8 Touch up with sandpaper

- Thanks to sharp blades and consistent pressure, the molding shown here is just as it emerged from Steps 1–7
- If your molding has saw marks or rough spots, remove them with sandpaper
- Don't round over sharp angles if they are part of the design

Router Tips

Old-time woodworkers made molding with hand planes. Today, most homemade molding is created with a router mounted on a router table.

- Think of a router as a touch-up tool. Remove most of the waste material with a table saw, then make multiple passes with the router and cut off only a little material each time.
- Use featherboards to keep shapes consistent and guard against kickback.
- If you must hold stock close to a blade, use a push stick with surface grip or a heel that fits over the wood.
- If you are making thin molding, shape the edge of a wider piece and then trim it to the correct width.
- Make extra pieces, especially on early steps, so you have test material for checking adjustments later.

Trimwork & Built-Ins

In this chapter, we go beyond trimwork to show you how to build a few basic built-ins, which you can visually connect to the rest of your home through the use of baseboard, crown, and other molding. Projects include bookcases and shelves, wall and base cabinets, and a lovely window seat (pictured on the opposite page) that uses a lot of the same techniques that you'd use to build a shelf.

Chapter Contents

Trimming Shelves
page 144

Building a Bracket Shelf
page 146

Building a Basic Bookcase
page 148

Building a Plywood Bookcase
page 150

Recessing a Bookcase
page 152

Embellishing a Bookcase
page 154

Wall & Base Cabinets
page 156

Building a Window Seat
page 158

page 156

Trimming Shelves

Building and installing a shelf is probably the most common type of home-improvement project. Before you buy lumber, make sure it can handle the load; apply trim to the edges of sheet materials to give your shelves a finished look.

Shelf Basics

- The maximum height for a top shelf is 72 inches if you want most adults to reach it comfortably without using a stepladder. Leave at least a foot between the highest shelf and the top of your bookcase or other limiting enclosure, such as a ceiling.
- The depth of shelves depends on what you will store and where you will build. Above a kitchen countertop, shelves are usually 12 inches deep. Under countertops, they can be up to 24 inches deep to take advantage of the extra space.
- The thickness of the shelves themselves depends on the material and its ability to resist sagging. The chart below shows the maximum distance that will keep shelves from sagging more than 1/8 inch over 45 inches. It assumes that items on the shelves weigh up to 40 pounds per square foot, a heavy load.

Floating shelves have no visible means of support. Instead, they are suspended on rods that fit into studs.

Oak or Maple

Thickness	3/4"	1"	1 3/4"
Span	36"	49"	85"

Plywood

Thickness	5/8"	3/4"	1"
Span	29"	34"	46"

Cherry or Poplar

Thickness	3/4"	1"	1 3/4"
Span	34"	45"	79"

Soft Pine

Thickness	3/4"	1"	1 3/4"
Span	33"	44"	76"

MDF

Thickness	5/8"	3/4"	1"
Span	18"	21"	28"

Particleboard

Thickness	5/8"	3/4"	1"
Span	16"	19"	25"

 **Stuff to Buy**

LUMBER Iron-on edging or screen molding
BASIC SUPPLIES Wood filler, wood glue, wire nails

 **Time Commitment**

A few hours

Tools You'll Need

Hammer
Iron
Nail set
Putty knife
Square
Tape measure
Utility knife

Related Topics

Fillers & caulk, 216–217
Lumber for trimwork, 46–47
Sheet products, 48–49

Trimming Shelf Edges

Although plywood and particleboard make good shelves, most people don't want to see the ragged edges of these materials in finished projects. Edging covers the evidence. There are two basic types: iron-on and solid wood.

INSTALLING IRON-ON EDGING

Iron-on edging is a thin strip of wood or plastic with heat-activated adhesive on the back.

1 Iron edging

- Heat an iron as specified by the edging manufacturer
- Leave the water reservoir empty
- While the iron heats, cut oversize lengths of the edging with scissors or a utility knife
- Press straight down with the iron to activate the adhesive
- Pick up the iron, move it to the next section, and press down again

3 Trim the ends

- Neatly cut excess ends at the corners
- Use a sharp utility knife and a square

2 Roll edging

- Immediately put pressure on the edging to secure it to the board
- Use a roller designed for applying laminate

4 Trim the edges

- To trim excess width from the edging, hold the blade of a utility knife flat against the shelf
- Pull the knife toward you
- Stop and cut from the opposite direction if the wood begins to tear into the area where you want the edging to remain
- If you have a lot of edging to apply, purchase an inexpensive edging trimmer

INSTALLING SOLID WOOD EDGING

Screen molding, which is sold in flat and beaded styles, makes good edging for ¾-inch-thick plywood, MDF or particleboard.

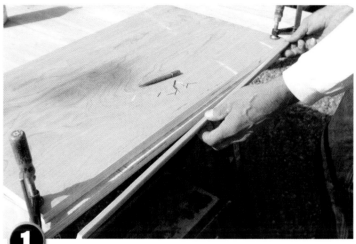

1 Cut and glue

- Place the shelf upside down on a flat work surface
- Cut the edging to length
- Apply glue sparingly to the back of the edging
- Press it against the shelf edge
- Press down on the edging to align it with the surface that will be the shelf's top

2 Tack the molding in place

- Use wire nails, which are thin and have small heads, to hold the molding to the shelf
- Set the nails with a nail set
- Fill the holes later with wood filler, if you wish

Building a Bracket Shelf

Bracket shelves are simple to build and are adaptable to a wide range of styles, including those of a home's trimwork. For design inspiration, look at crown molding—the cross section usually makes a handsome bracket shape.

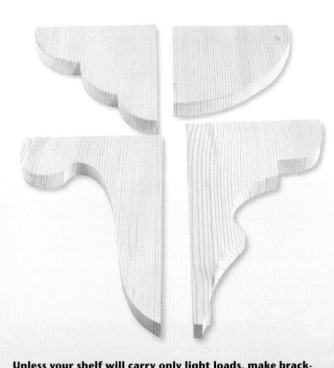

Unless your shelf will carry only light loads, make brackets taller than they are wide.

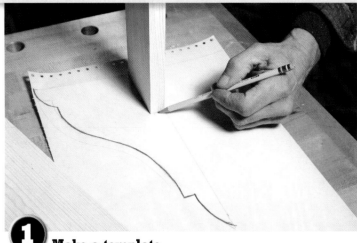

① Make a template

- Sketch your design on paper or cardboard; cut it out to make a template
- A bracket shelf usually has a brace that runs under the back
- If your shelf has just two brackets under each end, the brace can run between them
- If your shelf requires more brackets or cantilevers beyond the end brackets, notch the back of your template to accommodate the brace

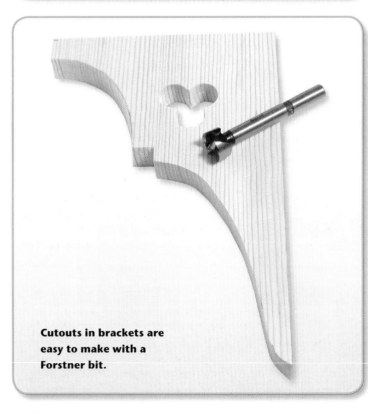

Cutouts in brackets are easy to make with a Forstner bit.

② Cut the brackets

- Using the template, trace the shape on solid wood, plywood, or MDF
- Brackets ¾ inch thick work well in most cases; if the shelf will support heavy items, use material 1½ inches thick
- Use a jigsaw fitted with a narrow blade designed for curves; a band saw or a scroll saw also works well
- Cut just to the outside of the line so that you can still see it

Stuff to Buy

LUMBER ³/₄–1¹/₂" solid wood or sheet material
BASIC SUPPLIES 2" finishing nails

Time Commitment

A weekend (to let finish dry)

Tools You'll Need

Drill
Hammer
Jigsaw
Putty knife
Rasp
Square
Tape measure

Related Topics

Fillers & caulk, 216–217
Lumber for trimwork, 46–47
Making curved cuts, 56–57
Sheet products, 48–49

3 Smooth the edges

- With a rasp or sandpaper, smooth the outside edge of each bracket
- If you use a rasp, pull it toward the center of your work; a back-and-forth motion can chip fibers on the outer edges
- Because the brackets won't be right next to each other, you won't notice slight variations in their shape
- If brackets are plywood, plug gaps in the outside edge with wood filler, allow it to dry, then sand again

4 Attach end brackets

- Unless you have notched all brackets so they fit around the brace, clamp the brace to a work surface
- Set one of the end brackets in place
- Drive 2-inch finishing nails through the bracket to attach it to the brace
- Repeat on the other end

5 Add the brace

- Place the brace with its back facing down
- Clamp spacers to your work surface to keep the brace from scooting away
- Set any notched brackets in place

6 Add the shelf, apply finish

- Nail or screw the shelf to the brace and to brackets
- If you want a smooth surface on the shelf, countersink the heads and cover them with wood filler or wooden plugs cut flush
- Tip the brace and shelf, and nail or screw through the back of the brace into brackets
- Apply the finish of your choice

7 Install the shelf

- With a carpenter's level and a pencil, mark the wall to show the bottom edge of the brace
- Use a stud finder or tap on the wall to locate studs; mark them with a pencil or low-tack painter's tape
- Attach the shelf by screwing through the brace into studs
- Or, if the shelf will hold only a light load, attach keyhole hangers to the back of the brace and slip them over screws driven into studs or secured with drywall hangers

Building a Basic Bookcase

Bookcases are basically just boxes. The simple design featured here consists only of a top, a bottom, sides, and shelves. You might want to include a back as well, especially if you opt to fasten shelves with nails or screws, rather than seat them in dados.

A Ladder-type Design

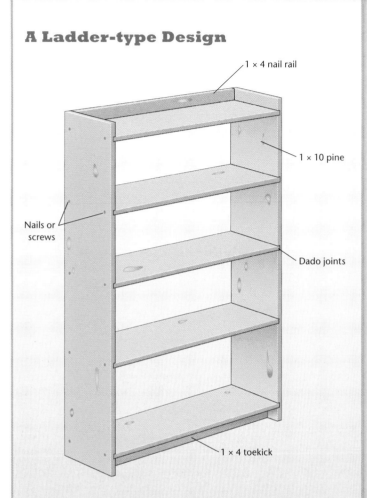

1 × 4 nail rail

1 × 10 pine

Nails or screws

Dado joints

1 × 4 toekick

The bookcase featured in this project uses a "ladder" construction, with fixed shelves nailed or screwed in dadoes. Dimensions are up to you, of course, but the bookcase shown uses 1 by 10 pine boards. The uprights are 48 inches tall, and the shelves are 29 inches long, making a total width for the cases of 30 inches after you allow for the two ¼-inch-deep dadoes. A 1 by 4 pine strip at the bottom closes in the base, and another at the top serves as a nail rail where you can secure the bookcase to a wall.

Cleaning Up Edges

With a belt sander, you can clean up the edges of your shelves so they match and are square. Mark low points in the edges with squiggly pencil lines. Stack the parts, secure them with clamps, and then fine-tune the edges with the sander until the pencil lines just begin to disappear. Make light passes and hold the sander flat so you don't round the edges.

① Make the uprights

- Cut the uprights and clamp them together so they lie flat
- Mark the shelf locations
- Secure a rabbet bit in a router; choose a bit matched to the thickness of the wood
- Cut a scrap of wood to match the distance between the edge of a router's base and the bit
- Using that scrap to measure up or down from the shelf locations, clamp a straight board across the sides to guide the router as you cut a groove for each shelf
- Cut grooves ¼ inch deep

Orienting Boards

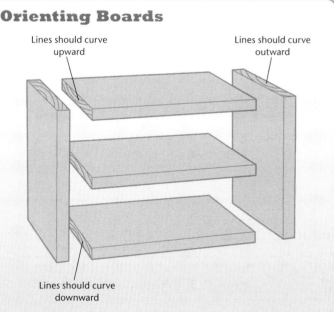

Lines should curve upward

Lines should curve outward

Lines should curve downward

If you build a bookcase from solid wood, orient the boards to minimize problems caused by cupping. Inspect the curved lines visible on the ends. These lines tend to straighten out as the wood dries.

$ Stuff to Buy

LUMBER 1 × 10 pine,
1 × 4 pine
BASIC SUPPLIES 1½"
finishing nails, wood glue

**🕐 Time
Commitment**

A day

**🛠 Tools
You'll Need**

Clamps
Drill
Hammer
Nail set
Power miter saw
Router with rabbet bit
Square
Tape measure

**◎ Related
Topics**

Fillers & caulk, 216–217
Lumber for trimwork, 46–47

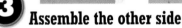

③ Assemble the other side

- Add glue to the dadoes in the other upright and to all the free ends of the shelves
- Fit the shelves so they're headed into the grooves
- Tap on the bookcase side to seat the shelves all the way; if the side will be visible, hammer against a scrap of wood so you don't mar the bookcase
- Turn the bookcase on the side you assembled first, predrill holes, and nail the shelves in place

② Cut shelves and glue one side

- Cut shelf boards to length
- Slide them into the dadoes to make sure all the parts fit
- Lightly mark the outside of the uprights to show the centerlines of the shelves
- Disassemble the pieces
- With a helper, spread wood glue in the dadoes on one side
- Coat one end of a shelf with glue and slip the piece into its dado
- Nail through the outside of the dado into the shelf with two 1½-inch finishing nails; drive each nail at least 1 inch from the edge of the upright
- Repeat for other shelves

④ Add toekick and nail rail

- Cut two 1 × 4 strips to the length of the shelves, minus ½ inch to account for the ¼-inch dadoes
- Place one strip at the bottom, 2 inches back from the front
- Nail it in place through the sides
- Place the other strip at the top, just above the top shelf and flush with the back
- Nail it in place through the sides
- If the sides will be visible, drive all of the nail heads ⅛ inch below the surface with a nail set to allow room for filler

Building a Plywood Bookcase

Most built-in bookcases are made of plywood, particleboard, or MDF. Sheet materials are flat and easy to work with. By trimming hardwood plywood with trim of the same species, you can create bookcases that look as if they are made of solid wood.

1 Rip the sides

- Ask the home improvement store or lumberyard where you buy your sheet to rip two pieces to the width that matches the depth of your bookcase
- Or make the cuts with a circular saw or even a jigsaw; use a straightedge clamped at the correct offset for the saw
- You can also use a tablesaw, but only if it has adequate support for a large sheet of material

2 Measure and rip the shelves

- Because this bookcase will have a back that's simply screwed on, the shelves are the same depth as the sides
- Make the shelves a little narrower if you want a recessed back
- Mark the width, then cut as you did the sides; if you're using a circular saw or a jigsaw, guide it with a straightedge

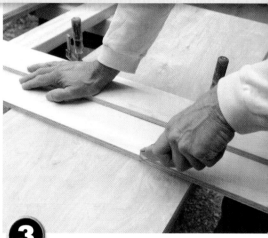

3 Score and cut to length

- Mark the lengths needed for the shelves
- If you're using a circular saw or jigsaw, clamp on a straightedge at a right angle
- Score the line with a sharp utility knife, then make the cut
- If you are using a miter saw or a table saw, you don't need to score first

4 Make a hole template

- The easiest way to support adjustable shelves is on pins; they come in two diameters, 5-millimeter and ¼-inch
- If you choose ¼-inch pins, a piece of pegboard makes a great template
- Draw circles around the holes that correspond to the spacing you want between shelves
- Turn over the pegboard and circle the same holes on the back
- On both sides, mark the top

5 Mark the holes

- Position the template on one upright
- With a ¼-inch bit, preferably a Forstner type, drill a short distance into each marked hole, just enough to mark the locations
- Use a block with a square edge as a guide if you're worried about drilling at an angle or too deep
- Flip the template horizontally and align it with the upright's other edge
- Mark the second row of holes, then mark the other upright

$ Stuff to Buy	🕐 Time Commitment	🛠 Tools You'll Need	◎ Related Topics
LUMBER Sheet material, pegboard **BASIC SUPPLIES** Wood screws, shelf pins	A weekend	Circular saw Clamps Drill Square Tape measure Utility knife	Embellishing a bookcase, 154–155 Recessing a bookcase, 152–153 Circular saws, 58–59 Sheet products, 48–49

6 Drill the holes

- Put tape around the drill bit to mark the depth of the shelf pins
- Remove the pegboard template and drill the holes to the proper depth
- Watch the tape; when it sweeps away sawdust, stop drilling

7 Assemble the frame

- On a flat work surface larger than the bookcase, set the sides on end
- Ease the bottom or top in place
- Use a clamp at the bottom to help keep pieces from tipping

8 Attach the ends

- Snug a second clamp higher up, then remove the first one, so you have room to attach the pieces permanently
- Predrill and countersink, then screw through the sides into the top or bottom
- Secure the other end in the same way

9 Add the back

- Cut the back panel and place it on the bookcase frame
- Don't worry if the sides angle out; just align the bottom edge
- Screw the back in place to the bottom edge

10 Square up the case

- Move to the other end of the bookcase
- Push or pull the parts until the back lines up with the frame
- Screw the back in place

Tool Tip

A Forstner bit, left, cuts the cleanest hole for shelf pins.

Recessing a Bookcase

By fitting a bookcase into a wall, you can add storage without losing precious floor space. This bookcase extended into the next room's closet, but the wall was opened up as if that wasn't an option so we could show you how to avoid damage to the back wall.

1 Check the wall

- Choose an interior wall
- With a hole saw, cut an inspection port
- Twirl a bent wire around to feel for obstructions
- If you find wires or pipes, reconsider the project
- If you will be cutting studs, check with your local building office to find out if you need a permit; also determine whether the wall is load-bearing (see opposite page)

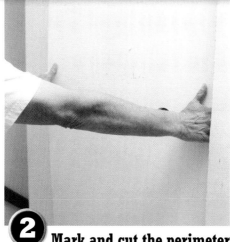

2 Mark and cut the perimeter

- With a level and a pencil, outline the shape of the opening; cut it slightly larger than your bookcase
- If the wall is load-bearing, add space to maneuver in a header (see Step 6)
- Score the line in the drywall with a utility blade; go over it several times
- When you have cut through all the edges, rock the drywall back and forth
- Pull out any nails or screws that pop loose and remove the panel

3 Cut the studs

- Cut a slot for a reciprocating saw blade 1½ inches below the bottom of the opening you made in Step 2
- Saw through the studs
- Angle the blade so you don't cut through the drywall on the opposite wall
- This wall has two studs because of a closet on the far side

4 Loosen nails, remove studs

- Slip a pry bar behind the cut studs to open a little space next to the drywall at the back
- Cut through the nails
- If the opening extends nearly to the ceiling, twist the studs free at the top; use wire cutters to clip off framing nails
- If the opening is lower, cut studs at the top the way you did at the bottom

5 Add cripples and a sill

- Cut short studs, known as cripples, so they fill the bottom of the opening, minus 1½ inches
- Cut a 2 by 4 sill that spans the opening
- Nail or screw it across the cripples

 **Stuff to Buy**	**Time Commitment**	 **Tools You'll Need**	**Related Topics**
LUMBER 2 × 4s, 2 × 6s, molding **BASIC SUPPLIES** Wood screws, finish nails	A weekend	Drill Hole saw Hammer Nail set Pry bar Reciprocating saw Tape measure Utility knife	Building a plywood bookcase, 150–151 Mitered trim for doors, 94–97 Sheet products, 48–49 Trimming a window, 102–107

6 Cut a header and a trimmer

- Cut a 2 by 6 header as wide as the opening, plus a hair
- Cut off a bit of one top corner, then hammer the header into place
- Screw at an angle to attach it to studs
- Cut a 2 by 4 trimmer the same length and install it under the header to trim out the top of the opening
- If the wall is a load-bearing wall, sandwich two headers and a spacer so they are as thick as the wall framing (usually 3½ inches)

7 Add trimmer studs

- On each side of the opening, install a vertical 2 by 4 between the sill and the top trimmer just behind the drywall
- Screw these in place at the top and bottom

8 Position the bookcase

- With one screw through the center, attach a scrap stick to each side of the opening and at the center on top
- Muscle the bookcase into position
- Pivot the sticks to keep the bookcase from tipping
- Tuck shims between the case and the framing to make it level and plumb; insert a shelf in the bookcase so its sides don't bow
- Screw through the shims to attach the bookcase to the framing

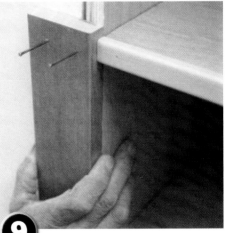

9 Trim edges

- Install casing as you would for a doorway or window
- Here, screen-door molding was nailed to the edges of the plywood shelves and window casing will be nailed to the bookcase and stud-backed drywall

Recognizing a Load-bearing Wall

Walls that run in the same direction as floor and ceiling joists don't usually carry a structural load, but ones that run crosswise often do. Even if a wall is load bearing, you can usually cut one stud without a problem, but you may need to brace the ceilings on both sides of the wall until you have installed a header, the horizontal framing at the top of the opening. If you're not sure about loads or bracing needs, consult a structural engineer or an experienced builder.

Here, a ceiling is being braced before a stud is removed in the adjacent wall. First, a smooth 2 by 4 that crosses under several ceiling joists is held against the ceiling. Then, two more 2 by 4s, cut slightly too long, are wedged between the 2 by 4 on the ceiling and a scrap of plywood on the floor.

Embellishing a Bookcase

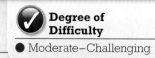
Now it's time to fine tune the bookcase design featured on pages 150–151 by adding details to the top, front, or bottom. Recess the back, if it will be visible. Or add a fixed shelf to stabilize a tall bookcase.

Making a Bookcase Look Built-in

With simple molding, you can make a bookcase or cabinet look like part of a room. Take style cues from elements nearby, but don't worry about matching every detail. In a room with elaborate crown molding, for example, you might choose a more streamlined version to crown a built-in bookcase. Or you can move in the opposite direction and dress up the molding on a built-in so that the piece becomes the star attraction.

If baseboard, chair rail, or other trimwork is already in place where the bookcase or cabinet will sit, consider removing the molding so you can snug the case to the wall. If you want to leave the trim in place, cover the gap with molding. Or, if only baseboard is in the way, consider setting the case on a slightly shallower base that's high enough to clear the baseboard.

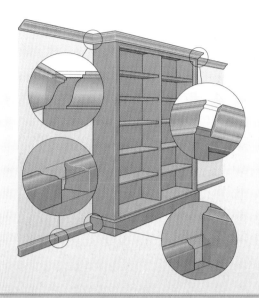

Trimming a bookcase so it looks built-in involves the same basic joints as other trimwork. Cope inside corners and miter outside corners.

Adding a Face Frame

A face frame gives a bookcase or cabinet the look of solid wood on the front and serves as a base for doors or drawers that partially overlay it. It's the traditional way of trimming the front of a cabinet, so it looks great in classically styled houses.

❶ Make the face frame

- Select solid, knot-free wood ¾ inch thick by at least 1½ inches wide
- Use pieces with square edges; rounded edges don't make tight-looking joints
- Consider making the frame a little wider than the cabinet so you can use the frame overlaps on the outside as scribing strips
- For frame joints, drive screws at an angle from the back using a pocket hole jig
- Biscuit joinery also works, if the framing is wide enough to hide the biscuits

❷ Install the face frame

- Spread glue on the front of the box and set the face frame over that
- Check the alignment to make sure it's square with the cabinet
- Before you secure it with finish nails, drill pilot holes with a bit that's skinnier than the nails

Making a Bookcase Look Like Furniture

If you want a bookcase to resemble furniture, consider additions to the top, front, or bottom.

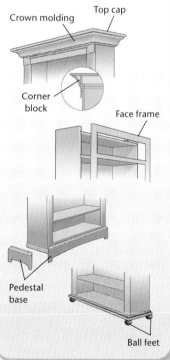

Crown molding
Top cap
Corner block
Face frame
Pedestal base
Ball feet

| **Stuff to Buy**
LUMBER Molding, face-frame stock
BASIC SUPPLIES Wood screws, 1" brads, #20 biscuits, wood glue | **Time Commitment**
Varies with project | **Tools You'll Need**
Biscuit joiner
Clamps
Drill
Hammer
Nail set
Pocket-hole jig
Router or table saw
Tape measure | **Related Topics**
Building a basic bookcase, 148–149
Building a plywood bookcase, 150–151
Mitered trim for doors, 94–97
Sheet products, 48–49
Trimming a window, 102–107 |

Recessing the Back

To recess the back of a bookcase, alter the basic design so that the sides, top, and bottom are deeper than the shelves by at least the thickness of the back. A back can be ¼-inch-thick plywood, hardboard, or MDF. For a stronger cabinet, use ½-inch-thick material. If the back will be exposed—for example, where a bookcase doubles as a room divider—use material ½ to ¾ inch thick.

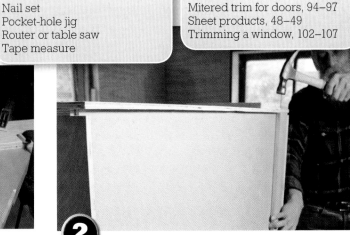

1 Rabbet perimeter pieces

- Cut a rabbet, or groove, on the inside face of the back edge of each perimeter piece
- Use a router or a table saw with a dado blade
- Use a zero-clearance (tight-fitting) throat plate, plus a featherboard for the first cut; for the second, position the rip fence so the cutoff falls away from the fence
- Make the rabbet half as wide as the edge is thick; the depth should match the back panel's thickness, or a little more

2 Add the back

- Screw or nail the sides to the top and bottom; also attach any fixed shelf (see below)
- Slip the back into place; you may need to push or pull on the perimeter pieces to get the case square
- Clamp across the back near the middle to prevent the sides from bowing out
- Nail the back to one side with 1-inch brads
- Measure diagonally across the bookcase in both directions; the distances should be equal
- Nail along the other side, the top, and the bottom

Adding a Fixed Shelf

A tall bookcase can't consist of just a top, two sides, and moveable shelves or it is likely to turn into an out-of-square parallelogram. A fixed shelf near the middle adds rigidity. You can support the shelf in dados (see pages 148–149), in which case it needs to be longer than shelves supported on pins or brackets. To avoid cutting a dado and having to make one shelf longer, connect the shelf by gluing oval-shaped plywood wafers, commonly called biscuits, into slots cut with a biscuit joiner.

1 Slot the sides

- Cut the parts like on pages 150–151
- Adjust a biscuit joiner to cut slots for #20 biscuits
- Clamp plywood scrap to one bookcase upright at the bottom of the fixed shelf
- With the joiner's handle pointing up and the fence against the straightedge, cut slots centered 2 inches from each edge and in the middle

2 Slot the shelves

- Clamp the shelf to a flat surface with the top up
- Turn the joiner so the handle is horizontal, facing you
- Resting the joiner's base on the same surface as the shelf, cut matching slots the same distances from the edges
- Don't worry if the slots aren't exactly on the marks; the slots are longer than the biscuits to allow for this

3 Assemble the case

- Test the fit of all parts
- Spread wood glue in slots on the uprights, insert biscuits, spread a little more glue, then push the shelf onto them
- Position the pieces so they are resting on their edges
- Attach the top and bottom to one upright, then do the other
- Clamp or drive finish nails through the uprights to hold pieces while the glue dries; avoid nailing into the biscuits

Wall & Base Cabinets

Building wall or base cabinets is a lot like building bookcases, except that cabinets usually also include doors and perhaps drawers. Each type of cabinet also has a few special features that are easy to deal with, as long as you plan ahead.

Wall-cabinet Components

A key feature of a wall cabinet is its nail rail—a strip across the back where you can sink nails or screws to secure the cabinet to a wall. Cabinet backs are usually too flimsy to support the weight directly.

Wall Cabinet

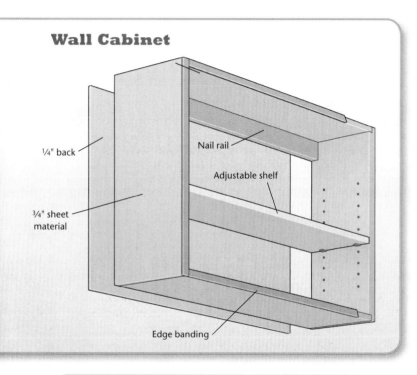

¼" back

Nail rail

Adjustable shelf

¾" sheet material

Edge banding

A Simple Nail Rail

A hardwood strip ¾ inch thick and 2 inches wide makes a good nail rail. Predrill through each side, then drive finish nails or trimhead screws to attach the strip. Don't nail without predrilling into hardwood, or it may split.

A Recessed Nail Rail

If you don't want a nail rail showing on the cabinet interior, recess the back of your cabinet deeply enough so you can tuck the rail behind it. Consider cutting angled edges into the rail and a ledger so they mate to each other. This simplifies installation. Instead of struggling to keep the cabinet steady and level while you screw it into studs or drywall anchors, just hold the ledger level as you attach it to the wall. Then lift the cabinet into place. The ledger's bevel tip should point up and out; the nail rail's tip goes down and out.

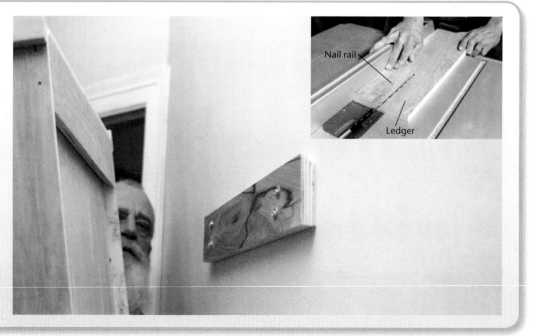

Nail rail

Ledger

Base-cabinet Components

The key issue for a base cabinet is whether to build it so it rests directly on the floor or on a separate base. Either way, you'll probably want to recess the bottom to create a kickspace, a gap that keeps people from banging their toes when they stand close to the countertop. Kickspaces are often about 4½ inches high and 3 inches deep. Some cabinet companies use taller kickspaces, though, so if you are coordinating with existing cabinetry, check before you build.

Base Cabinet

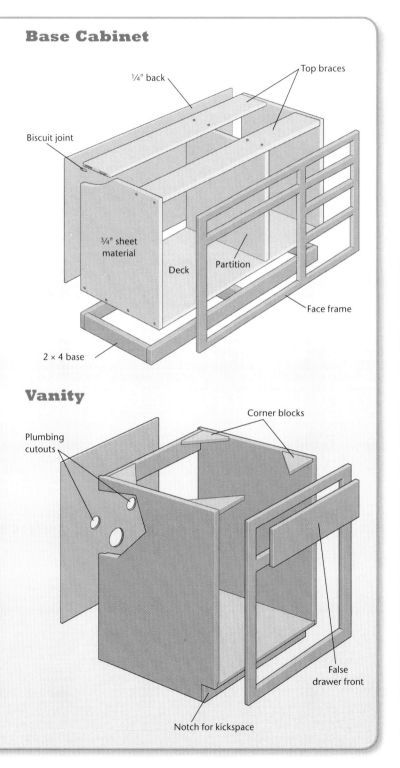

- ¼" back
- Top braces
- Biscuit joint
- ¾" sheet material
- Deck
- Partition
- Face frame
- 2 × 4 base

Vanity

- Corner blocks
- Plumbing cutouts
- False drawer front
- Notch for kickspace

Base-cabinet Shortcut

If you will be adding a countertop, you can omit a solid top on a base cabinet. Install braces instead to save on materials and weight. Plus, the braces double as handles when you move the cabinet into position.

Design Tip

There's an easy way to add doors and drawers to cabinets you build, as long as you order the correct parts from companies that specialize in cabinet components (see Resources, page 236). Before you build, make sure you know what hardware you will use and what offsets you must provide. Traditional hinges (bottom row) are designed for face-frame cabinets, just as frameless cabinets and Euro-style cup hinges (below) are designed for each other. Cup hinges, which can also be used on face-frame cabinets, are hidden when the doors are closed. The best ones are adjustable and clip on and off, so you can remove doors without a screwdriver.

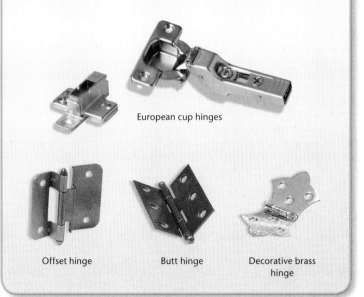

European cup hinges

Offset hinge   Butt hinge   Decorative brass hinge

Building a Window Seat

There are two basic ways to build a window seat: as a low cabinet or as an enhanced shelf. The cabinet approach works best when you are starting with an open wall. But if you have a bay window like this one, a shelf-style seat is easier to build.

1 Determine the angle

- Place a straightedge across the opening of the alcove or along a line that is at a right angle to an adjoining wall
- Use an adjustable bevel gauge to determine the angle between that line and one side of the alcove
- Transfer the angle and a line showing the back wall to cardboard
- Leave the front edge oversize as you cut along the lines

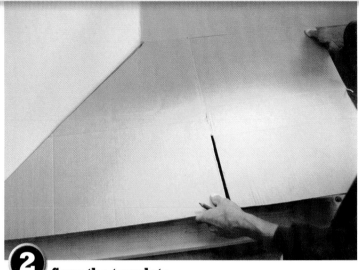

2 Copy the template

- Flip the rough template
- Snug it into the opposite side
- Most bay windows are symmetrical, so it's likely to fit
- If it's at least close, copy the template

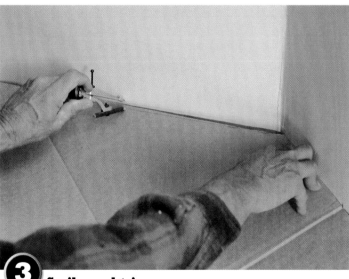

3 Scribe and trim

- If you see gaps between the rough templates and the wall, fine-tune one edge at a time
- Set a scriber to the widest gap and trace along the wall to mark the cardboard
- Then trim the cardboard to fit
- Fill in with other cardboard pieces if the two end templates don't span the whole alcove
- Tape the pieces together

4 Establish a line

- Draw a level line showing the top of the ledger strips that will support the back of the window seat
- Window seats are generally most comfortable if they're about 18 inches high
- Make the ledger that height minus the thickness of the bench seat and any cushions

 **Stuff to Buy**

LUMBER Plywood, 2 × 4s, molding
BASIC SUPPLIES 3½" wood screws for 2 × 4s, piano hinge with screws, recessed ring pull, cardboard for template

 **Time Commitment**

A weekend

Tools You'll Need

Bevel gauge
Circular saw
Drill
Hacksaw
Hammer
Level
Nail set
Utility knife

Related Topics

Circular saws, 58–59
Sheet products, 48–49

5 Install ledgers

- To create a solid base for the seat, cut a frame of 2 by 4s for the back, sides, and front
- Use the template to help you determine lengths and angles
- Screw the back and sides to the wall along the level line, then attach the front
- At each stud, use two screws at least 3½ inches long
- Use a level to make sure the frame is horizontal

6 Add cross braces

- Add 2 by 4 braces between the front and the corners at the back
- If you want storage underneath, place the braces so they will support the sides of a lift-up door
- Cut a notch ¾ inch wide and 1 inch deep on the bottom front of each brace so you can slip in the front panel (see Step 14 on page 161)
- Attach braces by screwing through the front framing and at an angle into the back ledger

7 Trim the front edge

- Set the template on the ledgers; push it back against the walls
- Mark the front edge flush with the outside face of the framing
- Cut the cardboard along that line
- Check the fit one more time

8 Transfer the shape and cut

- Place the template on the bench material; on this bench, it's ¾-inch-thick maple plywood
- Tape down the cardboard
- Using a pencil, trace the edges onto the plywood
- Guide a utility knife along a metal straightedge to score along the lines
- Cut along the lines with a circular saw or a jigsaw

⑨ Mark the braces

- Place the seat on the framing
- At the front and back, mark the bench to show the centerline of each brace underneath

⑩ Define the door

- Extend the marks you made in Step 9 to make lines that run the back to the front on both sides
- Between those lines, draw a perpendicular line about 3 inches in from the back edge
- Score these lines with a utility knife

⑪ Cut the door

- Clamp a straightedge along the back line, which establishes the back of the door
- To begin cutting at the start of the line, you'll need to make a plunge cut, as shown above
- A few inches forward of the start of the line, place the saw at an angle so the front of its base touches the straightedge but the blade doesn't contact the plywood
- Retract the blade guard with one hand, and switch on the saw with the other
- Carefully lower the spinning blade into the wood and cut forward
- Before you reach the end of the door line, switch off the saw
- When the blade stops, lift and reposition the saw, and cut the sides
- Finish the corner cuts with a jigsaw or a handsaw

⑫ Make the back lip

- Place the cut seat back on the frame
- Make a lip to support the back of the lid by fitting a length of ¾-by-2-inch wood or plywood between the cross braces
- Position it under the seat and press it back against the back ledger
- Clamp it to the seat
- Then remove the seat, turn it over, and screw on the lip

⑬ Attach a hinge

- With a hacksaw, cut a piano hinge so it's slightly shorter than the lid is wide
- Screw it to the seat and the lid

Tool Tip

Piano hinges use numerous screws, which need to be perfectly centered. Use a self-centering drill bit or hole punch to make pilot holes in exactly the right spots.

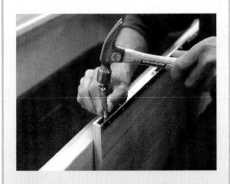

14 Add the front

- Cut the front panel so it spans the width of the seat at the front
- Or cut two panels and design a decorative detail to hide a center seam
- Make the panel tall enough to fit behind the front framing in the notches you cut in Step 6 on page 159
- Screw the front panel to the framing from the back

15 Attach the top

- Slide the seat into place
- Fasten it by driving a few nails or screws into the ledgers and framing

16 Add a front trim

- Make a lip along the top front edge to cover the bench's plywood edge and keep cushions from sliding off
- Nail a strip of wood about 3 inches wide by ¾ inch thick to the edge; elevate the strip by ¾ inch or so
- Miter the ends to fit against the wall, or cut mitered returns (pages 114–115) if the front extends out from the wall
- Also nail baseboard or other molding along the bottom edge

17 Add a door opener

- So you can open the door, install a recessed ring pull near the center front
- Or drill a hole about ⅞ inch wide, big enough to slip a finger through
- If you drill, clamp a scrap block underneath to prevent splinters; use a clean-cutting Forstner bit

7

Columns & Ceilings

In this chapter, we sets our sights high by showing you how to create decorative box beams. Unlike structural beams, box beams don't have to do any heavy lifting, but they still need to be properly secured. To that end, we take you step by step through the process of building support blocks, which can be attached directly to joists or, with toggle bolts, to a ceiling. Also included is a design for faux posts.

Chapter Contents

**Columns &
Ceiling Trim**
page 164

Box Beams
page 166

Faux Posts
page 168

page 166

Columns & Ceiling Trim

Vertical columns and horizontal ceiling beams often serve a crucial purpose—holding up a floor or roof above. In that case, they're designed into a house from the beginning. But exposed columns and beams can also be added later as purely decorative details.

Columns like these work great as a room divider when you want to define separate spaces for activities, such as cooking and dining, but still want to keep the spaces somewhat connected to each other. These columns are modeled after a classical design, with tall pedestals below and a multipart entablature above.

Regardless of whether a column actually carries a structural load, it should always look like it does. To help perpetuate the illusion, add bulk to the top and bottom of the column, as shown here.

Exposed ceiling beams, braced by ornate corbels at each end, are a signature feature of Southwestern adobe buildings. Corbels with mock beams create a similar look, with or without the exposed planking above.

Simple mock beams, running in either a single direction or crossing, are often found in Craftsman interiors, especially in the fanciest rooms in the house.

Ceiling trim doesn't need to extend across the full expanse of a room. When a room has a very high ceiling, you can install a rim of ceiling trim around the perimeter. This visually lowers the ceiling while still preserving some of its airy effect. With strips of intersecting molding (above, left), the feature looks like trimwork. Or skip the intersecting molding (above, right) to create a more structural look.

Box Beams

✓ Degree of Difficulty
● Moderate

Box beams on a ceiling create a look similar to exposed structural beams, but the pieces are lighter and easier to handle. If possible, install box beams so you can fasten their support blocks to ceiling joists, or use toggle bolts, as shown on page 169.

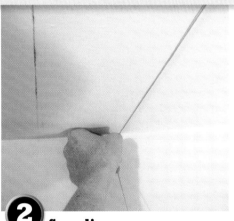

This box beam has been combined with faux posts (see instructions on pages 168–169) and low cabinets to create a room divider.

Design Tip

Because a real beam is strongest when its thickest dimension is vertical, a faux beam looks best when you use wider pieces for the sides. Don't try to line up the sides and bottom precisely; that's needlessly difficult. Instead, include a reveal, or offset, in your design.

1 Design the beam

- Cut short scraps to work out dimensions and offsets
- This design has a plywood support block, wrapped by a 1 by 4 on the bottom and 1 by 6s on the sides
- The sides overhang the bottom by ¼ inch

2 Snap lines

- Locate and mark ceiling joists
- Try to have the centerlines of the beams line up with those of ceiling joists, or run the faux beams perpendicular to the joists
- Snap chalk lines to mark the outside of each support block

3 Make support blocks

- Build inverted U-shape support blocks about 12 inches long from ¾-inch-wide plywood
- For each support, make two uprights that are the width of the beam's sides minus the thickness of the beam's bottom and the reveal
- Cut one top for the support block that's equal to the width of the beam's bottom minus 1½ inches
- Screw the pieces together
- Make enough supports to place one every 3 feet or so

 **Stuff to Buy**
LUMBER Plywood, 1 × 4 and
1 × 6 stock, molding
BASIC SUPPLIES Wood screws,
nails

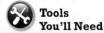 **Time
Commitment**
A weekend

**Tools
You'll Need**
Clamps
Drill
Nail gun
Table saw
Tape measure

 **Related
Topics**
Faux posts, 168–169
Use reveals, 82–83

4 Attach blocks

- Align a block between the chalk marks
- Screw through the top to attach the support to a joist
- Use screws 2½ to 3 inches long

5 Scribe end

- From ¼-inch-thick plywood, cut a template as wide as the support block
- Align the template with the block
- If you see a gap, get a small scrap of wood and place it under the template
- Trace along the side of the scrap to transfer the wall's angle to the template
- Trim the template along the line

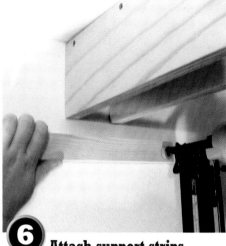

6 Attach support strips

- At each end, tack a support strip to the wall; drive at least one nail into a stud
- Leave enough of a gap between the strips and the ceiling so you can maneuver the beam's sides into place later
- If you're dealing with a long span, enlist a helper or rig up intermediate supports

7 Cut and attach bottom piece

- Measure the distance from wall to wall
- Using the template showing how the ends angle, mark the bottom piece and cut it to length
- Either work with the wrong side of the stock facing up, or flip over the templates before you use them
- Nail about ⅜ inch in from each outside edge into the edges of the support blocks

8 Attach sides

- Use a similar procedure to measure and fit each side
- If the ceiling dips, clamp the piece to keep an even reveal on the bottom edge; you can cover any gaps on the top edge later
- Nail through the side into the support blocks; use nails on the bottom piece as a guide to block locations
- Between supports, nail the sides to the edge of the bottom piece; place the nails about ⅝ inch up from the edge to account for the reveal

9 Cover gaps

- If you see gaps between the sides and the ceiling, cover them with thin molding
- Nail the molding to the faux beam, not to the ceiling
- Use cove molding (above) or 1 by 2 flat molding, as shown on opposite page

Faux Posts

Built much like the box beams on pages 166–167, these faux posts are anchored to nail pads at the top and bottom. Just preassemble three sides of the posts, install a nail pad at whichever end needs to be most precise, and slide the nearly complete post into place.

1 Determine the height

- Instead of struggling to keep a tape measure straight, use "pinch sticks"
- Grasp two straight sticks and hold them vertically within the space
- Slide the sticks apart until one end presses against the ceiling or top beam and one end of the other piece presses against the base cabinet or floor
- Keep the sticks pinched together as you mark their overlap; add arrows showing which ends point up

2 Cut parts and preassemble

- Decide how thick and wide to make the posts; include a reveal of at least ⅛ inch
- Set the pinch sticks on the stock; mark their top and bottom, then cut
- If the post is under a box beam, cut two sides slightly shorter if they need to tuck under a reveal
- Fit the post sides together; cut ¾-inch-thick plywood to plug each end
- Nail three of the sides together; nail both long pieces if the lengths aren't equal
- The end plugs are your nail pads

3 Install nail pads

- Here, the post's top must line up with the bottom of the beam above
- Use one of the plywood plugs as a nail pad for the post
- Use screws if you're fastening to a box beam or ceiling joist, or a toggle bolt if you're fastening a short post to drywall
- If there's no wood above a floor-to-ceiling post or a post of any length that someone might lean against, go into the attic and add wooden supports fastened to ceiling joists

4 Slide in the post

- Ease the three assembled sides into place over the nail pad
- Drive finish nails through the sides into the pad
- Predrill first if you're hand-hammering

5 Plumb it

- Slip the other nail pad into the end of the post
- Snug a level against one side of the post and nudge the post, as needed, until it is plumb

6 Attach base pad

- Screw through the pad into the cabinet or other surface below
- Drive finish nails though the sides into the pad

7 Add the final side

- Slip the final piece into place
- Secure it with clamps, then nail into edges of the two adjoining pieces
- If the edge has a reveal, factor it in before you nail

Stuff to Buy

LUMBER Plywood, stock
BASIC SUPPLIES Wood screws,
nails

**Time
Commitment**

An hour or two per post

**Tools
You'll Need**

Circular saw
Clamps
Drill
Level
Nail gun
Miter saw
Tape measure

**Related
Topics**

Box beams, 166–167
Use reveals, 82–83

Using Toggle Bolts

Toggle bolts are the best alternative when there's no ceiling joist or stud where you need to anchor faux beams, posts, or other features. However, the bolt's holding power depends partly on how securely the drywall is attached, so always be cautious. If you're unsure, go into the attic and install a wooden support between the joists. Or cut through the drywall from underneath and add the framing from that side. For short beams, though, toggle bolts should be fine.

❶ Drill a small hole

- Position the piece you want to fasten on the wall or ceiling
- Drill through both layers with a bit sized to the bolt part of a toggle bolt

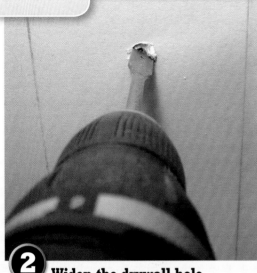

❷ Widen the drywall hole

- Set aside the piece you are fastening
- Drill a wider hole through the drywall; size it for the toggle's wings when they are pressed shut

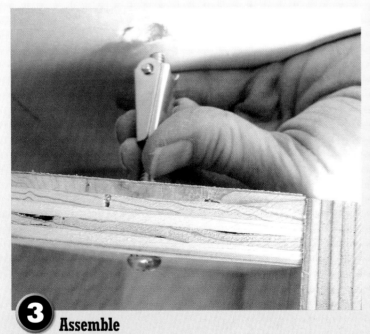

❸ Assemble

- Unscrew the wings from the bolt
- Push the bolt through the hole in the piece you're fastening
- Reattach the wings
- Spread construction adhesive on the back of the piece
- As you place the piece, close the wings and guide them through the hole in the drywall

❹ Tighten

- Out of sight, the wings should spring open
- Turn the bolt clockwise until the connection is tight
- If the bolt does not seem to be tightening, pull down or out as you tighten to put tension on the wings

Custom Trimwork Projects

In this chapter, we get into projects and techniques that are sometimes a little bit complicated but extremely rewarding. We start with bead-board wainscot, which we show you how to install below and around windows. Wall frames are also covered, as are fireplace surrounds and mantels. We also cover doors (from basic ones to pocket doors) and finish with a section on installing a handrail for a stairway.

Chapter Contents

Bead-board Wainscot
page 172

Installing Bead-board Wainscot
page 174

Bead Board Around Windows
page 176

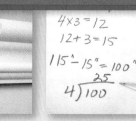

Other Bead-board Techniques
page 178

Planning & Sizing Wall Frames
page 180

Installing Wall Frames
page 182

Trimming a Basement Ledge
page 184

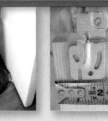

Trimwork for Fireplaces
page 186

Fireplace Surround & Mantel
page 188

Prehung Doors
page 192

Hanging a Door
page 196

Installing Bypass Doors
page 198

Installing a Pocket Door
page 202

Handrails
page 206

Bead-board Wainscot

Bead board is one of the most enduring and adaptable styles of wainscot, supporting everything from Victorian to modern looks. Traditional bead boards have interlocking edges and a bead milled into the face, but sheet materials are also available.

Reasons to use bead-board wainscot aren't just visual. The material also creates a tough, dent-resistant surface, so it's an ideal wall covering behind a bench or hooks where people will hang objects that might gouge drywall.

In this bathroom, an elaborate cap gives bead-board wainscot a traditional look. Note how the trim around the shower has a thick back band on the outside edge. This allows it to project into the room a little more than the baseboard under the wainscot, an aesthetically pleasing detail.

Sheets of plywood milled to resemble bead board work well as wainscot. You can also use them to enhance the look of furniture or built-ins, such as this headboard and bookcase. Furniture that matches the wainscot looks like a custom built-in, even if it's not attached to the wall.

If you're trying to create a modern look, consider topping bead-board wainscot with a very simple cap.

Bead-board wainscot always needs a cap to cover the top edge, as well as baseboard or base shoe to neaten out the bottom edge and help with the transition to the floor. In a room with a high ceiling and tall wainscot, you might also want a third band of horizontal trim. Besides giving your eye a break from the long verticals, this band can also be put to practical use as a plate rail or, as in this mudroom, a coat rack.

Installing Bead-board Wainscot

Bead board is one of the easiest kinds of wainscot to work with. Installation is especially straightforward when the wainscot is low enough to ring a room below the window stools, as shown here.

How to Do It

Before construction adhesive was invented, attaching bead board to a wall took considerable preparation. There's too much space between studs to fasten all of the boards to them, so installers had to cut horizontal strips out of the drywall or plaster to fill them in with nailing strips fastened between the studs. This approach is still preferred by some carpenters, but most choose to glue bead boards to the wall and nail the ends, which get covered with trim boards that are fastened to studs.

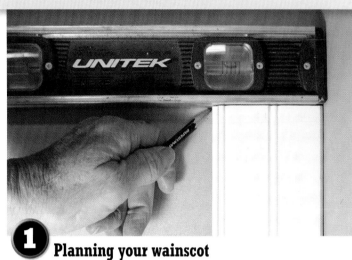

❶ Planning your wainscot

- Measure the width of the first wall in inches
- Divide wall length by the exposed width of the bead board; don't include the tongue
- The leftover is the width of the final piece; if it's too skinny, trim from the first piece and add it to the last
- Cut a piece; use it and a level to mark the wainscot height
- Mark studs on the wall above the wainscot

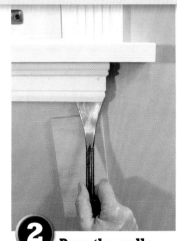

❷ Prep the walls

- Assuming the bead board reaches at least as high as the stools, remove window aprons
- Also remove baseboards

Before You Install

If you plan to paint bead board, paint the tongues before you install the boards. If you don't, you'll see slivers of unpainted wood or MDF when the pieces inevitably shrink in dry or cold weather.

About Outside Corners

Preassemble outside corners and install them first so you can shim the assembly as one piece. Some designs influence the direction of the tongues and grooves—another reason to install outside corners first.

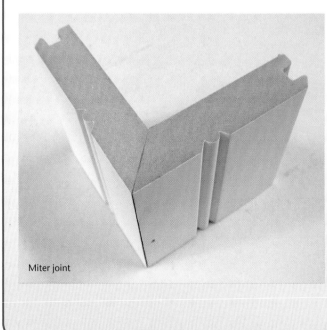

Miter joint

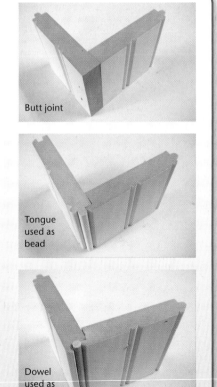

Butt joint

Tongue used as bead

Dowel used as a bead

Stuff to Buy

LUMBER Baseboard, bead board, cap molding, trim below cap
BASIC SUPPLIES Construction adhesive, nails, trim-head screws

Time Commitment

A weekend

Tools You'll Need

Drill
Hammer
Level
Nail gun
Power miter saw
Tape measure

Related Topics

Baseboards, 122–127
Bead board around windows, 176–177
Other bead-board techniques, 178–179

3 Attach the first board

- If there is an outside corner, start there, otherwise, start at an inside corner
- Squirt construction adhesive on the wall
- Set the first piece in place and plumb it
- To keep the level free of adhesive, rest it on the bead-board's tongue
- A thin gap next to the wall is okay; the bead board on the other wall will cover it
- If it's an outside corner, shim as necessary to make the corner assembly plumb

4 Nail the board

- Boards need to be secured while the adhesive cures
- Fasten through the face at the top and bottom where horizontal trim will cover nail heads
- Or nail at an angle through the tongues
- On outside corners, predrill and hand-hammer because there's probably a metal corner under the drywall mud

5 Install additional boards

- Place several more boards; nail them in the same way
- Work your way across the wall; periodically check that the boards are still plumb
- If they tilt, space out the next few boards to make up the difference
- Don't worry if the boards are slightly out of line across the top

6 Attach a cap

- Cut chair rail or the top part of a built-up cap; miter or cope the ends
- Position the rail over the wainscot and make sure it is level
- Attach the molding to studs with sturdy finish nails or trimhead screws; drive them straight into chair rail or at an angle if the cap is wide
- The gap at the back of this cap is from molding with a rounded edge; fill with caulk or install with the rounded edge down if you can

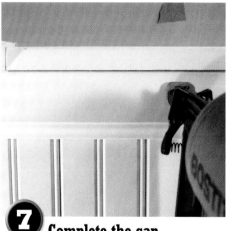

7 Complete the cap

- Below the cap, install one or more layers of horizontal trim, recessed behind the cap
- If the top cap piece lines up with window stools, the lower layers can double as apron trim

8 Install baseboard

- Install baseboard in the usual way; nail it where studs lie underneath
- If a baseboard would look too thick in proportion to the room's door casing, see pages 178–179

Bead Board Around Windows

You'll appreciate the practical benefits of working with bead board over sheet materials if you need to notch pieces so they fit part way up a window. Because you're dealing with small boards, it's easy to dry-fit and mark them to get just the shapes you need.

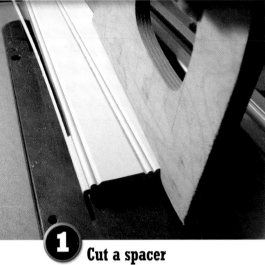

❶ Cut a spacer

- Adjust the fence on a table saw so you can cut off just the tongue on one piece of bead board
- If you don't have a table saw, slice off the tongue by scoring several times with a sharp utility knife

❷ Dry-fit and mark

- As you near the window, do not spread adhesive behind at least the last full board
- Instead, just dry-fit a piece; slip the leading edge behind the notched-out stool
- Place the spacer on the stool, with the groove side against the window casing
- Trace along the tongueless edge, as shown

❸ Mark stool depth

- Move the spacer block so its flat edge is against the bottom of the stool
- Trace against the dry-fit piece
- Slip out the dry-fit piece
- Draw a second line about 1/8 inch below the first one and mark it as the line to cut; this will give you some wiggle room during Step 5 below

❹ Cut the notch

- A table saw works best for long, straight cuts; stop before you reach the horizontal line and finish with a jigsaw
- Or use a jigsaw to cut the entire notch
- In either case, cut on the waste side of the lines

❺ Install notched piece

- Test the fit, then disassemble the notched and dry-fit pieces
- Spread adhesive and position the notched piece

❻ Install dry-fit piece

- Slide in the dry-fit piece from the top
- Make sure the channel is free of dust so it doesn't jam

$ Stuff to Buy

LUMBER Baseboard, bead board, cap material, chair rail
BASIC SUPPLIES Construction adhesive, nails, trim-head screws

Time Commitment

A few hours per window

Tools You'll Need

Chisel
Hammer
Handsaw
Jigsaw
Nail gun
Table saw

Related Topics

Installing bead-board wainscot, 174–175
Other bead-board techniques, 178–179
Trimming a window, 102–107

7 Fitting the other side

- Install bead boards under the window; dry-fit the last one
- Dry-fit a full-height piece beyond that
- Repeat Steps 2 to 4 to mark the notch lines and cut the notch

8 Install

- Remove the dry-fit piece under the window
- Glue and nail the notched piece in its place

Prepping Window Stools

If you are installing wainscot in a room with window trim already in place, notch the back of the stool so the bead board can slip behind it.

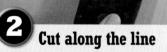

1 Mark the stool

- Place a scrap of bead board against the wall and casing
- Face the back out because it's flat
- Trace the depth onto the stool

2 Cut along the line

- To start the cut, position one hand on the saw blade above the stool and one below
- Cut only as far as the casing
- Near the end, angle the saw so it does not nick the casing

3 Chisel out the waste

- Use a sharp chisel no wider than the strip you need to remove
- Cut down, then slice sideways
- Remove only a little wood each time

Other Bead-board Techniques

Although bead board is basically very easy to install, you may confront a few finicky details when you go to install it in your house. Luckily, there are easy work-arounds for the most common complications.

Overlapping a Rail or Cap

When chair rail or a wainscot cap is thinner than window and door casing, you can end it in a simple butt joint. But if the horizontal trim is thicker, it looks best if it overlaps the casing by a little bit. For flat trim, this is easy: Just notch the horizontal piece in the back so it overlaps the casing by the same amount on the front and the edge. If the chair rail has a profile, creating the overlap is a little trickier. Create a mitered return (pages 114–115) or shape the end, as shown here.

1 Trace the profile
- Cut a thin slice of the chair rail
- Set it over the end of the molding that you want to shape
- Trace against the slice with a pencil; hold it as vertical as possible

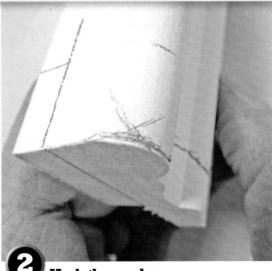

2 Mark the overlap
- Mark the casing depth on the end of the chair rail
- Extend the line around the top
- Measure from the top edge to the outside edge of the rail
- Measure back from the end of the rail by the same distance and draw a perpendicular line; this is the amount the rail will overlap the casing

3 Cope the shape
- With a coping saw, cut the profile you drew in Step 1
- Try to cut as vertically as possible or even slanted in at the front
- Make a relief cut at every sharp bend for crisp details

4 Smooth the shape
- With a rasp and sandpaper, smooth the cut end
- Use a backsaw to cut the notch on the back

5 Install
- The final result shows how the chair rail wraps over the door casing

Stuff to Buy

LUMBER Bead board, molding
BASIC SUPPLIES Sandpaper

Time Commitment

A couple of hours

Tools You'll Need

Backsaw
Hammer
Nail gun
Rasp

Related Topics

Baseboards, 122–127
Bead board around windows, 176–177
Bead-board wainscot, 172–175
Creating mitered returns, 114–115

Simple Solutions

If you don't want to overlap or create a mitered return for a thick chair rail, just miter the part that extends past the door casing.

Another technique is to build a two-part chair rail. Round over the top piece where it projects out from the casing, but keep a crisp corner next to the casing so you get a tight fit. Attach a thin apron below the top piece, butt the end, and then paint.

Avoiding a Proud Baseboard

When you install wainscot, the extra thickness may result in a baseboard that stands too proud (i.e., it sticks out farther than the door casing). Here's how to avoid this.

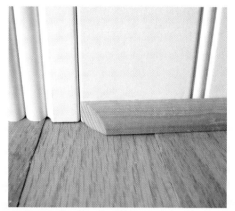

Omit the baseboard

- Install base shoe or quarter-round
- Cope inside corners and miter outside corners of the base shoe
- Miter the base shoe where it meets the door casing or a plinth

Add a back band

- Around the outside edge of the casing, add molding that's as thick or thicker than the wainscot plus the baseboard
- For consistency, also add a back band to all windows in the room

Apply a trim strip

- Replace the baseboard with a piece of wood as thick as the bead board; rest the wainscot on it
- Once the bead board is in place, add horizontal trim that hides the line where the wood and bead board meet
- At the door casing, overlap the trim as you would for chair rail, or miter the end as you would for base shoe

Planning & Sizing Wall Frames

Degree of Difficulty
● Easy

Wall frames break up and define open walls, but they can look awkward if you don't plan for them properly or give them the right proportions. Fortunately getting it right is as simple as following the Golden Rectangle rule.

A Sense of Proportion

The Golden Rectangle rule of proportions states that the most visually pleasing rectangle has a ratio of 1:1.618. For practical purposes, a rectangle with sides that have a ratio of 5:8 is about right.

Try to adhere to the Golden Rectangle rule for basic frames that repeat around the room, but realize there will always be exceptions with individual frames and situations. Here are some basic strategies to keep in mind:

When to go horizontal. In rooms with a chair rail at 36 inches or lower and/or an 8-foot-high ceiling, horizontal frames usually look best.

When to go vertical. If the chair rail is at 60 inches, or if the ceiling is 9 feet or higher, vertical frames are better.

Irregularities are okay. The frames do not always have to be of equal size. Indeed, if there are other elements in a room such as doors, a fireplace, or windows of different heights, you will need to vary the frame sizes.

Pay attention to spacing. Try for uniform spacing between frames and between bottom pieces and the baseboard. However, you might want to leave wider gaps at the ends of a wall, and the gap between the frames and the baseboard can be a little taller than the spacing between the tops of the frames and, say, a chair rail.

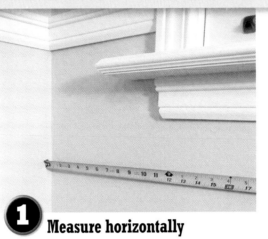

❶ Measure horizontally

- Measure the width of the space
- Tentatively decide on the number of frames and the gap between them

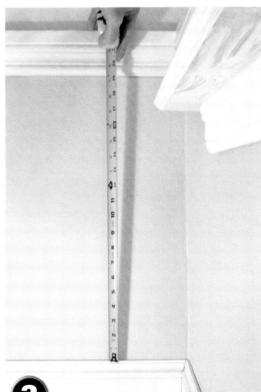

❸ Find the tentative height

- Measure from the top of the baseboard to determine the available height
- If there is a chair rail, use its bottom edge as the other end point and then subtract by two gaps to calculate the tentative height of each frame
- If there is no chair rail, repeat Step 2 to calculate vertical dimensions

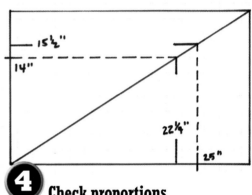

115" width
4 frames
3" spaces
$4 \times 3 = 12$
$12 + 3 = 15$
$115" - 15" = 100"$
$4\overline{)100}$ = 25

❷ Do the math

- Multiply the gap in Step 1 by the number of frames
- Add one extra gap width to allow for gaps at both ends of the wall
- Subtract that number from the overall width; this is the space available for frames
- Divide by the number of frames across the wall
- The result is the tentative width of each frame

❹ Check proportions

- Scale down the dimensions so you can sketch the frame; for example, make ¼ inch represent 1 inch
- On the same base lines at the bottom and one side, draw a rectangle 5 by 8 inches
- Draw a diagonal line through the second rectangle
- Adjust the size so the scaled-down frame is close to fitting along the diagonal
- In this example, the size was 14 by 25 inches; making it 15½ inches tall or 22¼ inches wide would look better
- If you don't like either of those sizes, try a different number of frames or vary the size of the gaps

$ Stuff to Buy	🕐 Time Commitment	🔧 Tools You'll Need	◎ Related Topics
LUMBER Molding **BASIC SUPPLIES** Paper and pencil, construction adhesive	An hour or two	Chalk line Level Tape measure	Check every angle, 76–77 Trouble-shooting mitered trim, 98–99

Wall Frames on Stairways

To determine the size of wall frames along a stairway, ignore the slope while you are working out the math. Measure the total horizontal distance in segments and add them, if necessary. Once you settle on a basic frame size, measure up at the top and bottom of the stairs and snap chalk lines to show the top and bottom of the frames. With a level, mark the verticals for one frame. Measure the frame lengths directly from the marks. Use the folded paper technique on page 99 to determine the angle for the miters; the tip on page 76 shows how to convert it to degrees.

Varying Wall Frames

Frames need not be equal in width, but they do need a clear design principal to guide their relationship. For example, you might want to group three frames and make the middle one wider than those flanking it. Or you can alternate wide and narrow frames. Try to make the most dominate frame size fit the Golden Rectangle.

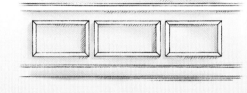

Upper wall frames show off artwork and decorative paint panels in this dining room. The symmetrical arrangement uses a single wide panel on the bottom and one wide panel between two narrow ones on the top.

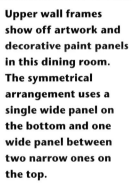

Wall frames along a stairway can be level on top if there is no handrail on that side. The bottoms of the frames should follow the slope of the stairs.

Vertical or Horizontal?

On tall walls or ones with a high chair rail, vertical frames look best. Horizontal frames are a better choice under a low chair rail.

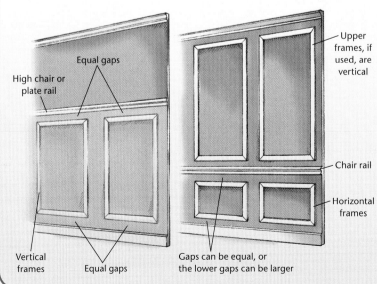

Installing Wall Frames

Although it's possible to install wall frames piece by piece on a wall, preassembling the frames and installing them as a unit is much easier. You can clamp the parts before you get out the glue, and you minimize mess on the wall.

How to Do It

The visual impact of wall frames varies depending on how beefy the molding is and whether you paint it to match the walls, the trim, both, or neither. Wall frames with a color of their own are most prominent, especially if you choose a flashy finish, such as metallic paint. You can also apply separate colors to different shapes of the molding. Whatever design direction you choose, here's how to get it done.

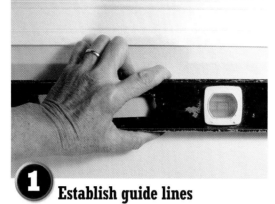

① Establish guide lines

- Follow the procedure on pages 180–181 for determining the size of the wall frames and the spaces between them
- Measure up from the floor or baseboard and mark the top of the frames; allow for the gap needed above the baseboard
- Use a long level to establish other marks at the same height

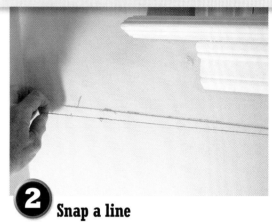

② Snap a line

- Connect the marks by snapping a chalk line
- Snap another along the bottom edge if you are assembling the frames in place
- If there is a wall covering that the chalk might mar, see the tip on the opposite page
- Mark along the top line to show where each frame will lie, or cut a spacer block as wide as the horizontal distance you want to leave between frames

③ Cut the frame

- Adjust a miter saw to cut at 45 degrees
- If the molding is thin, keep it from bending as you cut it by using a jig, as shown on pages 114–115
- To ensure that pairs are equally long, place opposite pieces side by side; the long tips should line up precisely

④ Assemble the frame

- Cut a rectangular plywood scrap and screw it to a base that's bigger than the frame; make sure the outside corner of the scrap is square
- Rub candle wax on the base below each corner of the frame; this keeps glue from sticking
- Starting at the corner with the scrap, clamp each section to the base
- If everything fits, remove one piece and spread wood glue on its mitered ends; also paint glue on the adjoining end, but leave that piece clamped
- Replace the loose piece and clamp it; glue the opposite piece the same way
- If the molding is thick enough, drive one or two brads through each corner; don't nail thin molding or it might split
- Wipe off excess glue

Stuff to Buy

LUMBER Molding, plywood
BASIC SUPPLIES Wood glue,
   panel or construction
   adhesive

**Time
Commitment**

About 30 minutes per frame

**Tools
You'll Need**

Clamps
Power miter saw
Tape measure
Utility knife

**Related
Topics**

Creating mitered returns,
   114–115
Picture-frame windows, 112–113
Planning & sizing wall frames,
   180–181

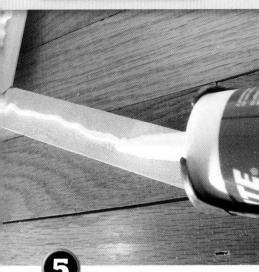

5 Glue frame to wall

- Let mitered corners dry completely before you unclamp the frame
- Because wall frames don't always line up with studs, glue them to the wall
- Use panel adhesive or construction adhesive

6 Place the frame

- Line up the top of the frame with the blue line
- Place the side closest to the corner at the mark showing where the first frame goes
- You can use a spacer

7 Nail the top

- Nail the frame to hold it while the adhesive dries
- Use finish nails or brads, depending on the thickness of the frame
- Don't nail through the miter joints
- Nail only the top strip at this point

8 Plumb the sides

- Check with a level to make sure each side is plumb
- Once it is, nail it to the wall
- Then nail the bottom edge
- Repeat this procedure for the other frames

Alternative to Chalk

It's easy to wipe blue carpenter's chalk from a painted surface. But if you're worried that the color might stain a wall covering or other surface treatment, use spacer blocks or push pins as markers instead. Simply align a spacer block against other trim, such as a window apron, chair rail, or baseboard.

Trimming a Basement Ledge

When daylight basements are converted into living spaces, an awkward ledge may exist where the thick insulated foundation meets a thinner partial wall with windows. Converting this partial wall into an attractive shelf is relatively simple.

This finished basement ledge betrays none of its unattractive concrete-and-foam interior.

❶ Mock up shelf

- Use scrap to help you work out pleasing proportions
- Make the shelf wide enough to overhang trim about 1/2 inch
- Be sure to factor in the adjoining window trim

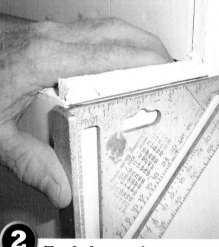

❷ Check the opening

- Determine whether the drywall projects into the shelf space
- At a corner, use a speed square to show where to cut
- Keep the vertical cutoff line square with the front edge of the wall

❸ Trim the drywall

- Pare away excess drywall with a utility knife
- Brush or vacuum off the debris

$ Stuff To Buy

LUMBER Shelf material
BASIC SUPPLIES Construction adhesive, 100-, 120-, and 180-grit sandpaper

🕐 Time Commitment

Four to five hours

🔧 Tools You'll Need

Caulk gun
Power miter saw
Power nailer
Sander
Speed square
Tape measure
Utility knife

◎ Related Topics

Choosing materials, 40–41
Lumber for trimwork, 46–47

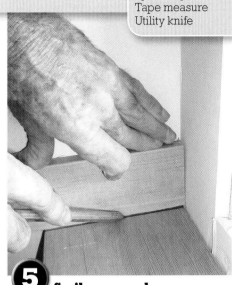

4 Check alignment

- Place the shelf board on the ledge
- Check whether top surface is level
- Use a speed square to check the angle with the wall

5 Scribe one end

- Press scrap piece against wall
- Trace along its bottom edge
- If wall isn't straight, scribe with a compass
- Cut board using a power miter saw

6 Sand shelf

- Smooth top face and front edge
- For quickest results, use a random orbit sander
- Use 100- or 120-grit, then 180-grit

7 Glue shelf

- Load construction adhesive into caulk gun
- Spread a liberal amount over the foam and concrete exposed on the ledge
- To prevent a mess, avoid getting adhesive on drywall edge

8 Position and attach shelf

- Note location of foam layer and set shelf on ledge
- Press board down and tight to back edge
- To keep the shelf in position, nail into the foam
- Stack several 2 by 4s on the shelf; leave undisturbed for several hours

9 Add the apron

- Cut and sand the apron
- Clamp it to the shelf
- With a power nailer, shoot fasteners through the shelf into the edge of the apron
- Also nail through the front face, aiming alternately right and left

Trimwork for Fireplaces

People are drawn to warmth and light, so it's no surprise that a fireplace is often the centerpiece of a room. Like a costume on an actor, the right trimwork helps a fireplace serve in this starring role.

Panels on the mantel resemble those on shutters elsewhere in this room, helping to create a unified look.

You can link fireplace trim with other trimwork in a room. Here, the top shelf continues past the fireplace and becomes the stool for the windows.

A fireplace surround like this would work well in a Craftsman-style house because wainscot in this style traditionally consists of battens over flat panels. The fireplace surround includes a similar detail, topped by a geometric design and crown molding.

Elements of a Fireplace Surround

Because fireplace surrounds are often quite elaborate, it might seem daunting to design one yourself. The task is easier if you recognize that there are several basic approaches.

The mini temple

- Review the parts used in classical Greek and Roman buildings on pages 12–13
- Flank the firebox with rounded columns or flat pilasters that sit on bases or plinths
- Top those with the equivalent of an entablature
- Add decoration to the entablature's frieze
- Top the entablature's cornice with a shelf

Layered molding

- Surround the firebox with trim, much as if you were trimming a door
- Miter the corners (as shown here) or use butt joints
- Add layers of molding above, each of which can project out a little farther on the sides and front from the layers below
- Create mitered return on these layers
- Add a shelf on top

A hanging shelf with no surround

- Make a thick shelf from two layers separated by molding
- If you want the top shelf to be bigger than the bottom one, separate the layers with crown molding
- Fasten the shelf on cleats or hangers; use masonry or drywall anchors if required

A bracket shelf on masonry

- Pick a bracket shape that's compatible with the room's style
- Build a bracket shelf like the one on pages 146–147
- Make the shelf as thick or thicker than the brackets
- Secure the shelf to the framing behind the masonry

Fireplace Surround & Mantel

Trimwork elevates a fireplace from a heat source to a focal point. Though the end result looks complex, the woodwork around the stone surround is relatively simple: two tall, three-sided boxes on the sides, plus a wide, shallow three-sided box with a shelf on top.

How the Pieces Go Together

With its proportions rooted in classical architecture, this handsome fireplace surround and mantel was installed in a corner, with TV and sound components tucked into a built-in cabinet above. This required a few extra steps that you won't need if you are trimming a fireplace on a flat wall with no cabinet above it. The step-by-step instructions on the next few pages focus on the basic installation.

Mantel shelf

Undershelf

Crown molding

Applied trim

Lintel box

Stone surround

Legs

Simplify with Solid Wood

This fireplace surround was made out of veneered plywood, so a table saw was required to cut the mitered joints along the long sides of the legs and the corners of the lintel box. To simplify construction, use solid wood and make butt joints.

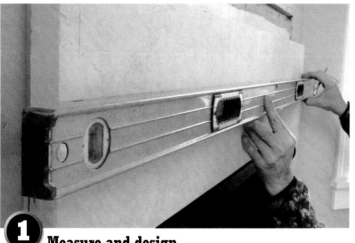

① Measure and design

- The setback for wood must be 6 inches when a surround projects into a room ¾ inch or less
- Add 1 inch of setback for each additional ⅛ inch of projection
- From the opening, measure up and out based on your surround's projection
- Draw level and plumb lines to mark the clearance area
- The height of the top clearance line equals the length of the legs
- The legs should be wide enough to cover the stone beyond the side clearance lines, plus at least 3½ inches
- Make the legs 2 inches deep, plus the width of the stone

② Make the legs

- From hardwood plywood, cut a piece as long as the legs and as wide as their total widths, plus several inches
- On a table saw, rip two strips as wide as the legs; bevel both long edges to the inside at 45 degrees
- Rip four strips to the leg depth on the wall side; the two strips that rest on the stone get trimmed in Step 6
- As you cut each leg piece, bevel one long edge and straight cut the other
- Assemble the legs with glue and finish nails

$ Stuff to Buy

LUMBER Hardwood plywood and stock, 2 × 4, molding
BASIC SUPPLIES Wood glue, finish nails, construction adhesive, wire brads, sandpaper, finishes

Time Commitment

A weekend, or two

Tools You'll Need

Belt sander
Drill
Nail gun
Power miter saw
Table saw
Tape measure
Utility knife

Related Topics

Trimming shelves, 144–145
Fireplace surrounds, 18–19
Mitering outside corners, 136–137
Table saws, 60–61

3 Make the lintel box

- The lintel lines up with the legs in front and on the sides, so its depth is the same as theirs; its width equals their widths plus the distance between the side clearance lines
- This lintel box is 8¾ inches high, but looks about 2 inches taller because the top shelf rests on a drywall ledge (see Step 14)
- Making the box is similar to making the legs
- To make the wood grain wrap around the sides, cut one side piece from each end of the main piece, as shown
- You can apply finish at this point, if you like

4 Install nailers

- Cut two 2 by 4s to the height of the legs
- Locate studs or other framing in the wall next to the surround
- Spread construction adhesive along the back of one nailer
- Screw it into wall framing
- Repeat for the other nailer

5 Scribe legs to the surround

- If you applied finish, spread painter's tape along the leg sides facing the fire; make scribe marks on that
- Set the legs against the wall on either side of the stone surround
- Trace along the stone edges to mark where each leg needs to be trimmed
- If you are working in a corner, measure the stone's projection from the wall in several places and mark the legs

6 Trim each leg

- If the scribe line is virtually straight, clamp a straightedge along it
- Trim off the excess with a circular saw or a jigsaw
- If the scribe line curves, don't use a straightedge; cut freehand with a jigsaw
- Cut on the waste side of the line, not through it

7 Fine-tune the fit

- Place each leg in position
- Check the bottom edge first
- If you see gaps, mark places where the joint is tight
- Remove these high spots with a belt sander; or use a rasp that you direct away from the edge
- Bevel the edges slightly; the long point is the edge that will show
- When the bottom fits, repeat these steps for the rest of the edge, then the edge against the wall

8 Drill for control knob

- If either leg lies over a control knob for gas or electricity, mark its location
- Drill the hole needed for the shaft
- Set the leg over the shaft
- Check that you can secure the knob

9 Install the legs

- Slip each leg over its nail strip
- Measure the gap between the nailer and the inside of the leg
- Find scrap material to plug the gap; 1/2-inch-thick plywood should work
- Check that the legs are plumb and that they are level across the top
- Drive finish nails through the sides to secure them

10 Make the lintel shelf

- From solid wood, cut a lintel shelf 2 inches longer than the lintel box
- The width is the box's depth, plus the thickness of the stone, plus 1 inch
- Set the shelf on the legs so each end projects 1 inch
- Mark where the surround ends, and measure the gap between the shelf and the wall
- At each mark, draw a perpendicular line as long as the gap is wide; then draw a line connecting the end points
- With a jigsaw, cut along the lines so the shelf fits around the stone

11 Install the lintel shelf

- You don't need to scribe for a perfect fit
- Just make sure the final inch at each end fits tightly to the wall
- Spread wood glue on top of the legs and nailers
- Set the shelf in place, and nail it down

12 Add lintel nailers

- At each end of the shelf, measure 3/4 inch toward the center
- Just inside of each mark, screw on a vertical nailer that matches the lintel box's height
- Add a horizontal nailer just below the top of the lintel box

13 Install the lintel box

- Set the lintel box in place and check that it fits
- Remove it and spread wood glue along the bottom edge
- Reposition it and make sure it's tight against the wall
- Nail up through the lintel shelf, 1 3/8 inches from the shelf's front edge
- Immediately wipe off any glue that oozes out

14 Plan next steps

- An undershelf extends over the lintel box
- The mantel's top shelf extends into the wall
- Usually both shelves rest on the lintel, but a gap was required for this installation
- Position a scrap of the crown molding against the undershelf
- Mark how far the crown projects on the bottom of the undershelf

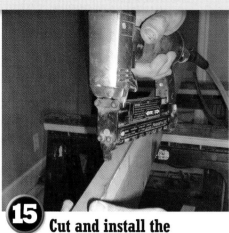

15 Cut and install the undershelf

- The width of undershelf is the distance you marked on the scrap in Step 14, plus ¾ inch for overhang
- It's as long as the lintel box, plus twice the distance in Step 14, plus 1½ inches
- Cover the outside edges with ¼-inch-thick solid wood edging; miter the front corners
- Check the fit, then spread wood glue on the top edge of the lintel box
- Position, nail, and wipe off glue

16 Add the spacer and the top shelf

- Make the mantel shelf the same way
- It is the same size as the undershelf
- Nail or glue the layers together before you add edging
- For edging, use a strip 1¼ inches high and ¾ inch deep; miter the outside corners

17 Cut first crown piece

- Cut a scrap piece first; line up the miter with the corner of the lintel box and mark where the outside edge of the molding fits against the undershelf
- Then cut the front miter; from short tip to short tip it should be as long as the lintel box

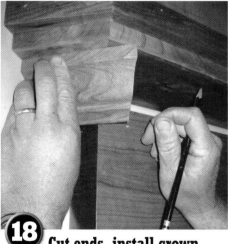

18 Cut ends, install crown

- Cut a short piece of crown with a straight cut on the wall side
- Mark the back where it intersects the outside corner of the lintel box
- Mark where the front top edge lines up with the mark you made in Step 17
- Cut the miter a short distance beyond the marks
- Nail on the front crown through the flat surfaces that fit against the lintel box and the undershelf
- Apply glue to the miter ends, then nail the side pieces

19 Shape the applied trim

- This surround has applied trim 1 inch wide and ⅜ inch thick
- To lay out the curve with an improvised compass, tie a pencil to a string
- Cut the curve with a jigsaw; sand the edges smooth
- To get the angle for the ends, mark two lines showing the edges of the straight pieces
- Draw a line between the parallel lines at the ends of the curves and cut

20 Install applied trim

- Remove the painter's tape, if you used it
- Spread wood glue on the back of the curved strip
- Tack it in place with wire brads or 32-gauge pins; wipe away excess glue
- For the side pieces, cut a trim strip that fits against the wall and ends in a miter that lines up with the corner
- Cut pieces for the remaining space on the front
- Install all short strips as you did for the curved strip, but instead of nailing, tape them in position until the glue dries

Prehung Doors

The easiest type of door to install is one that's been "prehung" at a factory. You get not just the door but also the hinges and the jambs, and everything lines up perfectly. However, you still need to make a few adjustments to get a perfect fit in your doorway.

Prepping Before You Buy

If you want to replace a door, it's often easier to remove not only the old door but also the jambs. That way you can install a prehung door, rather than trying to fit a new door into an old opening (as shown on pages 198–199).

1 Remove the old door

- Don't try to unscrew the hinge; instead, remove the pins
- If you can't slide up the pins, tap with a finish nail from the bottom
- Raise all of the pins most of the way before you remove any of them all the way
- Then move the door sideways as evenly as you can so you don't bend the lower hinge

2 Remove molding and cut nails

- Carefully pry off the casing on both sides of the door
- See the tips on pages 84–85 if you want to reuse the molding
- Cut the nails holding the old jamb to the framing; run a reciprocating saw along the back edge of each side jamb

3 Tip out the jamb

- Tap along the side of each jamb; if it doesn't budge, run the saw along the top edge to cut any nails there
- When all the nails are cut, just pivot the jamb assembly out of the way

Before You Order a Prehung Door

MEASURE THE EXISTING DOOR
- Determine its width, height, and thickness
- List the measurements in that order

MEASURE THE JAMB
- Note its width and thickness
- Typical widths are 3½ to 4⅝ inches for interior doors and 5½ to 6⅝ inches for exterior doors
- The jamb you get may be 1/16 to 1/8 inch wider; this helps the casing fit well against the jamb

DETERMINE THE SWING
- Stand on the side where the door swings away from you
- Open the door
- If the hinges are on your right, you need a right-hand door
- If the hinges are on your left, you need a left-hand door

CHOOSE THE HARDWARE
- Hardware includes the hinges as well as the knob or lever assembly

Even a prehung door may need to be adjusted. For tuning tips, see page 195.

 **Stuff to Buy**

LUMBER Door, lath
BASIC SUPPLIES Hinges, door knob, wood screws, nails

 Time Commitment

A day

Tools You'll Need

Square
Drill
Hammer
Nail gun
Reciprocating saw
Tape measure
Utility knife

 **Related Topics**

Hanging a door, 196–197
Installing a pocket door, 202–205
Installing bypass doors, 198–201

Installing a Prehung Door

① Clean up the opening

- Scrape off any drywall mud on the framing around the doorway
- With a utility knife, cut back any drywall that protrudes past the framing

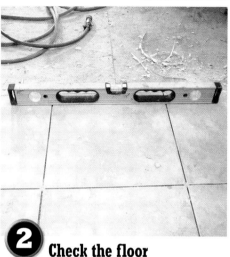

② Check the floor

- Use a level to check the floor
- If it slants, you might need to shim the low side so the jambs sit level
- If you need clearance for flooring that will be installed later, cut a spacer
- In this doorway the tile is level; the room beyond will have carpet, so the rough floor is lower

③ Place the door

- Get a helper to stand on the hinge side of the doorway
- The main installer should lift the door and jambs, and muscle the package into the doorway

④ Place the first shim

- Ask the helper to insert one shim between the framing and the jamb
- Place it directly behind the bottom hinge
- The shim's thin end goes in first

⑤ Plumb the hinge side

- On the other side of the door, wait for the shim to emerge
- Slide in a second shim next to the first one, slim end first
- With a long level, check whether the jamb is straight and plumb
- Tap in the second shim, if necessary

⑥ Even up the front edges

- Make sure the jamb is even with the drywall
- The edge of a square helps you check this

7 Fasten the jamb

- Drive a single nail into the framing through the jamb and shims
- Repeat this process at each other hinge

8 Check the gaps

- Open the door and thank your helper
- Stand on the hinge side and check whether gaps along the top and the hinge side look reasonably straight
- They don't need to match, but they should not taper significantly
- If they do, you may need to trim one side jamb or shim under it

9 Add fasteners

- Drive a second nail alongside each hinge, but this time on the other side of the jamb
- Or, remove one of the hinge screws and replace it with a screw that has the same head shape but a shaft long enough to bite into the stud behind the jamb

10 Attach the latch side

- Once the hinge side is straight, focus on the latch side
- Insert a pair of shims, each with its thin end pointed in
- Push in the shims only far enough to fill the gap behind the jamb; do not hammer
- Nail through the jambs and shims into the framing

11 Position bottom shims

- Add a pair of shims at the bottom
- Push them in just far enough so the space between the door and the jamb is even at the top and bottom
- Because the shims aren't wedged, you may need to press the jamb to keep the shims from falling
- Nail through the jamb and shims into framing

12 Shim the middle

- Just above the latch, shim the middle of the jamb in the same way
- Stand back and check whether the gap between the door and the jamb is even
- If not, shim in another place or two, until everything looks straight
- Nail these shims in place, too
- Score the shims at the drywall edge and break them off

Tuning a Sagging Door

1 Find the gaps

- On this door, the side gap disappears at the bottom
- The top gap is wider on the latch side
- This indicates the door needs to move in toward the hinge at the top

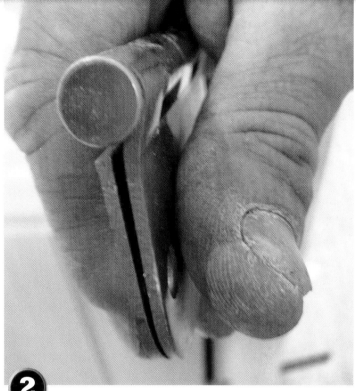

2 Check the top hinge

- Remove all of the screws on the top hinge
- Close the hinge and note the spacing between the leaves

3 Open and bend the hinge

- Fold the leaves back as far as they will go
- Step on the opened hinge
- You don't need to flatten it, though

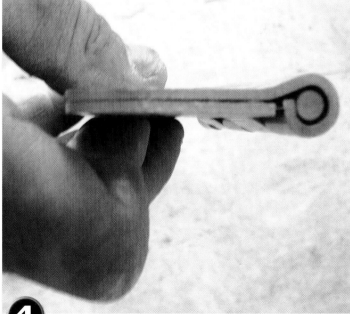

4 Check the hinge again

- Close the hinge as it would normally close
- The gap between the leaves should be smaller or gone, which should close the gap at the top of the door
- If the gap still shows, fold the leaves back and step on them again
- Reattach the hinge

Hanging a Door

Changing a door without disturbing trimwork is trickier than installing a prehung door. Making a template streamlines the job and saves you from lifting a heavy door on and off hinges as you shave it to fit an opening that might be out of square.

How to Do It

The project shown here features a door from a company that specializes in used building materials, but you can use a similar procedure to install a new door. The replacement door must be as thick as the original and as tall and wide, or a little bigger.

If you are buying a new door and know that the existing door opening is square, consider ordering a "partially machined door," if it's available from your retailer. The door comes without jambs, hinges, or stops but with recesses for hinges and the latch and handles. It also has a bevel already cut on the latch side.

1 **Make a template**

- Cut two strips of lath that almost match the doorway's height and three strips a little shorter than its width
- Clamp the strips into a rectangle with one cross piece; use your door on sawhorses as a workbench
- Set the frame into the doorway on the hinge side
- Shim under the bottom cross piece to create floor clearance, typically 1 inch
- Adjust the pieces to leave gaps of about ⅛ inch on the top and sides; if the jamb bows, you may need to scribe

2 **Glue the template**

- Hold the frame in position by clamping against the door stops on the back
- Heat a hot glue gun
- One joint at a time, release the clamp, squirt in hot glue, and press the parts back together

4 **Use the template**

- Set the template, marked side up, on top of the door with its hinges facing up
- If the template is bigger than the door, you need a different door
- If the hinge marks aren't on the same side as existing hinge recesses, you'd be very smart to get a different door
- If the template is just a tiny bit smaller than the door, align the hinge side and either the top or the bottom
- If the template is much smaller than the door, plan to trim all of the edges
- Trace along the template on edges that you need to trim, then set it aside

3 **Mark the hinges**

- Mark the top and bottom of each hinge on the adjoining template piece
- Use a combination square and a sharp utility knife so the marks line up precisely
- Draw arrows between the marks so you know which side of the template faces up and out

> **Time Saver**
>
> Don't try to remove a door by unscrewing the hinges. Remove the pins instead. If they don't slip out easily, tap a finish nail up from the bottom. Get all of a door's pins most of the way out before you remove any of them all the way.

 **Stuff to Buy**

LUMBER Door, lath
BASIC SUPPLIES Sawhorses, hinges, door knob

 **Time Commitment**

An afternoon

 **Tools You'll Need**

Chisel
Circular saw
Combination square
Drill
Glue gun
Tape measure
Utility knife

 **Related Topics**

Installing a pocket door, 202–205
Installing bypass doors, 198–201
Trimming a pass-through, 92–93

5 Trim to shape

- Clamp a straightedge like the one on pages 58–59 to the door
- If you are trimming the hinge side, top, or bottom, cut straight down with a circular saw
- Trim the latch side with a 2-degree bevel ($1/16$ inch, angled in, on an interior door)
- If you had to scribe the template, cut to the biggest dimension and then remove excess material with a belt sander

6 Mark hinges

- Place the template back on the door and line up all the edges
- Transfer the hinge marks to the door, again using a square and a sharp utility knife

7 Make a Dutchman

- If your door's hinge recesses are too big or in the wrong place, create a patch, often called a Dutchman
- Cut a replacement piece that's the same length but a little wider and thicker
- Glue and clamp it into the recess
- When the glue dries, plane off excess wood, then re-mark the hinge locations

8 Cut a hinge recess

- Set the door on edge on the latch side
- Place a hinge between one set of marks; the flat edge next to the barrels should project $1/4$ inch beyond the face of the door
- Predrill and then screw the hinge into position; it's fine to use only two narrow drywall screws at this stage
- Trace around the hinge edges with a sharp utility knife
- Unscrew the hinge and set it aside
- Using a chisel, make a series of straight-down cuts across the hinge space; then hold the chisel parallel to the door edge and pare off the fibers you just cut
- If you cut too deep, fill in under the hinge with tar paper or cereal-box cardboard, but don't use corrugated cardboard

9 Hang the door

- Screw the hinges to the door, through the same holes you made earlier
- If necessary, install knobs or a latch according to the manufacturer's instructions
- Stack tapered shims on the floor; lift the door upright and rest the bottom edge of the door on them
- Use your foot to nudge the shims in or out so the hinges line up
- Slip the hinge parts together; insert the pins partway, then tap them all the way down

Installing Bypass Doors

Common on closets, bypass doors are usually installed in pairs and occasionally as triplets. The doors slide on side-by-side overhead tracks, which means you don't need to allow any space for the doors to swing open into a room.

The bypass doors on the right function just as well as the ones on the left, but the doors on the left feel more like a built-in thanks to their trim, which hides their metal hardware.

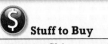

Stuff to Buy

LUMBER Shim material, doors
BASIC SUPPLIES Bypass hardware, finish nails

Time Commitment

Four to five hours

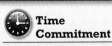

Tools You'll Need

Drill
Hacksaw
Hammer
Level
Nail set
Tape measure
Utility knife

Related Topics

Installing a pocket door, 202–205
Mitered trim for doors, 94–97
Trimming a pass-through, 92–93

① Prepare opening

- Trim the doorway as in Steps 1 to 11 on pages 92–93
- Measure remaining opening across top

② Cut rail

- Mark Step 1 measurement on metal rail
- Use a hacksaw to make the cut
- Make rail a little short

③ Place rail

- On top trim, make a few marks 1 inch in from the back edge
- Place back edge of rail on marks
- Orient rail so the J shapes open at the back

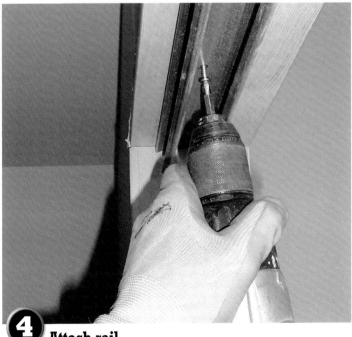

④ Attach rail

- Drill through holes in rail
- Drive screws

5 Place rollers

- Place door on sawhorses with its back up
- At each corner of top edge, align roller as hardware instructions specify
- Here, the center hole is $1\frac{1}{2}$ inches from the door's edge

6 Drill holes

- Predrill for one screw in each oversize slot
- Leave small round hole undrilled for now
- Follow instructions that came with door hardware if different from steps shown here

7 Attach roller hardware

- Drive screws in slots
- Leave them barely snug
- Don't overtighten; you need to adjust alignment later

8 Attach back door

- Position yourself inside the closet or door opening
- Tilt the door out at the bottom as you lift it into place
- Hook rollers into the J track

9 Attach front door

- Stand outside the closet or opening
- Push the first door to one side
- Lift and tilt front door to fit rollers in track

10 Check alignment

- Stand inside closet and close doors
- Inspect the shadow lines at both sides of doorway
- If lines are thin and even, the doors fit fine

11 Adjust alignment

- If a door tilts, loosen screws on one roller
- Move door position up or down slightly, then tighten screws all the way
- If door still appears tilted, adjust the other roller
- If tilt is fixed, tighten screws on other roller

12 Lock in the rollers

- When doors are aligned, predrill through remaining holes in hardware
- Drive screws through holes

13 Attach trim strip

- Cover roller track with a trim piece that spans the top of the doorway
- This job needed a strip ¾ inch thick by 1½ inches wide
- Predrill, then nail finish nails through the strip into door header

14 Attach bottom guide

- Push both doors to one side
- Position bottom guide so both doors hang straight
- Drill holes and drive screws

Fine-tuning the Fit

If adjusting the roller screws doesn't align bypass doors, the problem could be humps and valleys in the trim that lines the doorway. A carpenter's level is a good tool for finding the source of the problem. Once you've identified variances, hammer in a pair of shims, one from the front and one from back, until the trim is straight. Cut any excess shim material with a utility knife. You don't need to nail the shims; nailing on the doorway trim will lock the jamb in position.

Installing a Pocket Door

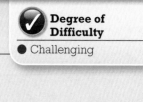
A pocket door slides into a wall cavity, eliminating the need to leave a clear area for the door to swing. The hardware is sold in a kit that includes an overhead track and jamb stiffeners, which are vertical metal plates that define the pocket opening.

Pocket Door Hardware

Hardware for a pocket door needs to be installed before the wall is covered with drywall. Instructions vary depending on the brand of hardware that you purchase. Follow the manufacturer's recommendations if steps differ from those shown here and on the following pages.

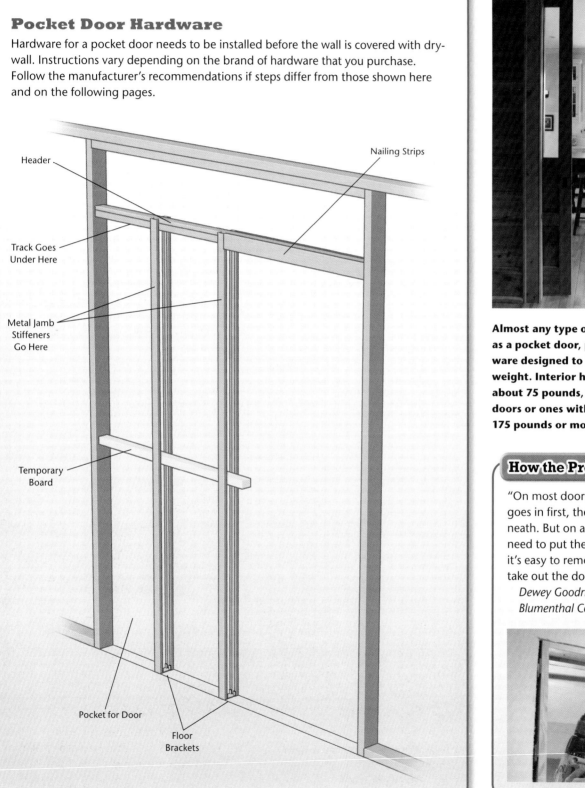

Header

Nailing Strips

Track Goes Under Here

Metal Jamb Stiffeners Go Here

Temporary Board

Pocket for Door

Floor Brackets

Almost any type of door can be installed as a pocket door, provided you buy hardware designed to handle the door's weight. Interior hollow-core doors weigh about 75 pounds, while solid hardwood doors or ones with glass panes may weigh 175 pounds or more.

How the Pros Do It

"On most doors, the top jamb piece goes in first, then the sides fit underneath. But on a pocket door, you need to put the top trim in last. Then it's easy to remove if you ever need to take out the door."

Dewey Goodrich,
Blumenthal Construction

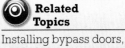

 Stuff to Buy
LUMBER Shim material, door
BASIC SUPPLIES 2½" finish
nails, door hardware

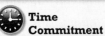 **Time Commitment**
A weekend, including time to
cover wall framing with
drywall, paint, etc.

 **Tools You'll Need**
Drill
Hammer
Jigsaw
Level
Tape measure
Screwdrivers

Related Topics
Installing bypass doors,
198–201
Mitered trim for doors, 94–97
Trimming a pass-through,
92–93

1 Prepare opening

- Make the initial framed opening twice the door's width plus 1¼ inch
- Install track and jamb stiffeners as manufacturer specifies
- When you hang drywall, avoid overlong fasteners that protrude into cavity

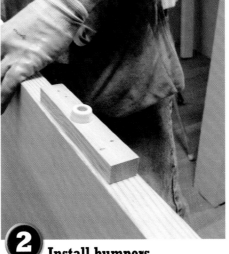

2 Install bumpers

- If Step 1 was done by someone else, measure depth of opening and door's width
- If measurements are equal, tack trim scraps to door's back edge so the door won't slip too deep into cavity
- Install bumpers (included in hardware kit) or spacers on the door's back edge

3 Add hangers

- At top edge of door, measure hanger setback specified by manufacturer
- Predrill through openings for screws
- Attach screws

4 Slip in rollers

- At open end of track, fit both roller sets into track
- Place the bolt ends down

5 Position door

- Enlist a helper, if possible
- Lift the door and snap one bolt into a hanger
- Push in the locking tab
- Repeat for the other hanger

6 Adjust door

- Use wrench included in the kit
- Turn bolts until door is level and plumb
- Do not loosen so much that post falls out
- If you need to remove the door, release the locking tabs

7 Make template for jamb

- Rip trim board and a scrap piece to width of jamb on side where door closes
- On the scrap piece, mark the gap needed for track
- Measure and mark the distance trim should extend up into track opening
- Cut tongue on scrap piece and test fit

8 Cut the jamb

- From one end of the jamb, measure up to show height of the doorway
- Above that, trace tongue shape
- With a jigsaw or handsaw, cut the tongue

9 Install the jamb

- Slide jamb in place
- With a level, check whether the jamb is plumb
- If the jamb is not plumb, slip in pairs of shims from both sides
- When the jamb is plumb, nail it in place with 2½-inch finish nails

10 Install floor bracket

- Slide the door into the wall
- Slip bracket (from hardware kit) over exposed bottom corner of door
- Attach bracket by nailing through the openings in the jamb stiffeners

11 Mark openings in jamb stiffeners

- Pencil lines to show where metal jamb stiffeners are perforated
- Mark both sides of the wall with the pocket

12 Add trim over jamb stiffeners

- Rip two trim pieces to the width on each side of the wall pocket and cut to length
- Align one trim piece by temporarily shimming both sides of door
- Predrill where you marked perforations, then nail trim in place
- Repeat for other trim piece

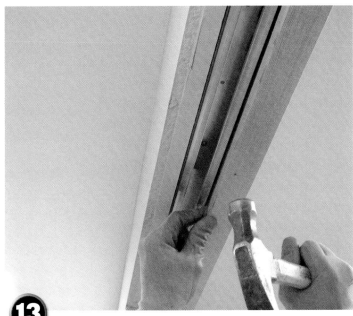

13 Trim top of doorway

- Cut two trim pieces to fit below track
- Predrill, then nail in place
- Align nails so they penetrate into wood, not drywall

14 Add face trim

- Install casing, such as mitered door trim on pages 94–97
- On the pocket side, use short nails
- Aim the nails where you marked in Step 11

15 Attach door pull

- A pull-out handle fits into recess on edge of the door
- Hardware usually isn't included in the installation kit
- Choose hardware whose style complements other hardware in your house

The final door offers easy access into a walk-in closet. If a regular door had been installed, opening it inward would have consumed closet space. Opening it outward was not really an option since it's located in a narrow hallway.

Handrails

Some staircase jobs are best left for pros, but installing a handrail is a good DIY project, especially as a retrofit for a rail that runs in a straight line. If you're replacing a rail or have a short stairway, you can skip some of the steps shown here.

Installing a Handrail

1 Attach brackets

- Tap or use a stud sensor to locate studs in the wall
- Just past end studs, drive one nail at the rail height (30 to 36 inches) minus the rail thickness
- Snap a chalk line between the nails
- Attach handrail brackets so they touch the line and are equally spaced over studs

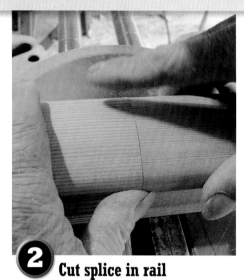

2 Cut splice in rail

- If you need to join pieces to make a long rail, cut the mating ends at a 90-degree angle
- Measure the pieces so the joint will lie over a bracket
- Fit the pieces together to check that the joint is tight and smooth

3 Miter the ends

- Adjust a miter saw to 45 degrees
- With the rail sections right side up, mark the lengths needed on the sides farthest from the wall
- With those marks as the long points, cut the miters
- On each mitered scrap piece, draw a diagonal line in the opposite direction for the short pieces that return to the wall

4 Make the returns

- Center a rail scrap lengthwise over a bracket
- Measure the offset from the wall to the outside edge of the rail
- Cut the miters you marked in Step 3
- Reset the saw to cut at 90 degrees and trim the returns to the offset distance

5 Bolt rail sections

- Buy a 3 by 1/4-inch hanger bolt (machine threads on one end, wood threads on the other), plus a washer and nut
- On a scrap of rail material, drill a 1/4-inch-diameter hole centered 7/8 inch up from the base
- With a miter saw, slice off about 1/2 inch of the scrap end with the hole to make a template
- Center the template on each rail end and drill holes 1 5/8 inch deep
- Be careful to drill straight in, not at an angle

How the Pros Do It

"Threading the nut onto the hanger bolt before you use the locking pliers gives you a way to repair the threads if you crush them. Just unscrew the nut, and it will smooth out any little nicks."

Dewey Goodrich,
Blumenthal Construction

Stuff to Buy

LUMBER Rail stock
BASIC SUPPLIES Brackets;
3"-long, ¼"-thick hanger
bolt with nut and washer;
wood glue

Time Commitment

Several days (so glue can set)

Tools You'll Need

Chalk line
Chisel
Drill
Hole saw (1 inch)
Pliers (locking, long nose)
Power miter saw
Power nailer

Related Topics

Check every angle, 76–77
Power miter saws, 52–55

6 Drill for access to nut

- Tip one rail section upside down.
- At the center, measure back 1⅜ inch
- With the pilot bit of a 1-inch hole saw on that mark, drill a hole 1¼ inches deep
- With a narrow chisel, break off and pry out the plug

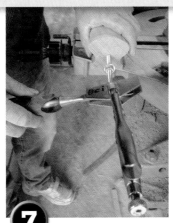

7 Insert hanger screw

- Thread a washer and nut onto the machine-screw end of the hanger bolt
- Attach locking pliers (sheet metal type is shown) to that end
- Twist the wood-screw end into the rail section that you did not drill in Step 6
- For extra torque, slip a chisel or screwdriver sideways into the pliers

8 Attach washer and nut

- Remove the washer and nut from the hanger bolt
- Slide rail sections together and make sure fit is correct; you may need to deepen the hole or trim the bolt
- Disassemble, spread wood glue on the mating surfaces, then slide them back together
- Slip on the washer and thread on the nut, through the 1-inch hole
- Tighten the nut with the tips of long nose pliers

9 Check alignment

- Stand at one end of the rail and peer down along its length
- If you see a bend in the rail, try twisting the rail sections slightly
- Wipe off excess glue with a damp cloth

10 Attach mitered returns

- One end at a time, spread glue on the miter cuts to join each rail end to its return piece
- Fit the pieces tightly together
- Drive one or two finish nails in on each side to hold the joint tight
- Wipe off excess glue with a damp cloth
- Leave the assembly undisturbed for several days

11 Mount the rail

- With a helper, carry the rail to the staircase
- Line up the rail with the support brackets
- Shift rail if needed so return ends butt tightly to the wall
- Predrill, then drive screws through the brackets to secure the handrail

The finish on this handrail matches the finish on other pieces of trim to create a cohesive look.

All About Finishes

In this chapter, we help you choose the right finish for your trimwork by showing you the effects you can achieve with a range of popular finishes—from clear shellac to metallic paint—as well as the best techniques to apply them. Primers, fillers, and caulk are covered in detail; masking and the importance of working in sequence are fully explained. The chapter also highlights the differences between painting windows and doors.

Chapter Contents

Choosing a Finish
page 210

Primers
page 214

Fillers & Caulk
page 216

Preparing to Paint
page 218

Prefinishing
page 220

Masking Surfaces
page 222

Working in Sequence
page 224

Painting a Window
page 226

Painting a Door
page 228

Applying Clear Finishes
page 230

Metallic Paint
page 232

Patching Drywall
page 234

Resources/ Credits
page 236

Index
page 238

Choosing a Finish

Clear coatings, stains, paints, and even metallic and faux finishes give trimwork a final flourish. The type or combination you choose will have a big impact on whether your trim stands out or blends in, and on whether it looks cozy or cutting-edge.

A monochrome color scheme, especially in white or a soft pastel, lets wainscot or other trimwork add background texture to a room rather than being the center of attention.

Clear finishes on natural wood make the material itself the focus. Warm wood tones create a timeless look that makes people want to linger.

Painting trim with bands of color emphasizes the sculptural qualities of the molding—especially when certain curves are painted with shiny metallic paint. Although the effect mimics the look of gold leaf, this kind of paint is as easy to apply as any other water-based formula. The shiny, shimmering look comes from tiny bits of mica, or fool's gold, incorporated in the paint.

It's possible to combine painted and clear finishes on trimwork. Visual harmony results when an underlying logic determines the finish for each part. On this staircase, the vertical elements are painted while the horizontal features—treads, rails, post tops, and a few molding details—are not.

Paint changes the apparent nature of trimwork, depending on the color you choose for it and the background parts of a room. For example, you can make wall frames appear to be part of the wall by using one color for both (left). Or you can emphasize that wall frames are trim by painting them and other trim one color and walls another (above). Painting wall frames a different color than either walls or other trim (above, left) makes the wall frames a distinct element—especially if you choose a metallic paint, which catches light as you walk past.

Clear vs. Opaque

Finishes for trimwork fit into two broad categories, clear and opaque. Within these, finishes also vary by the type of solvent they use, how easy they are to wipe clean, and many other factors. The type of trim material you use may narrow your options, since clear finishes are suitable for solid wood and veneers only. Choose opaque finish for finger-jointed trim or molding made of MDF, composites, or plastic.

Finish	What It Is	Effect	How to Apply	Cleanup
Clear finishes				
Penetrating oil	A drying oil, meaning it does not stay sticky once it cures by reacting with oxygen in the air. Tung oil is most durable; linseed adds more color	Soaks in and seals wood. Adds amber color and some water- and stain-resistance. Retains the natural texture of the wood	Wipe or brush on, let stand, then wipe off excess. Apply several coats. Times between steps vary because some products are pure, raw oil, while others have been heat-treated or contain solvents or driers	Clean tools with mineral spirits. Don't leave rags in a pile (see Safety on opposite page)
Alkyd varnish	Formed by modifying a drying oil and resin, then mixing with mineral spirits	Penetrates and forms an amber surface film that resists scratches and stains	Usually applied with a natural-bristle brush, sometimes with a foam applicator or a roller with a nap of 1/4 to 3/8 inch. With wipe-on products, use a lint-free cloth. Available in quick-dry and standard versions; standard allows time to finesse the finish and results in a tougher finish	Mineral spirits
Solvent-based polyurethane	Alkyd varnish plus polyurethane (a plastic)	Forms a slightly amber surface film that's tougher and more water-resistant than alkyd varnish	Use a natural-bristle brush or a lamb's wool applicator; or get a wipe-on type and use a lint-free cloth. Recoat within the time listed on the label. Sand between coats	Mineral spirits
Water-based polyurethane	Acrylic resin (a plastic) dispersed in water, plus other ingredients	Creates a clear surface film similar to solvent-based polyurethane, but without the amber color	Use a synthetic-bristle brush or a foam applicator; recoat within the time listed on the label or you may need to sand between coats to prevent peeling	Warm, soapy water
Shellac	A natural resin produced by insects, dissolved in denatured alcohol	Seals wood and creates a surface film with slight to deep amber color, depending on the product. Not as tough as other varnishes, and not resistant to alcohol-based stains	Use a natural-bristle brush, or pad on with a lint-free cloth. Dries hard as soon as solvent evaporates (less than 1 hour), but becomes liquid again if solvent is applied. This allows numerous coats in a day and easy spot-repair or recoating later	Denatured alcohol
Lacquer	Nitrocellulose resin (from cotton or other materials) dissolved in a mixture of petroleum solvents	Creates a clear surface film that's nearly as tough and stain-resistant as polyurethane	Usually sprayed, though some products can be brushed. Has the same quick-drying and easy recoating properties as shellac	Lacquer thinner
Opaque finishes				
Oil-based enamel	Pigment and resin mixed with mineral spirits or other solvents	Creates a tough, washable finish, but yellows over time	Apply only over oil-base primer or enamel undercoater; never over water-based paint. Use a natural-bristle brush or a sprayer	Mineral spirits
Water-based enamel	Pigment plus acrylic or vinyl-acrylic resin in water, with other ingredients	Creates a slightly softer finish that's a little harder to clean than oil enamel. Does not yellow	Apply over oil- or water-based primers or undercoaters. Use a synthetic brush, a roller or a foam applicator, or an airless sprayer	Warm, soapy water
Water-based paint	Similar to water-based enamel, but may have a lower percentage of resin	Might not dry as hard or be as easy to scrub. The glossier the paint, the more durable and washable it's likely to be	Same as above	Warm, soapy water

Using water-based paints or quick-curing clear finishes is particularly important in a child's room that must be occupied soon after it is painted.

Safety

Water-based finishes don't pose the fire hazard that some solvent-based products do, and they release far fewer fumes as they cure. However, most formulas still contain small amounts of solvents other than water, and some of these can trigger allergic reactions if you inhale them. The solvents can also dry out your skin if it is in contact with them for long periods.

Open windows while you paint, or consider wearing a suitable respirator, especially if you are coating a lot of trim, spraying, using a solvent-based finish, or working in a small room or ones with closed windows. The solvents in lacquer finishes are particularly hazardous.

For the least smelly, most environmentally benign finishes, look for low-odor products that are also low in VOCs (volatile organic compounds) and that have passed the certification standards of an independent organization, such as Green Seal. Avoid products with the words "warning" or "caution" on the label, or with hazardous materials listed on the manufacturer's safety data sheet, which the store should be able to supply.

Most oil- or solvent-based finishes are flammable. Drying oils, especially linseed, create so much heat as they combine with oxygen in the air that a pile of oily rags can spontaneously burst into flame. Hang rags individually to dry, or soak with water and wrap in plastic before disposing of them.

Work quickly when you're applying stain so it doesn't create streaks.

Stains

Stains and dyes aren't finishes, but they do have a dramatic effect on how a finish turns out. They change the color of wood without completely obscuring the grain or covering the surface with a film. Stains consist of finely ground pigment particles mixed into an oil- or water-based formula; the proportion of pigment and the particle size determine how much the stain masks the wood grain. Dyes are colored liquids, without pigment particles, so they don't cloud the wood grain. Some dyes fade when exposed to ultraviolet light, but that's less of an issue than it used to be because modern windows screen out most of the sun's UV rays. Stains and dyes don't protect against stains or scuffs; for that, you need to add a clear finish. A few tips ensure success:

- Always test stains and accompanying top coats on trim samples before you tackle the actual job. Keep every detail the same: sanding, application method, and number of coats.
- Many softwoods absorb oil-based stains unevenly. Pretreat with a wood conditioner.
- Some dyes lift or become mottled as you brush on a surface finish; to prevent this, you might need a middle layer of shellac.

Primers

Painting trim with a cheap coat of primer reduces the number of costly coats of paint needed for an even finish. Indeed, many of the horror stories you may have heard about people applying endless coats of paint to a surface can be traced to lack of a primer.

Primer vs. Finish

Primer paint and finish paint are formulated differently because they serve different purposes:

- Primer sticks, blocks stains, and seals so the surface is evenly porous
- Top coats add color, stand up to sunlight, and can be scrubbed clean
- Undercoaters are primers with even more body; they can be sanded smooth to create an ideal base for enamel

Hiding the Uglies

Paint stores can tint most primers, but not to deep shades because too much pigment interferes with curing. Even a pastel shade helps, though, if you're planning to paint trim or walls a color other than white. A little color helps you achieve an even shade in the finish paint.

Primer costs less than paint, so it's a wise first coat when you are painting over a vivid design or are switching from a dark color to one that's much lighter. This primer was tinted.

Using preprimed trim

- Spot prime after installation to cover bare spots, such as end grain or areas where you sanded
- Also prime over patched nail holes
- Top with water- or oil-based paint

Primer paint often seems to disappear into the end grain of trim pieces because wood fibers are open and much more absorbent on the ends than they are on their sides. You may need two coats of primer on the ends in order to wind up with smooth finish paint. An even better solution: Install mitered returns (see pages 114–115) so no end grain shows.

When to Use Primer

- Before you finish bare wood, MDF, composite, or new drywall
- To cover old paint that's glossy
- When using water-based paint over oil-based paint or paint of unknown type
- If you can see pitch or knots through old paint
- To spot-prime a previously painted or preprimed surface
- When you are dramatically changing a color

Cool Tool

Like a felt-tip pen but loaded with primer paint, an applicator designed for coating board ends comes in handy when you're working with preprimed trim. With a quick swipe, you can coat ends before you install trim pieces, without worrying about paint drying on a brush. The applicator has a screw-on cap that blocks evaporation, and if the foam tip does dry out, just rinse it and continue working. You can also spot-prime patched nail holes or areas where you sanded through the factory primer.

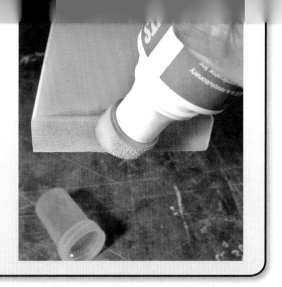

Choosing the Right Primer

Surface	Problem	Solution
Unpainted wood, MDF, or plywood	Standard paint tends to peel away from bare wood because the paint doesn't bond sufficiently to keep up with the wood's expansion and contraction as humidity changes. The end grains of bare wood absorb more paint than other surfaces, and water-based finishes have a tendency to raise some wood fibers. Some hardwoods, including oak, have open pores that absorb paint. These factors make it difficult to achieve an even top coat.	Use a general-purpose primer matched to the type of paint you plan to use. Go for an enamel undercoater and sand it smooth if you want an especially glassy surface. To counteract fiber-lifting by water-based primer, sand lightly once the primer dries. Or use an oil- or alcohol-based primer. If you are painting a hardwood with open pores, apply a paste filler and sand before you prime.
Pitch pockets and knots	Sticky pitch, common in knots but also found in isolated patches within wood, can bleed through paint and mar the surface.	Paint the entire surface with an alcohol-based primer that includes shellac. Or spot-prime knot holes and pitch pockets with this primer, let that dry, then prime the entire surface with a general-purpose water- or oil-based primer.
Different paint base	Oil paint continues to harden as it ages, while water-based paint remains somewhat flexible. When you want to use water-based paint over old oil paint, particularly when the oil paint is glossy, the different flexibilities can keep the layers from bonding properly. That may cause the top coat to peel off.	Clean and scuff up the surface or use an etching solution if you suspect the old paint contains lead. Then use a general-purpose water-based primer or one formulated for blocking stains.
Stained surfaces	You paint over stains and at first all looks good. But when the paint dries, the stains reappear. The reason is that water-soluble stains travel right through standard water-based primers and mar the finish. Oily stains are also problematic, as the new paint skids off.	For mild stains, use a water-based primer labeled as a stain blocker. Severe stains require an oil-based, stain-blocking primer, or an alcohol-based primer with shellac. To determine whether you can use a water-based primer, test a section by painting the dry primer with top coat. If the stain reappears, switch to a different primer.
Slick surfaces	Finish paint has a hard time grabbing onto a surface where there is no "tooth," so it doesn't adhere.	Scuff up the surface with sandpaper or use an etching solution if you suspect lead paint, then prime. Or paint with primer listed as suitable for slick surfaces.
New or patched drywall, and patched plaster	The paper face on new drywall and the joint compound over seams absorb paint at different rates. On patched drywall or plaster, patches are more porous than surrounding paint.	On new drywall, use polyvinyl acetate (PVA) primer, a water-based product. Over patches, use a general-purpose water-based primer, assuming the existing paint and the new top coat are both water-based.

Fillers & Caulk

Near the end of every trimwork project, a pesky task remains: filling nail holes. You may also want to caulk gaps along walls or the ceiling. Get different products for these jobs—nail holes change size little over time, while gaps tend to open and close with the seasons.

Fillers for Nail Holes

There are numerous kinds of fillers, most of which work fine if you plan to paint your trim. If you're using a clear finish, you need to consider carefully when to use filler. For example, plugging holes before you stain and finish the trimwork sounds like the obvious thing to do, but getting a good color match is easier if you wait until the wood is stained and perhaps even coated with finish.

SOLVENT-BASED FILLERS

These fillers contain real wood fibers, solvents, and plastic resin. Apply after sealing or priming, but before adding a surface finish. These fillers dry in about 15 minutes to the same consistency as wood. They can be sanded or used to fill oversize screw or nail holes. Solvent-based fillers can be stained, but they don't always turn the exact same color as the surrounding wood. Because the solvents in them evaporate rapidly, these fillers tend to get stiff and hard once a can has been opened a few times.

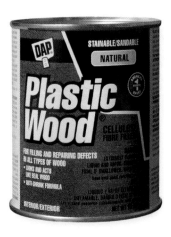

WATER-BASED FILLERS

These contain plastic resins plus fillers such as wood flour or limestone. Apply before adding a surface finish. The consistency is easy to spread, which makes these good choices for filling oversize nail or screw holes. Drying time varies; it can be as little as 15 minutes for shallow patches, after which you can hand sand. Some products can be stained, though not necessarily to the same color as surrounding wood.

Dry Powders

Similar to plaster that you mix with water as needed (unlike premixed fillers, the powder you don't use can be stored almost indefinitely). Powders can be tinted with dry pigments or water-based stain or paint. Use to plug large holes as well as small ones. Powders dry quickly (often in 1 hour or less) and they can be sanded and painted.

Caulk for Gaps

If you plan to paint trim, caulking the gaps between the trim and the walls or ceiling creates a tidy look that makes everything look like it fits just right. Use latex caulk that's labeled as paintable. But if you will use a clear finish for trim, it's usually better to leave the gaps unfilled unless you need to seal out drafts or block splashes from getting into the drywall. In those situations, use a clear caulk, but make sure it's a paintable type. Pure silicone formulas are not.

1 Get a good gun

- Make sure all of the controls work smoothly
- If you have an old gun that's gunked up, invest in a new one
- A standard-size gun is most convenient; it uses 10-ounce tubes of caulk
- Under the tip, this model has a useful feature: a wire that pivots out when you need to poke through the seal on a fresh tube
- The release button above the handles stops the flow of caulk; when you press it, pressure against the tube eases

2 Cut the tip

- Use a sharp utility knife to cut the tip of a new tube
- The closer to the tip you cut, the smaller the bead will be
- Match the bead size to the width of the gaps you want to fill
- If you aren't sure what size you want, cut off a smaller amount; you can always trim the nozzle farther back if you want a larger bead
- Some people like to cut at a steep angle; others prefer to cut straight across
- Practice to discover what works best for you

3 Let it flow

- With a new tube, squeeze the gun's trigger just until caulk begins to flow
- Depress the release button and wipe off the tip
- Place the nozzle tip at one end of the joint to be caulked
- Squeeze the trigger and move the nozzle along the joint
- Continue to squeeze to make a ribbon of caulk as even as you can
- Smooth the bead with your finger or a damp rag or sponge

Oil-based Putty

For small jobs, get the colored wax pencils and touch-up sticks; for big projects, choose putty in jars and tubs. Some types can be painted, while others must be applied after the final finish is on. Putty never completely dries, so it can't be sanded. Just stuff it into a hole and rub off the excess with a soft cloth.

Spackling Compounds

These vinyl and/or acrylic emulsions have the consistency of whipped cream. They fill small holes on trimwork that will be painted. Prime the surface, spackle, let it dry, then top with two layers of paint. You can sand spackle, but you might not need to.

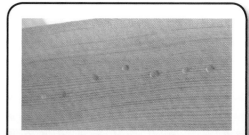

Testing Stainable Filler

Drill a series of small holes in one board. Put part of the filler into a new, sealable container, and mix in some stain. When the shade is still slightly too light, dab some of the material into one of the holes. Add a little more stain and plug the next hole. Continue doing this until you get a good match. If the filler gets too dark, lighten it by adding untinted filler.

Preparing to Paint

One secret to carrying out a great paint job is to work quickly. Working from an area that's still wet, rather than one where the paint has already dried, minimizes brush marks and results in a smooth finish. To accomplish this, you must be prepared.

Basic Tools & Materials

- Dropcloths
- Stepladder
- Paintbrush to use as a mini broom
- Low-tack painter's tape and paper tape
- Brush for cutting in along corners
- Bucket for paint when brushing
- Roller frame and two covers (one for primer, one for topcoats)
- Paint tray that fits roller
- Stir stick
- Paint key or flat screwdriver to open paint cans
- Painter's 5-in-1 tool
- Putty knife with flexible blade
- Clean white rags
- Plastic bags to cover tools and paint trays between steps
- Container with wash water or solvent
- Disposable plastic gloves
- Garbage can or trash bag

Drop Cloths

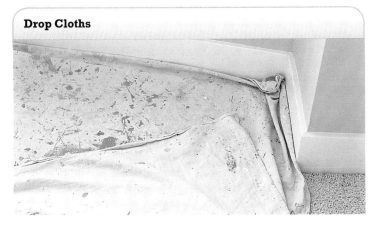

Plastic drop cloths are great for covering furniture in the center of the room but not so great on the floor—they're slippery and the plastic tends to tear. Canvas is what pros choose. Although paint can seep through the fabric, it rarely does; always use with the same side up (as shown above) so that clumps of semi-dry paint don't wind up against carpet. Brown paper drop cloths with a plastic layer in the middle are also a good choice.

Tool-toting Ladder

Good painting ladders have slots in the top so that you can stash tools when you scoot the ladder around. Get one with cushioned feet to protect floors.

Makeshift Stepstool

If you don't have a ladder or stepstool, find a 5-gallon bucket. Rightside up with the lid on (as shown) or even upside down, a bucket makes a perfectly decent stepstool. It lifts you high enough to see most trim at eye level, but it won't help you reach to the top of a cathedral ceiling.

On the job site, keep a few leftover plastic bags handy to wrap tools and paint trays between coats. This cuts down on wasted paint and reduces the time you spend cleaning tools.

Wear Your Tools

To save trips up and down a ladder, or just to keep moving, use your belt, belt loops, and pockets to keep tools close at hand. Carry a damp rag, a brush to use as a mini broom, and a 5-in-1 tool. And strap on a bucket filled with a few inches of paint when you're painting crown molding or cutting in paint where walls meet the ceiling.

One Handy Tool

Although it's called a 5-in-1, this enhanced putty knife does even more tasks.

Sharp edge scrapes off dried paint, removes small bulges, works as a chisel tip

Point cleans out cracks so you can patch them

Blunt edge opens paint cans, works in a pinch as a flat screwdriver

Teardrop works as a nail puller; the tip catches even small-head nails

Curved scraper removes dried paint from rounded edges

Curve scrapes excess paint from rollers

Handle acts as mini hammer to tap down nails or lids of paint cans

How the Pros Do It

"I screw a cup hook to the side of my brush so I can hang it over the inside edge of my paint can as I climb up and down a ladder. The bristles don't get overloaded with paint, and I don't risk dropping the brush."
David Schott, Interiors Only Painting

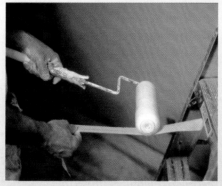

"I don't like finding small hairs from a roller in the paint I put on walls. So I remove excess lint first by rolling the pile across a length of tape pulled taut. I also dampen my roller and brush before I dip them in paint. This makes it much easier to clean the tools later."
Bruce Carter, Interiors Only Painting

Prefinishing Trim

Sometimes it makes sense to apply a finish before installing trim. You'll still need to fill nail holes and touch up any dings afterward. But you won't need to bother with masking or worry about drips, and you can keep most paint fumes outside of your house.

When to Prefinish

Prefinishing isn't always the right choice, despite its benefits. It makes installation trickier, since you can't sand trim to bring pieces into line. It also means the finish won't plug tiny gaps between the parts, which might be an issue if you are installing built-up trim. You can always decide to prefinish some parts and coat the rest once they are in place.

To Stay on Schedule

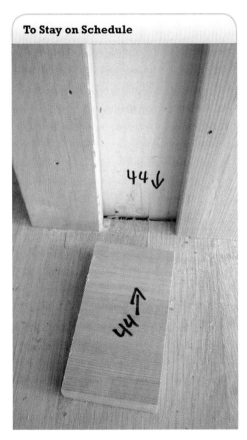

Sometimes you might want to cut trim first and prefinish just the pieces you will use. This makes sense where joints are simple or where trim goes against a surface that's not complete. This baseboard, for example, is against a floor that still needs work. Cutting and finishing the trim but installing it later keeps work on schedule. Label each piece on the back to show its location and orientation.

To Match Finishes

For some projects, it makes sense to prefinish the stock, then cut the parts. These cherry boards and plywood, for example, were finished at the same time as cabinets in another room. That ensured the finishes would match.

For Stand-alone Pieces

Doors and other easily removed pieces also make great candidates for prefinishing. Don't leave doors propped against walls for long, though, or they might warp.

When Not to Prefinish

This mitered trim was easier to install unfinished. That way, the pieces could be sanded in place to make them flush. The plan was to stain, then spray with lacquer, so lots of masking was needed.

Working Efficiently

With prefinished trim, there's even less margin for error than there is with standard trim. Paying attention to a few details helps ensure a good job.

1 Mark everything

- Don't count on remembering where each piece goes
- Stick to a number-and-letter system that identifies each room and part
- Write the code for each door on the bottom
- Write the same code in the hinge space

2 Plan your work

- Place doors or trim pieces on sawhorses or a workbench so you can work at a comfortable height
- Paint with pieces horizontal so there's less risk of drips
- Schedule your work so one side has time to dry before you paint the other
- Paint the edges when either side is up, or paint half of them each time
- With doors, seal all edges

3 Dry without dust

- Before you start applying finish, decide where to set pieces while they dry
- Clean both your work and storage areas well to reduces the chance that dust might settle on the damp finish
- Keep trim horizontal while the finish dries
- Elevate pieces so the finish along the back edge doesn't stick to the surface underneath

How the Pros Do It

"If I'm building with prefinished materials, I don't make pencil marks where they will show. Instead, I put down some painter's tape, and I make my marks on that."
Tyler Bloomquist,
Carley Construction

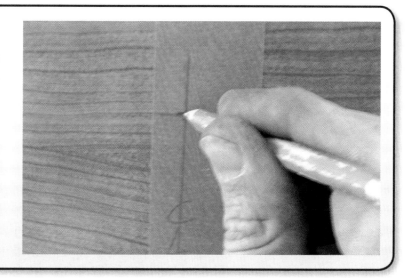

Masking Surfaces

A good paint job is as much about keeping paint off some surfaces as it is getting the finish onto others. Though it's possible to paint without masking anything, smart use of a variety of tapes makes the job easier.

Types of Tape

Masking tape is sold in blue, green, white, and even gray. Each color is supposed to signal how well the tape adheres, as well as which finishes it might damage. Unfortunately, what the colors really mean changes from one manufacturer to the next, so you can't use them as a guide without reading labels or checking store displays. If you're unsure, ask a clerk to make sure you buy tape that suits your needs.

CREPE PAPER TAPE

The original tan masking tape is a relatively high-tack tape. It works well where you are covering curves or bumpy surfaces. Remove it promptly, especially in direct sun, or it is likely to leave a stubborn residue. The ¼-inch width is particularly useful in some decorative paint projects.

Applying Tape

Smoothing tape along a surface seems simple enough, but aspects of the job can be frustrating. If you find a rounded corner, for example, it's unclear where the tape should go. Or you may pull off tape at the end of a job and find that paint seeped underneath and left a ragged edge. Several tips help ensure good results.

1 Dust first

- Dust collects on the top of doorway trim and other horizontal surfaces, such as baseboards
- If you don't dust, painter's tape won't adhere properly
- Keep a small, dry paintbrush handy to sweep these surfaces before you apply tape
- If the debris doesn't brush off, wash it off and let the surface dry

2 Avoid stretching tape

- Unroll a workable length, or cut a piece long enough for the section you want to mask
- Working in short sections, align the edge that will establish the paint line
- Gently press down the tape and smooth out any wrinkles
- Repeat for the next section
- When you're done, go over the tape again to seal the edges

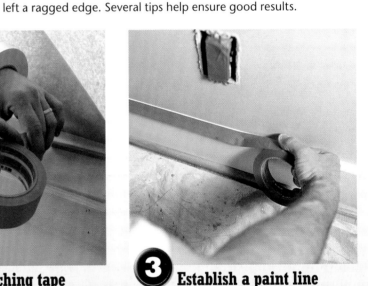

3 Establish a paint line

- If you've caulked between trim and a wall, the rounded caulk edge makes it unclear where trim and wall colors should meet
- Paint either the walls or the trim first; cover the whole bead and a little of the adjoining surface
- When the paint dries, apply masking tape so the inside edge is completely on either the wall or the trim
- Keep the tape slightly away from the rounded corner so you can establish a straight line
- Paint the other surface; go a little onto the tape
- Remove the tape immediately so you can wipe off any drips that seeped underneath

PAPER TAPE

Use it horizontally to deflect drips when you are painting overhead. Also use it to cover wide areas, such as when you're worried about spatters from spray paint.

Paper tape

Crepe
paper tape

PAINTER'S TAPE

This is a smoother tape. It's generally medium-tack, although low- and high-tack types are also available. Medium-tack tape works well for most situations. Remove it within the number of days that the manufacturer recommends.

4 Make crisp corners

- When you're taping off trim in a corner, use separate pieces of tape in each direction
- Extend the first piece all the way into the corner
- Cut off the next piece at a 45-degree angle so that you leave no ragged edges where paint might collect
- To cut the tape neatly, tear it along a sharp edge, such as the blade of a painter's 5-in-1 tool or a putty knife

5 Protect baseboards

- A single strip of painter's tape isn't wide enough to protect a baseboard from drips
- If the baseboard is already finished, use painter's tape along with a wider strip of brown paper
- Place the paper first so it's about half an inch from the edge of the wall
- Cover the gap with painter's tape
- Immediately after you apply each coat of wall paint, remove the painter's tape (but not the paper tape) to clean up seepage
- For the second coat, just put on fresh painter's tape since the paper tape is already in place

6 Think 3-D

- Masking doesn't always need to be flat against the surface it protects
- When tape projects from the wall, it blocks drips from above, as well as messy brushstrokes alongside
- This shadow box around a light-switch cover works particularly well

Working in Sequence

Because paint drips, it makes sense to start at the ceiling and work your way down. That's an obvious tip, but did you know that you don't need to mask when painting adjoining surfaces different colors until you get to the second color? Here are more time savers.

Principles of Painting

- If you are painting all surfaces in a room, coat the ceiling first, let it dry, then mask the ceiling and paint the walls. Finally, mask wall surfaces next to trim and paint the trim.
- If you are painting only the walls, mask the ceiling and the trim from the start.
- Although you should start at the top and work down when you paint, attach masking materials in the opposite order, beginning with the floor. This directs drips onto the masking material below rather than channeling drips behind.

This sitting room features a different color on the ceiling, walls, and trimwork, which makes adhering to a logical working sequence all the more critical.

How to Paint a Room

The following steps assume you are painting all surfaces and that the ceiling, walls, and trim are different colors.

1 Cut in the ceiling

- With a brush or a paint pad, apply paint to the edges of the ceiling
- Also paint any architectural detailing, such as a dropped edge
- If you are using ceiling paint or another flat paint, do all the edges at once
- If the paint is glossier, work in sections so the edge paint doesn't dry before you get to the next step

2 Roll on ceiling paint

- Work in relatively straight lines across the ceiling
- Roll in the direction where the room is shorter, if possible; this makes it less likely that the paint will dry before you get to the next section
- Let the paint dry before you apply a second coat

3 Mask the ceiling

- Place tape just beyond the corner, on the ceiling
- Brush some of the ceiling paint along the edge of the paint
- This keeps wall paint from seeping under the tape and marring the ceiling
- Paint may still seep under, but it will be the ceiling color; the line will look straight

4 Paint the walls

- With a brush or a pad, paint edges of one wall
- Then use a roller to paint the main expanse of the wall
- Create a zigzag of thick paint, then roll up and down to even out the finish
- Paint a section about 3 by 3 feet at the top of the wall, then immediately move down and do the lower part
- Run your roller down the wall to smooth where the paint overlapped
- Add a second layer after the first coat dries

5 Mask the walls

- When the wall paint is dry, protect it with masking
- Mask edges alongside trim
- If corners are rounded with caulk, keep the masking entirely on the wall paint, and keep the tape in a straight line
- If you are spraying a finish on the trim, install wide paper masking beyond the tape (as shown)

6 Paint the trim

- Apply your choice of finish to the trim
- If you want paint, you need primer plus two finish coats
- If you want a clear finish and a stain, rub on the stain first
- Let the stain dry, then apply a clear finish

7 Clean up

- Save at least some leftover finish for touchups
- Scrape excess finish from tools and trays; work brush bristles back and forth against newspaper
- Wash out remaining water-based paint with warm water and a little laundry detergent
- Unwanted water-based finish can go in household garbage if you stir in kitty litter so it's no longer liquid
- Call your sanitation department for rules about disposing oil-based finishes

Painting a Window

Many windows don't need paint except on the trim. Older wood windows are more complex. These steps cover windows with a movable bottom sash. If both sections of your window move, lower the top sash and raise the bottom one to paint hard-to-reach parts first.

Before You Begin

If you suspect the old paint on your windows might have been applied before 1978, test for lead. If it is present, avoid sanding, and remove any loose paint by wiping it away, not vacuuming.

1 Remove loose paint

- Scrape off any loose paint
- Pay particular attention to sections next to the glass at the lower edge of each pane; that's where moisture collects

2 Banish mildew

- If you see mildew, wipe off as much as possible with a damp rag
- Remove the remaining stain with a solution of 3 parts water to 1 part bleach
- Rinse with clear water; allow to dry

3 Lightly sand

- Sand the old paint just enough to scuff up its surface
- Or wash with an etching solution

4 Remove dust

- Vacuum or wipe off any sanding debris
- After you vacuum, your finger should stay clean when you run it across the trim

5 Fill holes

- Use lightweight or regular spackle
- Smooth with a putty knife
- Fill the hole but don't butter the trim

6 Caulk

- Apply a thin bead of caulk where the jamb and stop meet the stool
- Smooth with your finger, if necessary

Painting Vinyl & Aluminum Windows

Scuff up the surface with a green abrasive pad, but avoid scratching the glass. Then wash the frame. Use a TSP substitute on vinyl and water with a little vinegar on aluminum. Rinse with clear water. Paint with a water-based primer suitable for slick surfaces, then with a water-based topcoat. Because vinyl and aluminum both expand a lot as they get hot, and because dark colors absorb more heat from sunlight than light colors, stick with lighter shades.

7 Remove excess

- With a putty knife, remove whatever caulk bulges out
- Leave just enough caulk to seal the gap

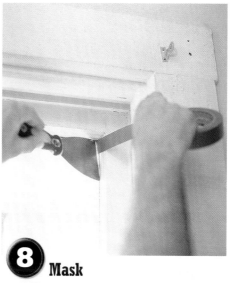

8 Mask

- Apply painter's tape to the glass
- Also smooth tape on the wall next to the window casing

9 Prime

- Brush primer paint over any bare spots or areas you filled with spackle
- If you are switching from oil- to water-based paint, prime the entire surface

10 Paint the sash

- When the primer is dry, begin applying finish paint
- The basic principal is to work from the inside out, so start with the beveled area next to the glass on the sash (the part that moves up and down)
- Open the sash so you can paint the top and bottom

11 Paint the casing

- Once you finish painting the sash, move on to molding strips (the stops) around the sash
- To avoid depositing globs of paint into the track where the window moves, start the brush at the edge of the track and pull the paint away

Painting a Door

Removing a door and painting it on a flat surface sounds like a good idea because it minimizes drips. But for most people, painting a door in place works better because there's
no heavy lifting or risk of damaging hinges.

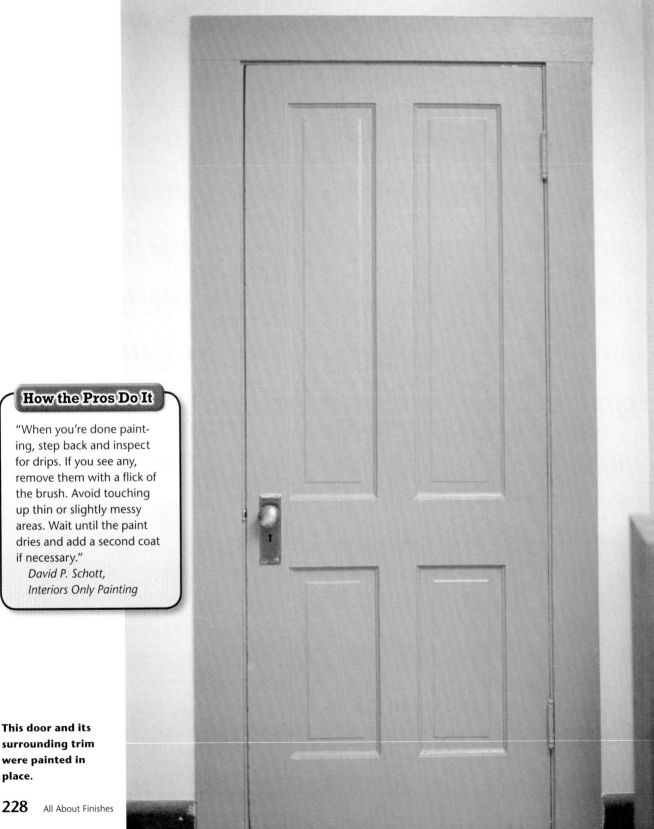

How the Pros Do It

"When you're done paint-
ing, step back and inspect
for drips. If you see any,
remove them with a flick of
the brush. Avoid touching
up thin or slightly messy
areas. Wait until the paint
dries and add a second coat
if necessary."
   David P. Schott,
   Interiors Only Painting

**This door and its
surrounding trim
were painted in
place.**

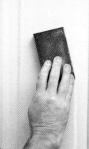

1 Clean and degloss

- Glossy paint is often found on doors because it stands up better to cleaning
- Apply a primer designed for slick surfaces, or etch the surface
- To etch, wash the door with a TSP substitute
- Wait for the surface to dry, then sand with 180-grit sandpaper or a sanding pad if you know that the old finish is lead-free
- Vacuum or wipe off sanding debris

2 Protect the doorknob

- Remove the doorknob and save all of the screws
- Or leave it in place and mask it with painter's tape
- The latter approach is easier and safer, especially with old-style hardware, which can be complicated to reinstall properly
- Apply tape in several pieces if necessary to ensure crisp corners

3 Paint the edges

- Slightly dampen a paintbrush and a small roller in water
- Remove excess water by rubbing the tools against a clean rag
- Stir paint and pour a workable amount into a separate container
- Dip the brush about a third of the way into the paint; tap brush against the sides of the container to remove excess paint
- Paint the top, right, and left edges of the door
- When you are done with each edge, run a dry brush along the corners to smooth out any drips

4 Paint a bevel

- Paint around the bevel on one of the upper panels
- Complete Step 5 (right) before you move on to the bevel in another panel

5 Paint a panel

- With the small roller, apply paint to the main part of the panel
- Using a roller is faster than brushing on the paint, and it helps ensure an even coat
- If you don't want the slightly pebbly texture that a roller leaves, brush over the paint immediately after you roll it on

6 Paint around handle

- Repeat Steps 4 and 5 for all of the panels
- Then brush paint around the door handle
- Feather the edges, especially across the grain, so you don't leave ridges

7 Paint frame

- Use the roller to apply paint to the door's flat framing; follow with the brush in the same direction as the wood grain, if you wish
- If there is a vertical piece in the middle of the top of the door, start with it
- Next paint the top horizontal piece
- Then coat the outside verticals down as far as the next horizontal
- Work your way down the door to the bottom horizontal piece

Brushing On a Clear Finish

The following procedure minimizes bubbles and guards against overworking the finish, which is an issue with water-based polyurethane, shellac, and lacquer. You can also apply alkyd varnish and oil-based polyurethane the same way.

How the Pros Do It

"When I'm painting a hand rail, I coat the bottom side first. Then I can focus on getting a smooth coat on the parts that will be noticed most. I use several thin coats, and sand them just enough to make them feel smooth, then add the coat. If a handrail has an indentation where people put their fingers as they grasp the rail, I'm careful to sand that part smooth as well."

Barry Ellis,
Interiors Only Painting

1 Prepare surface

- Sand, if necessary; use grit no finer than 220
- Vacuum or wipe with an electrostatic dusting cloth, or use an old t-shirt moistened with mineral spirits or denatured alcohol
- Do not use a commercial tack cloth if you are using a water-based finish; the residue might cause problems
- Apply a conditioner and stain (see page 213), if desired

2 Load brush or pad

- Gently stir the finish with a clean stir stick; do not shake the can or agitate
- Ladle or carefully pour a workable amount into a clean can, then reseal
- Dip your brush about one-third of the way into the finish; use natural bristles for oil-based finishes or shellac, or synthetic bristles for water-based finishes
- Do not wipe the bristles on the rim
- When the drips slow, tap the brush against the inside edge of the rim

3 Apply

- Hold the brush at an angle
- Beginning a few inches from one end, run the bristles down the trim in the direction of the wood grain
- Make one long, smooth stroke; use your tool like a squeegee
- Gradually lift your tool to end the stroke

4 Feather overlaps

- Go back to the start and coat the first few inches in reverse
- Feather the finish where strokes overlap
- On a mitered joint, end the second stroke just shy of the joint line, then reverse the brush again and lightly feather the finish back from the line
- Paint the other side of the miter as you did the first so you brush with the grain
- On narrow trim, make the second stroke parallel to the first; on wide trim, coat the full length before extending the finish across a wider area
- Resist the urge to touch up thin areas or brush out bubbles

5 Sand and recoat

- Read label directions about sanding and timing; products vary
- Even if sanding between coats isn't mandatory, you can sand if bubbles or drips dried in the finish, or if the surface seems rough
- Lightly sand with the wood grain, not across it; use 240-grit or finer unless there are large bubbles or drips, which may require 180-grit
- Wipe off dust with a dusting cloth; do not use a commercial tack cloth with water-based finishes
- Apply the next coat as you did the first; three coats gives excellent results

Creating a Faux Wood Finish

If you want the look of a clear finish but your trim material is MDF or other paint-grade material, it's surprisingly easy to create a fairly realistic wood look with paint and water-based stain. Practice first on scrap pieces.

1 Paint trim

- Apply masking along nearby surfaces
- Apply primer if it's not already on
- After the primer dries, paint the trim with the lightest color in the wood you are mimicking
- Allow to dry

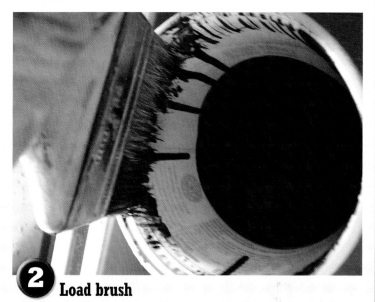

2 Load brush

- Pour a small amount of stain into a container that's not too tall, such as a cottage cheese container
- For an applicator, use an inexpensive chip brush; the sparse bristles help since they don't pick up too much stain
- Dip the bristle tips in the stain and tap them against the container's side to release any drips
- Don't get too much stain on the brush; a little goes a long way

3 Apply stain

- Tap and skid the brush along the trim so you get stain on only part of the surface, perhaps one-fourth
- With the brush perpendicular to the trim and with only the bristle tips touching, quickly work the stain back and forth
- Add a few swirls, if you want, to mimic grain lines
- Quickly go on to the next area; blend the beginning and end of each section

4 Tackle corners in two steps

- A two-step procedure helps you mimic the way miter joints slice crisply through wood grain
- Mask one side of the joint and apply stain to the other side
- When that's dry, mask the first side and work on the second

Metallic Effects

Metallic paints aren't merely shiny. They have a pearlescent quality that causes a surface to sparkle as you walk past. Mica-based finishes come in gold, silver, and brown to mimic various kinds of metal, as well as colors like purple and green.

The rich, golden wall frames in this entryway give the room an air of opulence.

With metallic paint, you often get more impact by using small amounts than you do by covering large areas. Think of it as painting in shadow lines, except that instead of painting on a bottom surface, where a shadow would be, metallic paint belongs on the top, where the highlights are.

A little gilding goes a long way in this elaborate composition of crown molding, stencils, and painted bands.

Silver-colored metallic paint pairs well with modern furnishings that feature similarly colored metal, such as aluminum or stainless steel.

Some metallic paints contain actual metal particles, so they tarnish and rust just like solid metal. You can let this happen over time, or accelerate the process by coating the paint with various patina formulas, as was done here.

Metallic paint works great as an accent. Two coats of copper paint turn a fence post topper into an elegant finial suitable for an interior stairway. Rubbing the final coat, once dry, with a scrub pad removed brush marks and created a surface with a more uniform sheen.

Metallic paint transforms a cardboard form for a concrete foundation pier into a column. Besides incorporating this kind of column in trimwork, you could also use it to make a plant stand, as was done here.

Patching Drywall

The best approach to patching drywall depends on the size of the holes. Nail holes are easy; dents and larger holes require several steps because you not only need to fill the hole, you may also need to match the surrounding texture.

Filling Dents

Use regular spackling paste for this, not a lightweight product.

1 Fill recess

- Stir spackling paste to a creamy consistency
- With a 3-inch drywall knife, press the material into the hole and the surrounding area
- Apply a layer no more than ¼ inch thick
- If you need a deeper layer, wait for the first one to dry, then apply another

2 Sand

- Wait for the final coat of spackle to dry
- Sand the material with 220-grit sandpaper or a sanding block
- Vacuum or brush off the dust

3 Texture

- If the wall has a textured surface, test a spray-on texture material on cardboard held vertically
- Vary the can's distance from the wall until you get a good match; hold the can at that distance as you spray the wall
- To keep the distance uniform, move your body; don't pivot the can
- Overlap passes by about one-third

Filling Larger Holes

When damage extends through the drywall, you can't just swipe spackle over the hole because there's no backing to hold the patch in place. An easy solution is to buy a drywall patching kit, which contains a small piece of fiberglass mesh and perhaps a stiff material that fortifies the patch. You can also make your own patch from a scrap of plastic window screen.

1 Clean edges

- With a sharp utility knife, cut away torn edges of the drywall paper
- Also remove any loose bits of the gypsum

2 Place patch

- Align the patch so it extends at least 1 inch beyond the hole in all directions
- Smooth out the mesh and press down the edges
- If you are making your own patch from window screen, hold it in place by dabbing drywall mud over the edges

3 Butter the patch

- Stir drywall mud to a creamy consistency
- With a 3-inch drywall knife, spread a thin layer over the patch
- When that's dry, run the knife over the area to knock off ridges, or smooth it with 150-grit sandpaper

4 Do it again

- Add a second layer of drywall mud over a larger area
- Wait for the final coat of mud to dry
- Sand the material with 220-grit sandpaper or a sanding block
- Vacuum or brush off the dust, then spray on texture

Resources & Credits

Acknowledgments

We'd like to thank the professionals who helped with this book:

Bob Stanton of *Stanton Specialties*, 360-297-3827

Richard Blumenthal, Larry Bell, Dewey Goodrich, and Michael Bow of *Blumenthal Construction, Inc.*, 206-842-3915

David Carley, John Tyler, and John Backland of *Carley Construction, Inc.*, 206-780-1248

Bo Blakey of *Finish Line*, 360-297-2337

Paul Venneman of *Fairbank Construction*, 206-842-9217

Billy Lounsbury of *Lounsbury Carpentry LLC*, 206-235-4096

Nick Green of *The Green Company*

Bruce Carter, David P. Schott, and Barry Ellis of *Interiors Only Painting*, 206-842-0296

Pat Rushon of *Refined Finishes*, 206-842-6174

Resources

Page 25
Decorative drywall
Trim-Tex Drywall Products
800-874-2333
www.drywallart.com

Page 36
Twig trim
Rustic Woodworking
218-384-9425
www.rusticwoodworking.com

Pages 40–41
Molding and other millwork
Architectural Millwork
800-685-1331
www.archmillwork.com

WindsorOne
707-665-9663
www.windsorone.com

Burton Moldings
888-323-8926
www.burtonmoldings.com

Homestead Hardwoods
419-684-9582
www.homesteadhardwoods.com

House of Fara
800-334-1732
www.houseoffara.com

Maurer & Shepherd Joyners Inc
860-633-2383
www.msjoyners.com

San Francisco Victoriana Inc.
415-648-0313
www.sfvictoriana.com

Superior Moulding, Inc.
800-473-1415
www.superiormoulding.com

Vintage Woodworks
903-356-2158
www.vintagewoodworks.com

White River Hardwoods
800-558-0119
www.whiteriver.com

Home Depot
800-553-3199
www.homedepot.com

Lowe's
800-445-6937
www.lowes.com

Menards
www.menards.com

Plastic molding
Flexible Molding International, LLC
801-852-0143
www.flexiblemolding.us

B.H. Davis Company
800-923-2771
www.curvedmouldings.com

Fypon, Ltd.
800-446-3040
www.fypon.com

Outwater Architectural Products
800-631-8375 (East); 800-248-2067 (West)
www.outwater.com

Royal Mouldings
800-368-3117
www.royalmouldings.com

Evertrue
Distributed by Axcess Inc. PTE Ltd.
905-326-8452
www.axcess-world.com

LP Moulding
888-820-0325
www.lpccorp.com/moulding

Pages 48–49
Applied moldings
Enkeboll Designs
800-745-5507
www.enkeboll.com

Castlewood
800-346-4042
www.castlewood.com

Pages 80–81
Horseshoe shims
Master Wholesale, Inc.
800-938-7925
www.masterwholesale.com

Page 91
Flexible drywall
National Gypsum Company
800-628-4662
www.nationalgypsum.com

Flexible plywood
Boulter Plywood Corp.
888-958-6237
www.boulterplywood.com

Pages 136–137
Spring clamps for miters
Collins Tool Company
888-838-8988
www.collinstool.com

Rockler
800-279-4441
www.rockler.com

Woodcraft
800-225-1153
www.woodcraft.com

Lee Valley Tools
800-871-8158
www.leevalley.com

Pages 156–157
Cabinet components
Scherr's Cabinet and Doors
701-839-3384
www.scherrs.com

Top Drawer Components
800-745-9540
www.topdrwr.com

Pages 196–197
Recycled doors and building materials
Building Materials Reuse Association
800-990-2672
www.ubma.org

Pages 216–217
Fillers
Color Putty Company, Inc.
608-325-6033
www.colorputty.com

Red Devil
800-423-3845
www.reddevil.com

DAP
800-543-3840
www.dap.com

Elmer's Products, Inc.
888-435-6377
www.elmers.com

Durham's Water Putty
The Donald Durham Company
515-243-0491
www.waterputty.com

Famowood
Made by Eclectic Products, Inc.
800-767-4667
www.eclecticproducts.com

PL
Made by Henkel Corporation
800-624-7767
www.stickwithpl.com

Minwax Company
800-523-9299
www.minwax.com

Photo Credits

T = *top*, B = *bottom*, L = *left*, R = *right*, M = *middle*

All photographs by Jeanne Huber unless otherwise noted.

Adobe/Beateworks/Corbis: 37; *Scott Atkinson:* 7BR, 46 all, 48 all, 49TL, 49BL, 50 2nd and 3rd from BL, 53BM, 54BL, 56TR, 58T, 60TR, 61BR, 144 all except TR; *Wayne Cable:* 208 3rd from BL, 217TM, 217TR; *Jason Carpenter:* 208 2nd from BR, 223TM, 223TR; *Corbis:* 7 4th from BL, 106TR, 119TR, 119BM, 186TR, 186BR; *Corner House Stock Photo:* 73BL, 108TL; *Courtesy DAP:* 216 2nd from ML, 216TR, 216BR, 217 2nd from BL; *Courtesy Durham's:* 216BM; *Courtesy Elmer's:* 216 2nd from MR; *Courtesy Famowood:* 216 3rd from MR; *Scott Fitzgerrell:* 40 all, 41 2nd from ML, 41 2nd from MR, 41MR, 44M, 44BM, 50 2nd and 3rd from BR, 53ML, 54BR, 55BR, 56TL, 57TR, 62TL, 64TL-TR, 65 all except BR, 69BR, 75BR, 85BR, 87BL, 87BR, 120L, 120R, 128R; *Tria Giovan:* 165TL; *Jay Graham/Corner House Stock Photo:* 130TL; *Jamie Hadley:* 143BR, 157MR, 157BR; *Douglas Johnson:* 144T; *Rob Karosis:* 7 3rd from BL, 7 3rd from BR, 23BR, 35TL, 35TR, 35BR, 36BR, 36 inset, 39BL, 94L, 118, 119TL, 165TR; *Muffy Kibbey:* 89T, 104, 129BR; *Chuck Kuhn:* 2TR, 5 2nd from TL, 57TM, 58B all, 59B all, 70BL, 71BL, 71BR, 73BR, 76BR, 79BR, 81TL, 81BL, 88 3rd from BR, 97BM, 98BR, 142 BL, 142 2nd from BL, 142 4th from BL, 142 3rd from BR, 142 BR, 143BL, 145–147 all, 150–153 all, 155 M, 155 MR, 156BR, 156 inset, 158–161 all, 208 2nd from BL, 208 4th from BL, 208 BR, 209T, 209BL, 209 2nd from BL, 209 2nd from BR, 209BR, 214BL, 218TR, 219TR, 219MR, 219BM, 222L, 223M all, 225 all except BL, 226–229 all, 233B all, 234–235 all; *David Duncan Livingston:* 211TL, 213T, 224, 232L, 232R; *Bob Manley/Corner House Stock Photo:* 16; *Courtesy PL:* 216ML, 216MR; *Eric Roth:* 2BR, 6 3rd from BL, 6 4th from BL, 6 2nd from BR, 6BR, 7T, 7BL, 7 2nd from BL, 8 all, 9T, 9BL, 10B, 11TL, 11TR, 13, 19BL, 19BR, 21 all, 22BR, 23TL, 23TR, 23BL, 24–26 all, 27TL, 31BR, 33 all, 39BR, 47B, 49T, 88BL, 90T, 90BR, 91R, 91BL, 94R, 108BL, 108R, 116BL, 116BR, 117T, 119TM, 119BR, 121B, 128BM, 128BL, 129TR, 130TR, 130BR, 131 all, 162BL, 164 all, 165BL, 165BR, 170BL, 171BL, 172–173 all, 181L, 181MR, 187TR, 187BL, 210 all except BL, 211BL, 211TR; *Andrea Rugg Photography/Beateworks/Corbis:* 106TR; *Mark Rutherford:* Cover, 50 4th from BL, 51BM, 52TM, 55BL, 60BM, 60BR, 61BL, 142 3rd from BL, 148TR, 149 all, 154BL, 154BR, 156TR, 157TR; *Alan Shorthall/Corner House Stock Photo:* 202TR; *Thomas J. Story:* 198R; *Brian Vanden Brink:* 1, 6 3rd from BR, 9BR, 18T, 23BM, 23TM, 27TR, 27B, 31M, 45TM, 186L, 187BM, 187BR, 119BL, 233TL; *Christopher Vendetta:* 116 2nd from BL, 120ML; *Jessie Walker:* 28T, 233TR

Illustration Credits

T = *top*, B = *bottom*, L = *left*, R = *right*, M = *middle*

All illustrations by Greg Maxson, www.gregmaxson.com, unless otherwise noted.

Dartmouth Publishing and Tracy La Rue Hohn: 148BR; *Bill Oetinger:* 142 2nd from BR, 148TL, 155T, 155BL, 156TL, 157TL, 157BL, ; *Rik Olson:* 6 2nd from BL, 17TL, 17BL, 18B, 19-20 all, 28B, 29–32 all, 34–36 all, 38–39 all, 45TR, 84T, 88 2nd from BR, 100 all, 116 2nd from BR, 121T, 128TR, 129 all, 139BL, 139BM, 139BR

Index

Angles
cutting, 60, 64, 136–137
measuring and marking, 64, 76–77, 99, 158
Aprons (window trim)
about, 11, 17
Art Deco and Modern, 38
installing, 110
Neoclassical, 30
Victorian, 32
Art Deco style, 38, 139
Arts and Crafts movement, 34

Back bevels, 80
Baseboards
about, 12, 14, 122
Art Deco, 38
Colonial and Colonial Revival, 28, 29
corner blocks for, 45
installing, 122–126, 179
Neoclassical, 30
Victorian, 32
Bead board, 21, 32, 47, 172–179
Beams, ceiling
box beams, 11, 24, 25, 166–167
exposed, 29, 165
Bookcases
basic, 148–149
Craftsman, 35
plywood, 150–151
recessed, 152–153
trim for, 154–155
Box beams, 11, 24, 25, 166–167
Bracket shelves, 11, 119, 146–147, 187
Built-ins
cabinets, 156–157
shelving, 144–147
trim for, 121
window seats, 158–161
Built-up molding, 45, 94, 122, 128, 138–139
Butt joints, 43, 81, 120
Bypass doors, 198–201

Cabinets, 158–159
Casing
Art Deco and Modern, 38–39
beveled, 39
clamshell, 39

Colonial and Colonial Revival, 28–29
Country, 36
Craftsman, 34
mitered returns for, 114–115
Neoclassical, 30–31
painting, 226–227
Victorian, 32–33, 100
See also Door casing; Window casing
Caulk and fillers, 87, 102, 111, 216–217
Ceilings
box beams, 24, 25, 166–167
exposed beams, 29, 165
painting, 225
trim for, 24–25, 165
Chair rails, 14, 29, 30, 32, 128
Chopsaws. See Miter saws, power
Circular saws, 58–59
Clamps, 65
Classical architecture, 10, 12–13, 15, 18, 30, 187
Colonial and Colonial Revival styles, 15, 27, 28–29
Columns, 12, 31, 164, 168–169
Coped joints, 120, 124–125, 134
Corner blocks, 18, 19, 32, 44–45, 100–101
Country style, 27, 36–37
Craftsman style
choosing trim for, 34–35, 108, 118
crown molding for, 139
mock beams for, 165
plate and picture rails for, 129
tall wainscot for, 21
Crown molding
about, 11, 12, 14, 130–131
Art Deco, 38
built-up, 138–139
Colonial and Colonial Revival, 28, 29
corner blocks for, 45
Craftsman, 35
for fireplace surrounds, 18, 19
installing, 84, 132–133, 134–135
miter joints for, 136–137
Neoclassical, 30
Victorian, 32
Custom molding, 41, 101, 140–141

Dentils, 11, 19, 31
Door casing
about, 12, 16–17
Art Deco and Modern, 38
Colonial and Colonial Revival, 28–29

corner blocks for, 44–45
Country, 36–37
Craftsman, 34
installing, 95–97
mitered trim for, 94, 114–115
Neoclassical, 30–31
for pass-throughs, 90–93
Victorian, 32–33, 100
Doors
bypass, 198–201
fitting and hanging, 196–197
painting, 228–229
pocket, 202–205
prehung, 192–195
Drywall, 234–235

Edging, 145

Faux posts, 166–167
Featherboards, 61
Files and rasps, 57
Fillers and caulk, 87, 102, 111, 216–217
Finger-jointed molding, 40
Finishes and finishing
choosing, 11, 27, 40–41, 210–213
clear, 212, 231
color schemes, 34, 119, 182, 210–211
faux, 230
filling nail holes, 85, 92, 102, 112, 216–217
metallic, 232–233
opaque, 212
prefinishing, 220–221
preprimed molding, 40
sequence of work, 224–225
surface preparation, 218–219, 234–235
See also Painting
Fireplace surrounds
about, 18–19, 186–187
Colonial and Colonial Revival, 28, 45
Craftsman, 35, 186
installing, 188–191
mantels, 35
Victorian, 32
Frame-and-panel wainscot, 20, 21, 28
Framing (studs), 17, 123, 132, 152–153

Glues and gluing, 97, 115, 174, 182–183, 185, 207

Hammers, 65, 81
Handrails, 22, 206–207
Hand tools, 54–57, 62–65, 70, 77, 81
Hardware
for cabinets, 157
for doors, 197, 198–199, 202
for handrails, 207
for window seats, 160, 161
Hardwood
lumber, 40, 46
plywood, 48
Horizontal trim. See Running trim

International Residential Code (2006), 18, 22

Jigs and templates
for built-up molding, 138
for circular saws, 59
for cutting brackets, 146
for cutting crown molding, 137
for cutting reveals, 83
for cutting small pieces, 114–115
for hanging a door, 192–195
for marking running trim, 72, 127
for measuring angles, 158
for spacing holes, 150
for tearing sandpaper, 56–57
Jigsaws, 56–57, 146
Joinery
butt joints, 43, 81, 120
coped joints, 120, 124–125, 134
dado joints, 148–149
scarf joints, 120
See also Miter joints

Ledges, basement, 184–185

M

Mantels
about, 18–19, 188
constructing, 190–191
Craftsman, 35
See also Fireplace surrounds
MDF (medium-density fiberboard),
40, 41, 48
Measuring and marking
angles, 76–77, 158
chalk lines, 65, 74
mitered trim, 97, 99, 136–137
prefinished trim, 221
prehung doors, 192
reveals, 82–83
scaling, diagonal, 180
scribing, 79, 105, 158
studs, 17, 123, 132
tools for, 65, 70–73, 183
See also Jigs and templates
Miter joints
for door and window casing,
94–97, 112–115
effect of humidity on, 94–95
filling gaps in, 112
fitting, 98
measuring for, 99
outside corners, 126, 136–137
for running trim, 120, 123, 134
for wall frames, 182
Miter saws, power
about, 52–55
cutting angles, 64
cutting back-bevels, 80
miter cuts, 52, 54, 126, 136–137
stands for, 66
Modern style, 27, 38–39, 119
Molding
adding to existing, 39
architectural roots of, 12–13
built-up, 45, 94, 122, 128,
138–139
carved and pressed, 49
choosing, 10–11, 42–45, 94
custom, 101, 140–141
flat, 24, 25
flexible, 41
laminated, 44
materials for, 40–41, 46–49
shapes of, 14–15
square stock, 43
See also Running trim; Standing
trim

N

Nail guns, 62–63, 81
Nailing, 62–63, 81, 85, 99
Neoclassical style, 30–31, 39, 100

P

Painting
bead board, 175
color schemes, 34, 119, 182,
210–211
doors, 228–229
filling nail holes, 85, 92, 102,
112, 216–217
masking, 222–223
prefinishing, 220–221
primers, 214–215
surface preparation, 218–219,
234–235
windows, 226–227
Panels and wall frames, 20–21, 28,
180–183
Pass-throughs, 31, 38, 39, 90–93
Picture-frame style trim, 16, 21,
112–113
Picture rails, 12, 14, 32, 119, 129
Plate rails, 34, 35, 129
Plinths
for columns, 11, 12
for door casing, 16, 17, 30, 44,
100–101
Plywood, 48, 58, 150–151
Pocket doors, 202–205
Posts, faux, 166–167
Power tools
belt sanders, 80
circular saws, 58–59
jigsaws, 56–57, 146
miter saws, 52–55, 64, 66, 80,
126, 136–137
nail guns, 62–63, 81
routers, 140
table saws, 43, 60–61, 83
Prefinished molding, 220–221
Prehung doors, 192–194

Q

Quarter-round (shoe) molding, 14,
24, 126

R

Railings, 22, 206–207
Rasps and files, 57
Returns, 10, 29, 114–115
Reveals, 82–83
Routers, 140
Running trim
custom molding, 140–141
defined, 10–11
design considerations, 118–119,
128–131
installing, 121
joints for, 120
See also Baseboards; Crown
molding

S

Safety
ear protectors, 52
for earthquake zones, 119
face masks, 52
for finishes, 213
for fireplace surrounds, 18
lead-based paint, 226
for power tools, 52, 58, 60, 101
safety glasses, 52, 66
for stairways, 22
for workspaces, 66–67
Sanding, 42, 56–57, 80
Saws
circular saws, 58–59
handsaws, 54–57
jigsaws, 56–57, 146
power miter saws, 52–55, 64,
66, 80, 126, 136–137
table saws, 43, 60–61, 83
Scarf joints, 120
Scribing, 79, 105, 158
Shelves and shelving
bracket, 11, 119, 146–147, 187
edging for, 145
face frames for, 154
for fireplace surrounds, 18–19,
35, 186–188, 191
specifications for, 144
See also Bookcases
Shims
about, 78–79
for door and window casing,
93, 98, 107, 111
for prehung doors, 193–194
Shoe (quarter-round) molding, 14,
24, 126
Softwood, 40, 46, 48
Sprung molding, 139
Stairways, 10, 22–23, 181
Standing trim, 10–11
See also Door casing; Window
casing
Stool-and-apron trim, 16
Stools (window trim), 11, 17, 105,
108, 177
Story poles, 73
Straightedges, 59
Studs, 17, 123, 132, 152–153
Styles
about, 17, 26–27
Art Deco, 38, 139
Arts and Crafts, 34
Colonial and Colonial Revival,
15, 27, 28–29
Country, 27, 36–37
Modern, 27, 38–39, 119
Neoclassical, 30–31, 39, 100
Victorian, 15, 26, 32–33,
100, 129
See also Craftsman style

T

Table saws, 43, 60–61, 83
Templates. *See* Jigs and templates
Tools
belt sanders, 80
carpentry, 54–57, 62–65, 70, 81
caulking guns, 217
cordless, 59
Forstner bits, 146, 151
nail guns, 62–63, 81
for painting, 218, 219
routers, 140
sliding T-bevels, 64, 77, 99
squares, 64
See also Saws
Trimwork
about, 8–11
based on classical architecture,
10, 12–13, 15, 18, 187
choosing materials for, 40–49
See also Molding; Styles

V

Valances, 36
Victorian style, 15, 26, 32–33,
100, 129

W

Wainscot
about, 11, 12, 20–21
bead board, 32, 47, 172–179
Colonial and Colonial Revival,
28
Craftsman, 34, 35
frame-and-panel, 20, 21, 28
Victorian, 32
wall frames for, 180–183
Wall frames and panels, 20–21, 28,
180–183
Window casing
about, 10, 16–17
Art Deco and Modern, 38–39
Colonial and Colonial Revival,
28–29
corner blocks for, 44, 100–101
Country, 36
Craftsman, 34, 108
fitting bead board around,
176–177
installing, 102–107, 109–111
mitered trim for, 112–115
Neoclassical, 30–31
painting, 226–227
picture-frame style, 112–113
valances for, 36
Victorian, 32–33, 100
Window seats, 158–161
Workflow, 67, 224–225
Workspace, setting up, 66–67

Sunset guides you to a fabulous home – inside and out

Sunset's all-new Design Guides have everything you need to plan — and create — the home of your dreams. Each book includes advice from top professionals, hundreds of illustrative photos and a DVD with planning software that will help you create 3D design options viewable from all angles. With an emphasis on green building materials and techniques, this entire series will inspire ideas both inside and outside of your home.

Includes interactive DVD with each book